Baranzan's People

An Ethnohistory of the Bajju
of the Middle Belt of Nigeria

SIL International®
Publications in Ethnography
46

The Publications in Ethnography series focuses on cultural studies of minority peoples of various parts of the world. While most volumes are authored by members of SIL International® who have done ethnographic research in a minority language, suitable works by others will also occasionally form part of the series.

Series Editor
Susan McQuay

Managing Editor
Eric Kindberg

Editorial Staff
George Huttar, Volume Editor
Diane Dix, Copy Editor
Newton Frank, Copy Editor
Carol Brinneman, Copy Editor
Gene Burnham, Proofreader

Production Staff
Lois Gourley, Composition Director
Judy Benjamin, Compositor
Barbara Alber, Graphic Designer

Cover photograph: Woman dances around a circle of horn blowers, circa 1974 by Norris McKinney.

All Bajju photographs 1968–2010 are used by permission of His Royal Highness Nuhu Bature on behalf of the Bajju people.

All C. K. Meek (1931) images are used by permission of the Meek family: Map 1.1, Figures 1.2, 2.1, 2.2, 2.3, 2.4, 3.1, 4.1, 9.2, 14.2, 14.3, 14.4, 14.5, 14.11, 14.13, 14.14, 14.15.

Baranzan's People

An Ethnohistory of the Bajju of the Middle Belt of Nigeria

Carol V. McKinney

Foreword by Samuel Waje Kunhiyop

SIL International®
Dallas, Texas

© 2019 by SIL International®
Library of Congress Catalog No: 2018953729
ISBN: 978-1-55671-399-6
ISSN: 0-0895-9897

Copies of this and other publications of SIL International® may be obtained through distributors such as Amazon, Barnes & Noble, other worldwide distributors and, for select volumes, publications.sil.org:

SIL International® Publications
7500 W. Camp Wisdom Road
Dallas, Texas 75236-5629 USA

General inquiry: publications_intl@sil.org
Pending order inquiry: sales@sil.org

Contents

Figures

Maps

Tables

Foreword

Dr. Carol McKinney's book, *Baranzan's People: An Ethnohistory of the Bajju of the Middle Belt of Nigeria*, is a comprehensive study of the origin, history, culture, religious beliefs, and practices of the Bajju people.

This is a study that started over forty years ago, which involves scientific research, personal interviews, and interactions. I was privileged to be a research assistant to the author on some of those research interviews as we rode on a motorcycle to various villages in Kajju land. Dr. Carol McKinney, before embarking on the research, had lived among the Bajju with her husband Norris and children. She learned to speak and write the Bajju language (Jju) and ate their food (*dituk, kpekpei, akam, ahywu,* etc.). She made friends among the sons and daughters of the Bajju. Speaking and writing the language gave her a deeper insight and understanding of the Bajju people, and this qualified her to write authoritatively on them. The original research work earned her a deserved PhD.

After receiving her doctorate in 1985, she then took another thirty years to further reflect on the study, which has now culminated in the two volumes, *Bajju Christian Conversion* (2019) and the present book. Over the years, she has written many journal articles in peer-reviewed journals on various aspects of the Bajju people. In this book there are a total of fourteen chapters: The Bajju; Baranzan, the Bajju Founding Father; The Men's Secret Ancestral Organization and Small-Scale Warfare; Bajju Legal System; Hunting and Horns; Witchcraft—*Nkut;* Illness and Medicine; God and the Spirit World; The Life Cycle: Birth, Marriage, and Death; Taboos; Values; Indirect Rule in the Precolonial and Colonial Contexts; The Christian Era;

and Bajju Cultural Change. The book also has appendices on Hausa and Jju terms for other ethnic groups, villages in Bajju sections, Jju numbers, and a list of glossary items. One can see that all the major aspects of the Bajju people as an ethnic group are covered. Though all chapters are very important, let me mention chapter 11 on values, which to me is the focal point in the book. The values, which include community, morality, hospitality, respect of elders, the supernatural, marriage and procreation, Christianity, etc., are decisive in understanding the Bajju person. These values are taught and transmitted through proverbs and stories. "He who has people is a happy person," is a fundamental concept of the importance of community among the Bajju. Also, "The one who speaks too often gets into trouble," is a clear warning not to be too quick to talk without thinking of the consequences.

For me as a Bajju scholar, this study is as important as E. E. Evans-Pritchard's classic study, *Witchcraft, Oracles and Magic among the Azande* (1937). For that reason, all Bajju sons and daughters must read this important work. It should be made available in all schools and homes in Bajju-land as a requirement, as it will enrich an understanding of who they are and what they should be. This book should also be a motivation and springboard for further studies in other neighboring ethnic communities in the Middle Belt of Nigeria, such as the Agorok, Atyap, Moroa, Ikulu, Kagoma, Ham, Kanington, Kadara, Chawai, Atakar, and Fantswan. Students of history, anthropology, sociology, political science, religion, and culture will also find this an invaluable work for further research. I must get myself a copy when it is released! Also be on the lookout for *Bajju Christian Conversion,* 2019.

Congratulations to Dr. Carol V. McKinney for an excellent study that will serve as a groundbreaker in Bajju-land.

Rev. Professor Samuel Waje Kunhiyop, PhD
Former research assistant to Dr. Carol McKinney
General Secretary of ECWA (2011-2017)
Executive General Secretary of Evangel Fellowship International

Preface

This book is an ethnohistory of the Bajju people, formerly known as the Kaje, in Nigeria. They live in southern Kaduna State; though they live in the cultural north, their home area is in the geographic center of the nation. They are one of several hundred Middle Belt ethnic groups that live between the Hausa and Fulani in the north, the Yoruba in the west, and the multiple ethnic groups in the south, including the well-known Igbo. The Bajju, as well as many other Middle Belt ethnic groups, have converted to Christianity.

The intended audience of this book includes the Bajju themselves; academics who are interested in the ethnohistory and culture of this and similar groups in southern Kaduna State or who are interested in Christianization, religious change, or conversion; missiologists; and development personnel. Much of the Bajju history is slowly being lost today. It is important for them to remember their history, to know what their ancestors believed and how they lived, and what led them as a people to become Christians. To that end I begin with a discussion of their apical (apex, foundational) ancestor, Baranzan and his sons. Their migration narrative allows us to know how they came to live in their home area, their farming activities, and how they were organized politically. I discuss what they believed and practiced in their precolonial society. I also discuss cultural change over time, bringing their story into the postcolonial era.

This book on the ethnohistory of the Bajju is based on data my late husband, Norris, and I collected over a number of years. Our fieldwork among the Bajju began in 1968, and we have continued off and on since then. After my husband's passing in early 2010, I continued working on this book. Hence, it represents the long relationship we have enjoyed with the Bajju. We began learning Jju, the language spoken by the Bajju, while living in Zaria, then at the end of 1968 we moved to Unguwar Rimi,[1] "the village of the kapok tree," in the southern part of the Bajju area. While there we immersed ourselves in their language and culture until 1976. We returned to Nigeria again in 1983–1984 when I conducted my doctoral research—and have continued in occasional contact with the Bajju since then, sometimes for as much as a month at a time.

My preparation for living among the Bajju and conducting fieldwork there was varied: after my undergraduate work in cultural anthropology at UCLA, I had one year of graduate study in anthropology and completed my MA degree in linguistics at the University of Michigan prior to going to Nigeria. I had also studied Christian Education at Biblical Theological Seminary in New York City. My husband and I attended a "Jungle Training Camp" in southern Mexico to gain experience living in an area without modern facilities (running water, indoor plumbing, electricity, etc.).

While living among the Bajju we first focused on language learning, then on phonological study, and then grammatical analysis. I focused on multiple action verbs (McKinney 1979) and Norris studied participant reference in Jju narratives (McKinney 1978). We also analyzed the noun class system. After this initial focus on language learning and analysis, we turned more of our attention to Bible translation, working with the Bajju Translation Committee, which hired Simon Waziri, a seminary graduate, to prepare a first draft of the New Testament. I entered that draft onto the computer and checked it exegetically. Norris took my exegetical notes and went over them with Rev. Iliya Ahuwan. Together they revised the text. Then Elisha Sambo, principal at the Baptist High School in Jos, read the draft to various groups of Bajju speakers to make sure that the translation communicated effectively. Elisha sent his comments back to us, and we entered the changes into the manuscript. The New Testament in Jju was launched in 1984. Since then the Bajju Language Board has been working on completing the Old Testament so that the Bajju will have the complete Bible in their language.

Our field trips were sponsored by SIL International, Wycliffe Bible Translators, the Sociology Department of Ahmadu Bello University, and the Nigerian Bible Translation Trust. My husband and I have been grateful for the generosity of these organizations, and I wish to express our appreciation to them on behalf of us both. Our work in Nigeria would have been impossible without the continual hospitality and help we received from the Bajju.

---

[1] Gunn (1956) stated that Unguari Rimi was earlier called Unguwar Tagwai. This name reflects an event in which Tagwai, a Hausa warrior, when in this area in the precolonial period, was killed by the Bajju in interethnic warfare. Hausa warriors came each dry season to raid this area for slaves and plunder. The Bajju vigorously resisted. (Note: "Unguwar Rimi" is Hausa, pronounced "Ungwar Rimi" in Jju.)

I would also like to thank the staff of the National Archives in Kaduna, who allowed me access to their archival material on the colonial era.

In writing this ethnohistory of the Bajju I am very aware that much of what is included is based on the recall of individual Bajju. I did not live among them when many of the things described were current. Yet what is described gives some understanding of this little-studied ethnic group. One of my goals in this study is for the Bajju themselves to better understand their background and to be proud of and enjoy their heritage. In the light of modernization and globalization, it is important that they not forget that heritage.

We thoroughly enjoyed living among the Bajju. It was a privilege to be called *ashong Bajju* (red Bajju, as our skin color falls within their red category). My husband often told people that living with the Bajju was the highlight of our lives.

There are many Bajju who shared their lives with us. I especially thank His Royal Highness Nuhu Bature, the paramount chief of the Bajju. His friendship has enriched our lives. We have had many long conversations with him about his people, and I hope that I have represented them well.

I thank Rev. Dr. Chidawa Kaburuk and his wife, Kande, who have shared their home, friendship, and lives with us. I also thank Rev. Iliyah Ahuwan and his wife, Asabat, who worked with us in Duncanville, Texas, in revising the Jju New Testament. Both Rev. Chidawa and Rev. Iliyah, together with other Bajju leaders, read through a draft of this book, correcting my misunderstandings and making suggestions for a more accurate text. I thank Dr. and Mrs. Abashi Ahuwan for sharing their home with us when we were in Zaria. I thank the late Rev. Dr. Musa Asake who read earlier drafts of papers I wrote, corrected my mistakes, and helped me write more accurately. I thank Dr. Haruna Karick who worked with me on several projects, including writing the stories for the Jju primers. In 1984 he helped administer an interview schedule in Kamarum Kaje and Television, a suburb of Kaduna, and again in 2009 he administrated it in the same places. The results of those interviews are in my companion book, *Bajju Christian Conversion* (2019). We initially worked with his late father Rev. Karick from Chenccuk on language learning and analysis.

I thank Rev. Dr. Samuel Waje Kunhiyop for his help in my fieldwork. I shared the backseat of his motorcycle with him as we went from place to place interviewing people. I was never sure whether or not that motorcycle would quit and we would have a long walk home. Thankfully it never did. He felt my misgivings about that motorcycle were unnecessary, and he was right! He made a wonderful research colleague. I also thank him for his facilitating informed consent approval for the use of the pictures including Bajju people with the Bajju chief.

I sought permission to use the Bajju photographs that were taken in 1968–2010. I sent copies of those I wanted to include in this book to the

Bajju chief, His Royal Highness Nuhu Bature. On behalf of the Bajju people he granted written permission to use them. I am very grateful to him.

The list of the Bajju who shared their lives with us goes on and on as we lived with them in Unguwar Rimi for years. I want to thank all of them, even those whose names I've forgotten or whose names I never knew. I left part of my heart in Nigeria with the Bajju. Among the Bajju I thank Phillip Allahmagani, D.K. Allahmagani, John and Martha Adive, Bulus, Yabo Yashim, the late Yabo Bayei, the late Daniel Hywa, Rev. Mika, the late Elisha Sambo, and numerous other unnamed Bajju.

In 1912 Charles Kingsley Meek was appointed as a government anthropologist in Northern Nigeria. He held that post until 1933. When he visited numerous ethnic groups, he took detailed notes on each group, and wrote a two-volume work filled with photographs. The ethnographic work, published in 1931, is entitled *Tribal Studies in Northern Nigeria*. One of the groups he visited was the Bajju; specifically he went to the village of Marsa. He also studied the A̲tyap people. Meek's photos of these people, taken in their cultural settings, illustrate their life and cultural practices during the 1920s, one of the eras described in his ethnohistory.

To receive permission to use these photos for my book, I did extensive investigation and finally learned that C. K. Meek died in 1965. His only two sons are also deceased. My son Eric helped me discover that Meek had five grandchildren. Each of the grandchildren has granted me written permission to use the photographs from Meek's book. They view the use of his photos as a way to honor their grandfather. I wish to thank Innes Meek, Charles Meek, Kip Meek, Nigel Meek, and Sheena Meek Brookman for their kind permission to use C. K. Meek's pictures.

My thinking and writing have been influenced profoundly by numerous invaluable comments on drafts of this manuscript made at various stages of its development, including those from Carolyn Sargent, the late Dennis Cordell, William Pulte, and John and Pat Hanne. I thank my late mother who helped fund my research. I also wish to thank Elinor Abbot, who accompanied me to the Bajju for the month of November 2010. I thank Barbara Moore, Johannes Merz, and George Huttar who helped with editing this manuscript.

Special thanks go to my late husband, Norris, who accompanied me on our field trips, who shared the joys and frustrations of fieldwork, and who gave me immeasurable support during the writing of this book until his passing. Finally, I thank our children, Mark, Eric, Susan, and Christy, who shared their mother with their Bajju colleagues as I conducted research.

A note on Jju

The Bajju, or "Kaje" (see chapter 1), speak Jju, a member of the Central Platoid group of languages within the Benue-Congo language family (Bendor-

Samuel 1989:364). It resembles several other languages and dialects spoken in southern Kaduna State. Hausa, the language of wider communication in the area, belongs to the Chadic branch of the Afro-Asiatic language family, a language family quite different from the family that Jju is in and, as such, is quite dissimilar. In the sociolinguistic environment of this area, it is almost inevitable that the spelling of the language of wider communication influences previously unwritten minority languages. While a CVCV (consonant-vowel-consonant-vowel) pattern is characteristic of Hausa, Jju has consonant clusters and a nearly complete set of fortis and lenis consonants that sometimes require two and three letters to represent a single consonant (McKinney 1984, 1990). Further, there is palatalization and labialization in Jju that are not present in Hausa (for example, *kpukpwei* 'thick bean soup', *kyang* 'thing'). The alphabet used for transcribing spoken Jju was approved by the Nigerian National Language Center in the early 1990s. It leaves out the extra "i"s and "u"s that the Bajju often insert because of Hausa influence. For example, I write the term for "father" as *ạtyyi* rather than *ạtiyi*. This spelling approximates Jju pronunciation more closely than does the spelling influenced by Hausa.

Jju orthography

Letters written double in Jju are phonetically long (for example, nn = [n:]). Sounds followed by 'w' or 'y' are labialized or palatalized, respectively, for example, 'tw' = [t^w] and 'ty' = [t^j].

Jju	IPA	Jju	IPA	Jju	IPA
a	ɑ	ky	kx	tw	t^w
ạ	ə	m	m	ty	t^j
b	b	mm	m:	tyy	t^j:
bv	bv *or* bz	n	n	tyw	t^ɥ
bvv	bv: *or* bz:	nn	n:	ụ	ɨ
c	tʃ	ng	ŋ	u	u
cc	tʃ:	nng	ŋ:	y	j
d	d	o	o	yy	j:
e	e	p	p	hy	ç
f	f	pf	pf	hyy	ç:
g	g̱	py	p^j *or* ps	yw	ʝ
gb	ɡ͡b	pyy	p^j: *or* ps:	yww	ʝ:
gg	gɣ	r	ɾ	w	w
i	i	rr	r	ww	w:
j	dʒ	sh	ʃ	hw	w̥
jj	dʒ:	ssh	ʃ:	hww	w̥:
k	k	t	t	hyw	ç^w
kp	k͡p	ts	ts	z	dz *or* z
'	ʔ	tss	ts:	zz	dz: *or* z:

The glottal stop appears only in the word *ba'* to mark the negative. Since the word /ba/ means 'they' and 'come,' the glottal stop has to be written. For example, *Baba* means 'father' so *Baba ba ba'* means 'Father didn't come'.

1

The Bajju

Everybody wants to be known. (Bajju proverb)

The Bajju are the largest minority ethnic group in southern Kaduna State[1] in the Middle Belt of Nigeria, West Africa. This book presents an ethnohistory of the Bajju, focusing particularly on their culture. It discusses how they became a separate ethnic group, beginning with their migration from the Jos Plateau to their present location in southern Kaduna State, in Kachia and Jema'a Local Government Areas. It describes their precolonial political-religious organization, their economy, their legal system, their social organization, including marriage, other beliefs and practices, and their values. There are also chapters on the Hausa-Fulani, the colonial contexts, the Christian era, and cultural changes that have occurred.

The Bajju (Kaje)[2] share many characteristics with other minority ethnic groups of the area, including the A̱tyap[3] (Ka̱taf, Ka̱tab[4]), A̱ngan (Kamantan), A̱gorok/A̱gworok (Kagoro), A̱sholyo (Moroa), Fanswam (Kafanchan),

---

[1] This area has been referred to as Southern Zaria, a term that dates from the precolonial and colonial periods.

[2] The names in parentheses after several of these minority ethnic groups are those that outsiders have called them and are often found in the literature.

[3] Jju distinguishes between [a] and [ə], with the schwa in the practical orthography written as "a̱." The high central vowel [ɨ] is written as "u̱."

[4] The name Kataf or Katab originally developed from the Hausa word *katambari*, meaning "camwood," as the A̱tyap were involved in trade in camwood, which was exported from this area.

1

Jijili (Koro), Tsam (Chawai), Kyung (Kaninkon), Yeskwa, Atakad (Atakar, Attakar), Bace (Rukuba), and Kachichere (Kachechere). They are also related to the Attakchirak, Gwom, Anemnuen (Numana), and Ninzo (Ninzam). Other minority ethnic groups in southern Kaduna State that are linguistically more distantly related to the Bajju are the Bakulu (Ikulu), Adara (Kadara), Gyong (Kagoma), and Ham (Jaba). These ethnic groups are all part of the same culture area.

As mentioned in the Preface, their language, Jju, belongs to the Central Plateau subgroup of the Benue-Congo language family, which is part of the larger Niger-Congo language family (Blench 2004:12). These languages have noun classes, some have fortis-lenis consonant contrasts, and subject-verb-object (SVO) clause order. Further, they have serial verb constructions that allow sequential information to be readily expressed through several verbs within one sentence.

These groups are part of what Meek referred to as the Katab group. He described the cultural complex of many ethnic groups in this area as follows:

> It has been said that the tribes mentioned display a remarkable cultural uniformity, the more conspicuous traits of which may be summarized as follows: (1) the use of a common language of the classifying type...; (2) the peculiar type of dwelling, oblong at the base, with a pinnacled overhanging roof; (3) the mushroom-shaped lumbar adornment worn by the women, the use of lip discs and of a similar pattern of tribal marks; (4) exogamy in some shape or form; (5) the practice of wife-stealing or sub-marriages; (6) the practice of marriage with the grandfather's widow[s] [other than one's grandmother]; (7) inheritance of father's widows [other than one's mother], and (8) headhunting. (Meek 1931:4)

Most of these characteristics are no longer observed.

All of these ethnic groups have experienced rapid religious and cultural change by adopting Christianity, living within the same political structure, experiencing economic changes, and in general, dealing with rapid cultural change as a result of their relationship with two Hausa-Fulani[5] emirates (Zazzau and Jema'a), colonialism, missionization, education, and globalization.

Most of these groups now have their own chiefs. They are no longer under the emirs of Zazzau or Jema'a, but rather they conduct their own

---

[5] I speak of Hausa-Fulani emirates as these were the two ethnic groups that formed the composition of the emirates following the jihad of Usuman dan Fodio in 1804–1811. He was a Fulani cleric who took over what he viewed as corrupt Hausa emirates. After that both the Hausa and Fulani worked together to govern the various emirates in northern Nigeria.

affairs. This contrasts with their position under British colonialism during which they had little political representation due to the British policy of Indirect Rule (see chapter 12) and specifically the application of the emirate model of governance to multiple minority ethnic groups.

Bajju in the literature

Until the last few decades the Bajju were known as the Kaje, a term first applied to them by the Hausa, which the colonial administrators and scholars later used as well (see Gunn 1956). Until recently, when asked their ethnic identity they responded that they are the Kaje. However, among themselves and now within Nigeria, they are the Bajju, their language is Jju, and their territory is Kajju. The term Kaje likely derived from Kajju. It also translates as "you go" in Hausa and may derive from this Hausa phrase. It may also relate to *kazwu,* a term that translates as a particular area or spot that has been cleared and readied for construction of a house (Asake 1991:4). In this study I use the indigenous terms; however, occasionally the term Kaje[6] occurs in quotations. This usage of indigenous terms is in line with the current practice by the Bajju and other ethnic groups in Nigeria who prefer to be known by their indigenous names. For example, the ethnic groups on the Jos Plateau formerly called the Sura now prefer to be called the Mwaghavul[7] and the Birom and Angas prefer to be known as the Berom and Ngas, respectively. Today to refer to the Bajju as the Kaje is considered pejorative by the Bajju.

The first mention of the Bajju in the literature was by Tremearne, a British colonial officer stationed at Jemaan Daroro (Tremearne 1912:61). During his time in this area he traveled to various ethnic groups, including staying for a short time at Marsa, a Bajju village. The book he wrote includes pictures, some of which he took at Marsa. When we showed the pictures to a young man from Marsa, he recognized his grandfather in one of them. Tremearne titled his book *The Tailed Headhunters of Nigeria.* This title reflects the Bajju practice in which women wore a mushroom-shaped lumbar ornament over their leaves, which hung from a rope they tied around their waists; the rope and ornament he termed a "tail." Women wore this ornament during the mourning period. The term *headhunter* derives from the precolonial practice of taking heads during warfare. Once they were

---

[6] Gunn (1956:110) asserts that Kaje, also termed Kurmin Bi, was a son of Baranzan. Kurmin Bi is the Hausa name for the village the Bajju call Dibyyi and not an alternate term for Kaje. *Kurmin* means "a forest or a wooded ravine" in Hausa. *Bi* means "to follow" in Hausa. So a literal translation of *Kurmin Bi* is "to follow into a forest or wooded ravine." The word Kaje does not refer to a specific person, such as Gunn suggests.

[7] Morrison (1982:141) and Isichei (1982:1) spell their name as Mwahavul. Here I follow Datok (1983:1), who is a member of this ethnic group.

cleaned out, skulls served as cups to drink out of in the men's secret ancestral organization.

C. K. Meek (1931), a British colonial anthropologist, provided a detailed description of the Bajju and other ethnic groups in the area. Ames (1934) also wrote extensively on this area. The material about the use of the hot oil ordeal to determine whether or not someone was telling the truth comes from Ames as well as from local Bajju sources. Harold Gunn (1956) wrote a more extensive description of the Bajju. He based his research largely on research materials from various sources, including published and unpublished material, mission archives, reports and records in government files, as well as field notes of anthropologists and others. Gunn is to be commended for the work he did in writing about a large number of ethnic groups in the area. His description of these ethnic groups follows basic ethnographic categories such as location, social organization, totemism,[8] the life cycle, religious beliefs and practices, and the economy. At the time of his research there were approximately 2,000 Christians in six different denominations (1956:116). He also mentioned the presence of mission schools, which he stated had greater influence than the number of Christians might imply.

More recently the Bajju have written a number of significant articles, theses, books, and dissertations on their own people, including those by Marcus Kato (1974), Samuel Kunhiyop (1984, 1988, 1993, 2005), Chidawa Kaburuk (1976), Iliya Usman Shemang, and Musa Nchock Asake (1991, 1998), among others. These provide emic views on their culture, which add significantly to our knowledge of the Bajju.

Setting

The Bajju live in former Southern Zaria Province, now in the southern portion of Kaduna State. Many continue to refer to this geographical area as "Southern Zaria," even though provinces no longer exist as political units. Today use of "southern Kaduna State" is preferable to use of "Southern Zaria" as the location of this Middle Belt people. They are located in the former Northern Region of Nigeria[9] and are in the geographic center of the nation.

The Bajju area is between 600 and 900 meters (2,000 and 3,000 feet) in elevation and, as such, the climate is not as extreme as further north

---

[8] A totem is an animal, plant, or feature of nature with which a clan has a special mystical relationship. A hunter would not kill or eat meat from his totemic animal. Totemism is the presence of totems. Among the Bajju each clan has its own totem. If the totem is an animal and a hunter captures such an animal, he talks to it as though it is a relative, then lets it go.

[9] When I refer to Northern Nigeria I capitalize the word Northern. Today formal regions are no longer governmental units but rather Nigeria has states. When talking about the north of Nigeria, I do not capitalize northern.

in Nigeria. It is an area with numerous granite inselbergs (isolated black bare-rock hills) and granite massifs, surrounded by undulating plains that formerly were partially forested, though during the 1930s the colonial administration cut down many trees in order to eliminate hosts for tsetse flies that carry sleeping sickness. Today the forests continue to grow along the Atacap River (Kogum River) that drains the southeast portion of the Bajju area. This all-season river is fed by numerous small streams and gullies that flow during and following heavy rainfall but tend to dry up during the dry season. There are no lakes in the area, with the exception of a small manmade lake at Dibyyi.

The Bajju home area is close to Plateau State, and in fact in their oral tradition they originated from the Jos Plateau. Other ethnic groups in this area also claim a Plateau origin, such as the Atyap, Asholio, Atakad, and Agorok. Thus in their history these groups are related to the Irigwe, Rukuba, Berom, and Afizare on the Jos Plateau. Linguistic evidence confirms their relationship.

An early sketch of ethnic groups in this area comes from Meek (1931:2). (See map 1.1. While it is not completely accurate, it gives some indication of the relative placement of ethnic groups. Map 1.2 has Hausa names for Bajju villages, and map 1.3 has local Jju village names.)

Map 1.1. Sketch map of the ethnic groups
in Southern Zaria (Meek 1931:2)

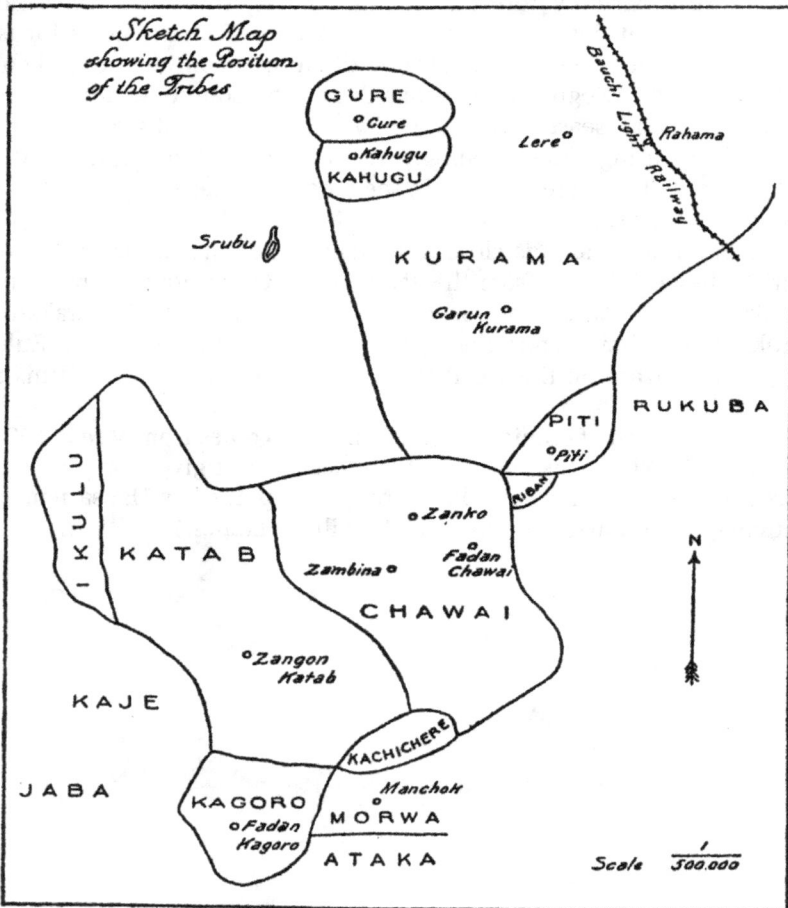

Map 1.2. Bajju area, with Hausa village names

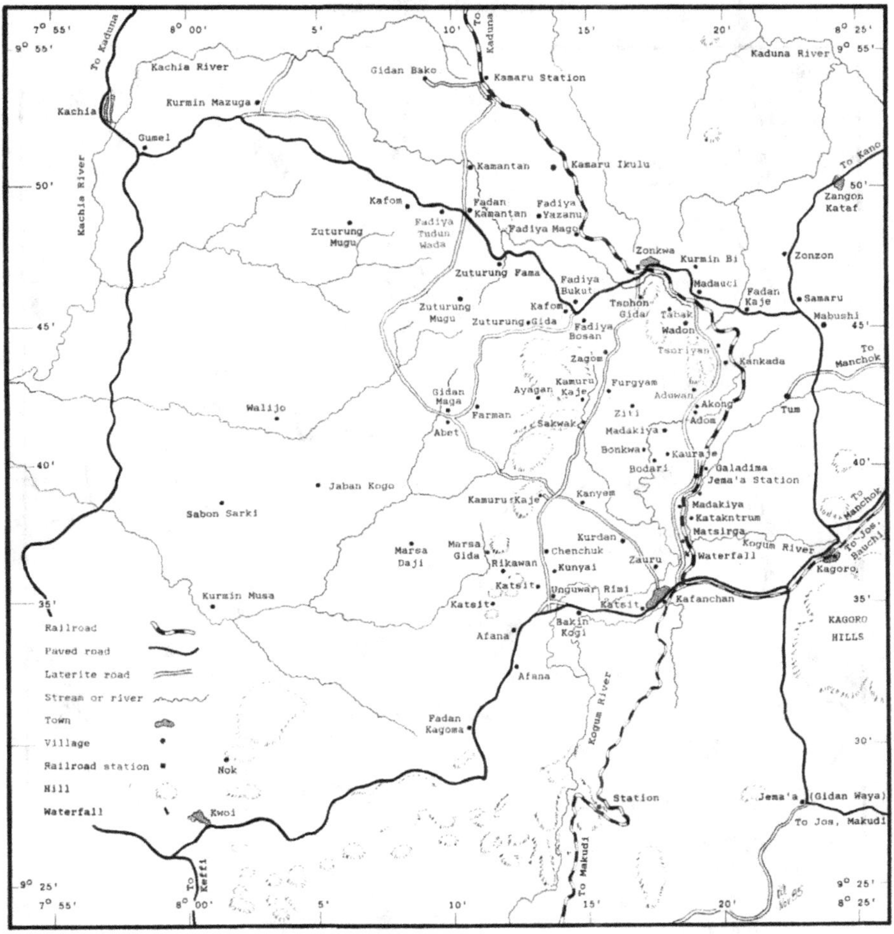

© Created by Norris McKinney and Carol McKinney.

Map 1.3. Bajju and surrounding ethnic groups, with Jju village names

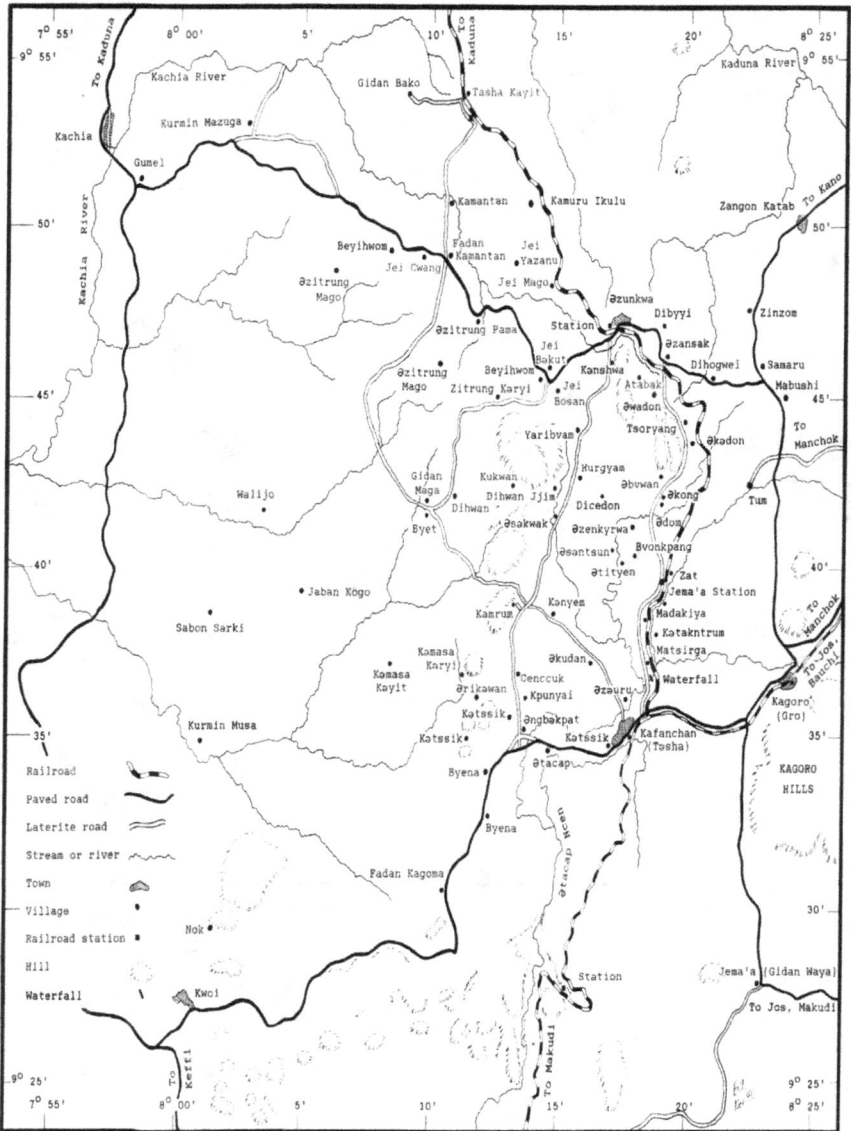

© Created by Norris McKinney and Carol McKinney.

The village of Nok, after which the Nok Cultural Complex is named, is located approximately twenty-two kilometers (fourteen miles) west of the Bajju village of Afana. In the distant past the Nok Cultural Complex covered the area where the Bajju now reside (Eyo and Willett 1980:2).

Demographics

Accurate census data are difficult to obtain in Nigeria. Census data available, though dated, give some idea of the number of Bajju. According to the 1963 census, the Bajju were the third largest ethnic group in Kaduna State, following the Hausa and Fulani (Kunhiyop 1984:10). The 1963 census figure was 148,459 Bajju in Zaria and Kaduna provinces, combined. Today there are between 480,000 and one million Bajju. The last few censuses have not included questions on the ethnic composition of the Nigerian population. They also have not included questions about religious affiliation of respondents, so data on these two areas are estimates only, based on the 1963 census data plus the annual rate of population increase in Nigeria. Data on the number of Christians in this area come from the interview schedule we administered twice, one in 1984 and again in 2009, as extended to the entire Bajju population.

Large numbers of the Bajju have moved to urban centers in Nigeria seeking education and employment opportunities. Some occupy positions in the local, state, and federal governments. Most remain in contact with people in their home area, and through education, economic success, and wisdom, some exercise considerable authority and influence within the Bajju home area, including within numerous Christian churches (today almost all the Bajju identify themselves as Christians). The Bajju who move to urban areas continue to worship in Christian churches.

Seasons

There are two seasons, a rainy season from April or May to October and a dry season for the other months of the year. The annual rainfall is 900 to 1,500 millimeters (35 to 60 inches) (Powell 1981:117). Since the rains are unpredictable, some years the rainy season is only six months long while other years it extends to eight months. One year the rainy season extended far longer than usual, and as a consequence some people came down with yellow fever. Doctors chose not to have a massive inoculation campaign because they reasoned that when the rains stopped, the mosquito population would decline significantly, and the epidemic would end. That is in fact what happened.

The dry season months of December and January are the coldest, when the dry harmattan winds blow in dust off the Sahara Desert. The fine red dust coats everything, making visibility a problem, especially for airplanes. On one occasion a pilot decided to land at the Kano Airport anyway and crashed. The fire engine took off for the wrong end of the field because they could not see the crash due to the thick harmattan dust suspended in the air!

Subsistence farming and farming rituals

The Bajju have been horticulturalists and many continue as farmers. Not to farm is to do nothing, to be lazy. When we first moved into our village home in December, my husband often asked children what their fathers did. The answer was predictable. They did nothing. During the dry season farmers were not out farming, so they were seemingly doing nothing.

Rural Bajju are excellent farmers. The measure of a good farmer was that he grew sufficient food to feed his family for a year.

Prior to beginning to farm in the early wet season (*kàtsìsèràng kà*), in the past the Bajju blew the bushbuck horn, which called people together to begin farming. At the beginning of the season they want rains to come. They asked a person who had not gone on a trip to sprinkle some hungry rice (a fine grain *tson; acca* H.[10]) into the bush near a road. Further, they soaked the hungry rice in palm wine, guinea corn beer, or water, then using some leaves, spread it at the corners of the field. The elders know the places where they were to make this sacrifice prior to the beginning of farming. This ritual was to help bring a blessing on them and their crops. It was used especially in the event of drought or excessive rain, both of which lessened the harvest.

A further ritual occurred prior to beginning farming when the rainy season was approaching. The ruling elder (*gado*) performed a ritual after which farming could commence. He first made some beniseed (sesame seed) paste. He gave some of it to the boys of his household and instructed them to scatter some on the stones where the elders usually sat for their deliberations. The elder then put some on all the rooms of the household and on the hoes. Finally, he said, "All sickness is put upon the hoe." After doing this, men should have been able to farm in health. He then took a hoe, farmed a small plot of land, and planted some beniseed. Then he declared that every man could farm and begin cultivating his fields (Kunhiyop 2005:7).

If crops were not doing well or there was no rain, people performed a blood sacrifice. It was a way to negotiate for rain to fall. Households prepared food and drink for the rituals that were performed outside the village. The elders talked first then shouted as though they were going to produce rain. They might have said, "If I am the one in charge of this place, then there is no reason rain shouldn't come." Everyone picked up a stone and threw them at the small spirits (*ngtanryang*) who were believed to be

---

[10] "H." following a word indicates that the word is Hausa; otherwise the words in italics are Jju, the language of the Bajju people.

preventing the rains from coming. Every village had a place where this type of ritual was performed. They took food and guinea corn beer to the ritual place to give to the spirits. They believed that rain would fall even before they reached their homes. After this ritual people returned to their homes to eat the food they had prepared.

Farming is a joint activity: men clear and prepare the soil by ridging it, men and women plant the seeds, men weed the ridges, men harvest the grain, and women carry the harvest home because carrying is a woman's job. Once the harvest is brought home, some of the crop may need further drying, which is done on drying racks, spread out on the ground or elsewhere where the chickens cannot eat it, or it may be placed on winnowing trays in some other safe place. Maize is attached to a rope that is then strung around a compound to allow it to dry.

The type of hoe used by the Bajju, Atyap, and other ethnic groups in this area is illustrated in figures 1.1 and 1.2. This type of hoe has been used in this area for a long time.

Figure 1.1. Bajju farmer with hoe, preparing ridges for planting (Norris McKinney).

Figure 1.2. Atyap farmer with similar hoe for preparing ridges for planting (Meek 1931:45).

Their main crops are millet, sorghum (guinea corn), soybeans, and maize (corn). In the Byet (Abet, H.) area seventy-five percent of all crops planted in 1983 were guinea corn, millet, maize, and soybeans (Powell 1981:65). These are the most important crops for Bajju farmers. Maize and groundnuts are planted in May and June. Millet is planted in late June and early July. Millet is a labor-intensive crop that is sown first in seedbeds. The field is then prepared by ridging it, and when the millet is approximately 30 centimeters (one foot) high in August, it is transplanted into the ridges. This contrasts with maize in which the farmer plants one seed into a hole with no transplanting necessary.

Cassava is also grown; it can be left in the ground until it is used on a particular day. Cocoa yams are planted in April and harvested in August and September. They are often planted near the river where the ground is moist. Other crops grown include ginger, hungry rice (*acca*), beniseed, rice, honey, various leaves, okra, tomatoes, broad beans, onions, garden eggs (eggplants), peppers, black-eyed beans, and yams. They also grow sponges and calabashes in these household gardens.

People placed medicine bundles in fields to frighten off those who might steal the crops. These bundles consisted of grass tied together and placed on a stick. The belief is that if a person stole from a field with a medicine bundle, it would make him unable to move.

At the end of the farming season, after the yams have been cooked and before eating them, they were first fed to the hoe in thankfulness for its help in their farming them. They smashed a cooked yam onto the hoe to feed it. This was termed *hyyu gnok,* to sprinkle or sacrifice to the hoe.

Figure 1.3. Bajju compound at Ayagan with a drying rack on right
(Carol McKinney).

Unguwar Rimi is known for its locust bean trees; women use its seeds to make locust bean cakes. In making these cakes they use lots of water, which is often thrown back into the river. Because of its toxicity, it can kill any fish in the river. Today they often use soybeans to make these small, flat, round cakes that are used in their stew.

After the harvest is dry, it is put into the granary. The left side of the granary is for guinea corn, with the right side for millet.

When building a new compound, the granary was built first. On the site that the granary was to be built, men put beniseeds, then covered the place with a basket. They slept overnight at that site. When they got up early, they checked the beniseeds to see if there was some animal fur among the seeds. If they saw some there, then the place had a blessing, and they could proceed to build there. However, if they did not see animal fur, then it was not a good place to build and they had to look for another place.

When building a new granary, they used (and many continue to use) the mud from a previous granary as they believed it was stronger. They build it up on rocks so that chickens can go under it to be protected from rain, to sit on eggs, and to eat any bugs that might get into the granary to eat the grain. A granary was smaller at the bottom and gradually became larger. There was a ledge near the top that the thatched roof rested on. This older style granary could last up to twenty years. After building the granary, they killed a white cock and put its blood and the soft feathers on the door of the granary to send evil away. Next they built their house. After building they took some beniseeds to eat together with a small amount of palm wine or guinea corn beer. They built a fire there and drank the wine. The purpose was for a blessing on their new compound. Many Bajju families have discontinued building granaries; rather, one room in their rectangular houses is designated as the storeroom for crops once they are harvested and dried.

When harvesting a field only the heads of the grain stalks are carried home, with the empty grain stalks left in the fields. These are often collected and used as fuel for cooking. They are also used as animal food for goats, pigs, and Fulani cattle to graze on. These empty grain stalks are termed *atakwo*.

There are numerous economically productive trees in the area, including citrus, mango, pawpaw, banana, plantain, and guava. In the early days of missionary work, Sudan Interior Mission (later renamed SIM) required its missionaries to plant a certain number of fruit trees each year, with missionaries having to sign a statement that they had done so (personal communication, Gerald Swank). Today the compounds of early Christians have large mango and citrus trees, especially grapefruit trees. When the citrus is ripe, this area provides citrus for Jos, Kaduna, and other places in the country as well as locally.

The colonial government introduced rice and ginger growing. After the Bajju harvest the ginger, women split it in order for the ginger to dry more rapidly by laying it out in the sun. The practice of splitting ginger means that it can only be sold locally, not internationally, as the international market purchases ginger that has not been split.

The Bajju raise goats, hogs, chickens, guinea fowl, ducks, turkeys, dogs, and occasionally cats. If the Bajju own any cattle, those animals are cared for by nearby Fulani pastoralists.

Missionaries introduced hog rearing. Today hogs are sent by rail, when available, or truck from the Bajju area to as far away as Lagos. Since pork was not part of their traditional diet, most Bajju still prefer to eat goat meat, chicken, or beef rather than pork.

Today with the availability of commercial fertilizer, fields are used over and over. This is less labor-intensive than clearing and preparing new fields. Before fertilizer became available, however, the fertility of a field would decline after a few years. Then the Bajju would allow it to lie fallow for a number of years. A fallow field was termed *dikwuk*.

Women prepare and plant the area (the *kạdak*) adjacent to their compounds where they grow broad beans, tomatoes, bathing sponges, gourds, and various types of edible leaves. Women's work includes finding firewood, chopping it, and carrying it home, hauling water, cooking, caring for children, housekeeping, carrying the harvest home, and selling produce in the market.

Other activities occur during the dry season. People remud and rethatch their houses, meet for church and community gatherings, celebrate marriages, travel, and in general do things that are crowded out by busy farming activities during the rainy season.

Methodology

My study of the Bajju reflects the eight and one-half years we spent in Nigeria beginning in 1967, of which a total of four years was spent living in Unguwar Rimi in the southeast part of the Bajju area. During our time in Unguwar Rimi, we gained a speaking knowledge of Jju that has proved an invaluable asset in conducting research. From mid-August 1983 to mid-May 1984[11] I concentrated specifically on collecting data on religious change, including data from the National Archives in Kaduna (NAK). These archives yielded a lot of material about missions and missionaries as they related to the colonial administration. There are colonial records of what occurred during the time the British governed Nigeria. I returned to the Bajju for the month of November 2010 to update my data.

While living in Unguwar Rimi we engaged in day-to-day participant observation. Since our family lived in the teachers' quarters of the senior primary school and since several paths went through our compound, people often stopped to greet us as they trekked along those paths. Further, the only road into the interior of the Bajju area was

---

[11] For 1983–1984 I had a Research Associateship with the Department of Sociology at Ahmadu Bello University near Zaria. I gratefully acknowledge their help in this research.

beside our compound. When we first moved there, we saw perhaps one car a day, and we often went out to greet whoever was driving past. By the time we left, a number of the Bajju had acquired cars and many passed by daily. Today roads throughout the Kajju area are paved, although many, especially the smaller ones, are not.

Our residence also lay on the cattle trail of the nomadic Fulani. During their annual migrations we saw hundreds of head of cattle go by together with sheep, dogs, donkeys, horses, and Fulani families. A herder went first, whistling and calling to his cattle, then the cattle passed by, and finally the women and children followed. Very young children were carried on their mothers' backs, and children who were a bit older were put on a horse or donkey. Newborn calves or calves that were too young to keep up with the herd were often carried on the shoulders of a Fulani herder.

In addition to participant observation I interviewed numerous persons. In 1984 my research assistant and I administered a structured interview schedule to 266 people (192 rural adult respondents and 74 urban ones). My research assistant administered the interview schedule again in 2009 to 63 persons. This research focused on the Bajju adoption of Christianity. Today almost one hundred percent of the Bajju are Christians, with most of their pre-Christian religious practices now abandoned, though many of their pre-Christian religious beliefs have been retained by Bajju Christians. The results from the two interview schedules are reported in *Bajju Christian Conversion* (McKinney 2019). Chapter 10 of this book briefly discusses the Christian era among the Bajju.

Kinship

The Bajju have patrilineal descent and patrilocal residence; it is women who move to the residences of their spouses following marriage, and women who leave in the event of divorce. The Bajju have an Omaha-type kinship system. In this system the terms for mother's brother and mother's father are the same for the generations above the person the kinship chart focuses on (ego) as well as lower generations (for example, for mother's brother's son). In other words, it does not apply to only one generation. Mother's brother is known as *angat*. Most of those in a wife's lineage are simply referred to as in-law. Kinship terms of reference are more developed for those within the patrilineage, as the Bajju have a patrilineal kinship system (see McKinney 1983, 1992).

Overview

This Bajju ethnohistory begins with a discussion of Baranzan, the apical ancestor of the Bajju, in chapter 2, which goes on to explain the precolonial political and religious structure of the Bajju that developed from Baranzan and his sons. As described in chapters 3 and 4, the Bajju were under a series of elders, including the one at Dibyyi who was over all the other section elders, the village elders, the elders in charge of the men's secret ancestral organization, the hunting elder, and family elders. The elders enforced the legal sanctions on the community that kept it free from the consequences of various transgressions of people. Blood sacrifice was necessary to atone for homicide, adultery, and certain other offenses.

The Bajju were excellent hunters. Each dry season the hunting elder of each village organized a communal hunt. Prior to leaving, the horn blowers blew animal horns in anticipation of the hunt. Thus in chapter 5 I discuss both hunting and musical instruments, especially horns, together.

The ideology of why people become ill and die, and in particular the witchcraft (*nkut*) beliefs that help to explain the ultimate spiritual cause of people's illnesses, misfortunes, and death, are presented in chapter 6, laying a foundation for chapter 7's description of illnesses and of the medications and other ways that diviners and herbalists sought to deal with them. In the past there were diviners who identified who was responsible for specific people's problems.

Chapter 8 deals with God and the spirit world: The Bajju believed in God and in various categories of spirits. These spirits made their wishes known through diviners and through the men's ancestral cult, the *ɡbvoi,* described in chapter 3. When the men decided the time was right, they selected the boys to initiate into this society. When the initiates emerged from their initiation, they were no longer classified with the boys but rather with the men. This rite of passage changed their status within the community.

The rest of the Bajju life cycle—birth, marriage, and death and reincarnation—is described in chapter 9. I discuss various types of marriage, including primary and secondary marriages. Many Bajju men were married polygynously (and some women were married polyandrously), and a few continue to take second and subsequent wives. This has led to problems in Christian churches, given the fact that church elders may have only one wife. Being married and having children to continue the patrilineage is an important value for the Bajju. A person who does not marry is considered a worthless person.

Chapter 10 deals with Bajju taboos and the possible consequences of breaking them, while chapter 11 addresses Bajju values. These values have allowed them to change their culture in response to the coming of Christianity, the topic of chapter 13. The Christian era began soon after the establishment of the Protectorate of Northern Nigeria in 1900; the history of the Protectorate is described in chapter 12.

Finally, chapter 14 discusses cultural change that has occurred among the Bajju. As Christians they are part of the global Christian community. Missionaries certainly contributed significantly to the cultural change that has occurred. Further, the Bajju are no longer under the rule of the two emirates that tried to control them before, but they have their own chief.

2

Baranzan, the Bajju Founding Father

Introduction

Baranzan is the founding father of the Bajju, their apical ancestor. Baranzan's ancestors originated in an area near Bauchi on the Jos Plateau where the Jarawa now live. From there Baranzan's father moved to Kwal via Fobur, an Irigwe village near Miango on the western edge of the Jos Plateau.[1] Because of famine, Baranzan, the son of Zamfara and Zambrang, moved from Kwal via Chawei and Kughang (Hurvang). They next went to the Atakad area where they stayed and daily went out hunting. From there the Bajju moved to Karyi Tibyyi, later named Karyi Dibyyi or just Dibyyi. The word *Dibyyi* means "grave"; the name change occurred when Baranzan died and was buried there. The Hausa originally named this area Bi, then later Kurmin Bi,[2] a term that means "to follow after into a wooded area or

---

[1] Some versions of the Bajju founding charter state that Baranzan moved from Miango, and others hold that he was born at Hugbang.

[2] Asake states that Achinge was the father of Baranzan (Asake 1991:5); Achinge left the Bauchi area in search of fertile farming and hunting areas. He went southwest and settled at Fambur; later he left there and went to Jere. From Jere he migrated to the hills of Kwang, and from Kwang three people left for Miango (Asake 1982:2). Asake further states that Baranzan left Miango because of famine. Baranzan and his younger brother stopped among the Atakad before arriving at Tibyyi. Gunn, who followed Reynolds (1950), also stated that the Bajju left Miango because of famine (Gunn 1956:110). Sankey presents a slightly different version when he states, "The Kaje tell the story of three brothers, who left the Jarawa area (Bauchi-Plateau State)

19

ravine." This was where Baranzan and his family settled. There Baranzan found good hunting with lots of African buffalo and other wild animals, fertile farmland, and the protection of thick forests and rocky hills.

Because the Bajju originated from the Jos Plateau, the Jarawa and Irigwe, two ethnic groups on the Plateau, together with the Bajju, refer to themselves as *dangi*, a term which translates as "people who are of the same stock" (Kunhiyop 1993:50–51). It is unclear when the Bajju migration occurred, but over the years the Bajju have maintained ties with their Plateau neighbors. The Bajju Development Association website links to Zitt Localization Project (2016), which states, "Today, the peoples of Southern Kaduna may be referred to as such, or as Nerzit. While they speak many different languages and see themselves as separate peoples, their unity as a group is also quite apparent to them, there being many of the tell-tale signs (that abound all around Nigeria) that let neighbors know they are both the same and different all at once. Indeed, Southern Kaduna is a culture area."

Bajju oral tradition relates that A̱kaat, Baranzan's brother, founded the Atakad, a related ethnic group.[3] Because of this close kinship relationship, traditionally the Atakad and Bajju did not intermarry (Kato 1974:17) as they saw each other as brothers and sisters; more recently this prohibition is breaking down. The Attakar also claim a Plateau origin and state that their name derives from a hill named Takar that is near the location where the sons of Attakar settled.

The Bajju similarly believe that the Chawai are descended from A̱nkwai, the younger brother of Baranzan. They too have a close affiliation with the Bajju (Kunhiyop 1988:6). Because of this close kinship relationship, they did not intermarry.

Baranzan had five sons,[4] each of whom founded a village, and over time these villages developed into larger territorial units or sections (*kwai*)[5]

---

and settled among the Miango (Plateau State). The senior became intorably [*sic*] oppressive forcing the two juniors to migrate southwards" (Sanke 1977:17).

Most Bajju origin narratives omit the names of Baranzan's parents; in particular the name of Baranzan's mother, Zambrang, is most often omitted. Kunhiyop attributes this to the Bajju practice of patrilineal descent (Kunhiyop 1993:51).

[3] The name Atakad is alternatively spelled Attaka (Isichei 1982:36, Ames 1934:222) or Ataka (Gunn 1956:103).

[4] This is the most commonly accepted number of sons cited in the numerous oral traditions about Baranzan, though in some accounts he had four sons, and in others, six sons. Gunn's (1956:110) account differs in that he considered all six of these to be grandsons, rather than sons, of Baranzan.

[5] Kato refers to these units as "subclans" (1974:51). Within a *kwai* there are smaller named totemic units (*sot*) that correspond to clans. Smith, who wrote on the closely related A̱gorok, defined *kwai* as "the localized clan or largest autonomous clan segment" (Smith 1982:5). The Bajju and A̱gorok had virtually the same structural units in their precontact societies. The *kwai* for the Bajju does not correspond to the localized clan. It is comprised of a number of clans. I suggest that the same applies to the A̱gorok. Meek alternatively translates *kwai* as a localized group, division,

(Gunn 1956:107) that are related to each other through kinship ties. Fission and occasionally fusion typified Plateau and related minority ethnic groups in southern Kaduna in the pre-1800 period and have continued into the present (Morrison 1982:136).

The five semi-autonomous Bajju sections within the Bajju federation are listed in table 2.1. (See Appendix B for a list of the villages within each *kwai*.) It also lists the sons[6] of Baranzan, together with the section each founded, the meaning of the term, and the village where each son and subsequent ruling elder resided.

Table 2.1. Sons of Baranzan in order of birth, the section each founded, meaning of the name, and the village where each son and subsequent ruling elders resided[7]

Sons of Baranzan	Section (*kwai*) of the Bajju	Meaning of name	Village where the ruling elder (*gado*) resided
A̱dwang (Yidwang)[a]	Ba̱yindwang (Ka̱tak A̱huwang)	People of *Dwang*, a stream	Ka̱ryi Dibyyi, Kurmin Bi
A̱kadon (Yinbyin)	A̱gbayinbyin	People of the drum	A̱ka̱don
A̱twan (A̱don)	Ba̱ta̱don	People of *Ta̱don*	Twan
Ka̱nshwa (Ka̱tson)	Ba̱yintsok (Ba̱itsok)	People of the hill	Ka̱nshwa
A̱kwak (A̱nkwak)	Ba̱nyehwan (Ba̱yinhuwan)	People of the mountain	Asa̱kwak, Sokwak

[a] Alternate spellings and names are in parentheses.

In another related version of the Baranzan origins narrative, Baranzan had a sixth son, *Ba̱itrung*, who founded the *Ba̱yintrung* section (Kunhiyop 1993:51; Ames 1934). The *Ba̱yintrung*, whose name translates as "people who put down their head-loads," was a sixth *kwai*. People in this section migrated into the Abet and Zitrung areas but at first did not trace their genealogy to Baranzan (Waters-Bayer 1982; Ames 1934). These people

---

or village-area confederacy (Meek 1931:101), though he notes that these were not clans in the accepted sense of the term.

[6] The youngest son of the father is usually the caretaker for the father as he ages and of his compound after the father passes away. All the older brothers build their houses adjacent to or as part of their father's compound as the Bajju are patrilineal and have a patrilocal residence pattern. After their father's death, the brothers go to the father's grave to show their respect. The oldest capable son becomes head of the extended family.

[7] Gunn (1956:110) lists Kaje or Kurmin Bi as a son of Baranzan. Neither Kaje nor Kurmin Bi was a son of Baranzan.

arrived independently from those who traced their ancestry to Baranzan. However, they spoke the same language and belonged to the same ethnic group. Waters-Bayer wrote concerning this Bajju section:

> The Kaje who live on the Abet Plains appear to comprise a sixth section which does not trace its history back to Kurmin Bi and is itself divided into two distinct groups, the Amabat and the Far- man (the 'Farman' elders refer to their group as the 'Duhuan'). These people seem to represent the most recent extension of Kajeland (Philipson 1979:13) and, according to present-day Kaje reports, have inhabited the Abet Plains for less than a century, although they have been using the area for hunting and some farming for a longer period than this. (1982:2–3)

This suggests successive migrations by small groups of Bajju from the Plateau. People who formerly called themselves *Bayintrung* have now been incorporated into one of the other Bajju sections and consider themselves descendants of Baranzan.

In an alternate tradition Baranzan had four sons: *Akwak, Akadon, Kanshwa,* and *Yidwang* (Asake 1982). *Adon* is omitted from this tradition. More recently Asake has included *Adon* as a son of Baranzan (Asake 1991:5); as mentioned above, the tradition that Baranzan had five sons is the most widely accepted account.

The Bajju also incorporate non-Bajju into their ethnic group. If a non-Bajju woman marries a Bajju man, their children are Bajju, given the Bajju patrilineal descent system, by which children belong to their father and his patriclan.

Ruling elders

Baranzan and the elders oversaw the wellbeing of the entire ethnic group. He, as the ruling elder (*gado*), was a political, religious, and judicial leader. The Hausa-Fulani emirates' officials, the British colonial administrators, and the Native Authority translated the term *gado* as "priest," yet this trans- lation highlighted his religious functions only and failed to recognize other functions he and the ruling elders of the other sections had within their communities. This failure to understand the Bajju religio-political struc- ture by these administrators became important during the colonial era. It contributed to the lack of recognition of the real leaders among the Bajju throughout the colonial era and eventually weakened their authority.

The ruling elder at Karyi Dibyyi was the *gado nkpang* (literally, "the ruling elder of stones"); he was the leader of all the Bajju, yet his position was that of the first among equals. He wore the skin of the leopard (*ccuk*) on his body and nothing on his head. Vansina (1990:74) states for western and central Africa, "The quintessence of leadership was the leopard." When a Bajju killed a leopard, that person brought the skin to the *gado nkpang*. If he did not have a leopard skin, he could wear the skin of the West African hartebeest, the *nnyo* or *kanki,* H. The use of the leopard skin is in line with other ethnic groups as the leopard symbolizes leadership in much of west and central Africa.[8] The second *gado* wore the skin of a goat, small calf, or whatever skin he had access to. The other elders wore whatever skins they found. Figures 2.2 and 2.3 illustrate the ruling elders of two neighboring ethnic groups, the Piti and the Chawai, wearing leopard skins.

The Anaguta, a Plateau people, also had a leader, the *Uja,* comparable to the *gado.* Diamond translated this term as "Priest Chief." He states concerning his functions in society:

> Prior to British occupation, he arbitrated disputes among clans, or villages involving witchcraft, homicide, incest or chronic feuding; the *Uja's* justice is sacred and, except in cases of witchcraft or repeated incest, is based on the principle of compromise. (1967:430)

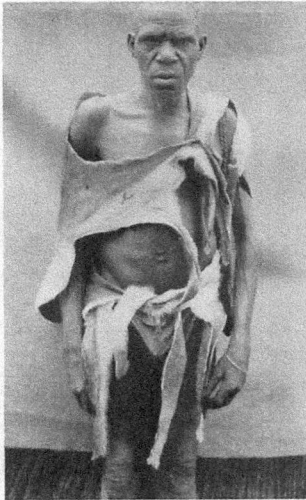

Figure 2.1. Bajju elder
(Meek 1931:105).

Figure 2.2. Piti elders with priest center, wearing a leopard skin
(Meek 1931:136).

---

[8] Another example is Mobutu Sese Seko, former head of Zaire (now DRC), who wore a leopard skin hat as a symbol of his leadership.

Figure 2.3. Chawai elders with the priest, center,
wearing a leopard skin (Meek 1931:148).

In addition to the *gado nkpang,* the Bajju had elders (*bạgado*) at other
levels within the society (see table 2.2).

Table 2.2. Elders and their units of authority

Elder	Unit of authority
Ruling elder of stones, father of the people (*gado nkpang, ạttyi ạkop*)	All Bajju
Elder of a section (*gado kwai*)	Section (*kwai*)
Elder of the village (*gado kạnkrang, gado kạpyyi*) (Sanke 1977:22)	Village (*kạnkrang*)
Elder of the clan, father of the clan (*gado sot, ạttyi nsot*)	Clan (*sot*)
Elder of the house, father of the house, man or husband of the house (*gado kạryi, ạttyi kạryi, ạntyok kạryi*)	Household, compound (*kạryi*)
Elder of the men's secret organization (*gado ạbvoi*)	Men's secret organization (*ạbvoi*)
Hunting elder (*gado kạpyyi*)	Hunting activities in each clan and village

The position of ruling elder was hereditary within the clan. Thus the *gado* of the Batadon came only from the Twan clan. This position passed to the oldest capable male, whether brother or son, within the clan upon the incapacity or death of the incumbent. In general, the Bajju preferred that a blood relationship exist between the former *gado* and the next person to occupy that position. Within the family the first son is second in command to his father, and he will succeed his father to the position of head of the family following his father's death. If the first son is not capable for any reason, the position of the next head of the household passes to the next son, and if there are no other sons, it passes to the closest male relative within the patrilineage. When there is no direct blood relative, there is more competition within the clan for this position. The position of elder was filled immediately following the death of a *gado*.

The ruling elder at Dibyyi[9] called the annual meeting of the other ruling elders from each section during the dry season. This meeting was held under a sacred tree at Dibyyi. It concerned the wellbeing of the entire ethnic group.[10] It allowed the ruling elders to meet each other and to work cooperatively. If the need arose, the ruling elder at Dibyyi could call special meetings to deal with natural disasters, locust invasions, epidemics, droughts, murder, homicide, incest, interethnic warfare, poor harvests, land disputes, a person hitting his mother or father, and any other issues not handled adequately at a lower level. In such cases the elders served as the final court of appeal. Some issues, such as murder and warfare, had to be handled at this level. The ruling elders also dealt with problems between clans and villages.

To call a meeting, the ruling elder sent messengers with a leafy branch from the locust bean tree (*kgron*) to each elder; each then cut off a branch or took some leaves. Messengers traveled along two routes:

1. Western route: Dibyyi to Azunkwa to Kanshwa to Asakwak
2. Eastern route: Dibyyi to Azansak to Akadon to Twan

The messenger delivered the message that announced the date of the meeting, and then each elder gathered the number of pebbles equal to the number of days remaining before the meeting. Each day he threw one pebble away until the date arrived for the meeting.

---

[9] Dariya (1983:1) claims that it was the ruling elder at Asakwak who called the meeting.

[10] The Anaguta had a comparable meeting about which Diamond states, "an annual ceremony that takes place under a sacred tree in Manza is attended by elders from all the villages, presided over by the Uja and his assistants" (1967:431). Reasons for calling special meetings also parallel those of the Bajju. He states, "A bad harvest, a famine, a recurrent disease, indeed, any social, natural, or physical misfortune, or a reason for thanksgiving may become the occasion for convening a special ceremony at a public shrine, under the direction of the Uja. Rainmaking is his most dramatic task" (1967:431).

When the Bajju desired to send a message other than by a messenger, they used other means. A person could call loudly from his home when he needed help; he could build a fire such that as the smoke rose, other Bajju knew that there was to be a feast there; he could put something on the road (used particularly to call men to participate in a hunt); or he could throw something at someone (used particularly when one wanted to give a gift to another person) (Asake 1991:7).

At the meeting each elder could speak, and the elder at Dibyyi spoke last. His words were those of the first among equals. He summarized the consensus of the discussion, thus presenting the consensus decision reached by the group. After this, he took his staff of office and beat the ground with it to indicate that the decisions made at this meeting were binding. No one would dare disobey a decision after the ruling elder had beaten the ground with his staff. At the end of the meeting each elder gently pulled the beard of the ruling elder of Dibyyi, while saying *gado, gado, gado,* thus blessing him (see figure 2.4). Then all the elders returned to their homes. When Baranzan was dying, he instructed his children through his son, A̱kwak, to always summon his other brothers at his grave for the annual meeting.

Figure 2.4. An elder pulling the beard of the ruling elder to bless him following the meeting (Meek 1931:81).

The ruling elders at Dibyyi, as remembered by the incumbent in 1984, beginning with the incumbent, are as follows:

1. Sanke Kahwei (see figure 2.5)
2. Asara Vonkwwat
3. Yamai Kahwei
4. Gwam Zwang
5. Atung Akoya

Asara, who died when quite old, was known to be very wise. Gwam Zwang, whose name translates as the "chief of war" or "warrior," lived up to that name as a good warrior and hunter. After one skirmish when the others involved presumed that he was dead, he eventually returned home alive. When a warrior was presumed dead, no one talked about him. The hope was that he would still return home alive. Gwam Zwang enjoyed immense popularity among his people.

Dating the above genealogy is problematic since the Bajju did not keep specific birth dates or dates when their elders reigned. However, names often represent events surrounding the birth of each person, and this can occasionally help assign birth dates. However, if one were to arbitrarily assign an average of twenty-five to thirty years' reign for each person, *Atung* would have begun his reign sometime between 1834 and 1859.[11]

The ruling elder at Dibyyi had sacred characteristics associated with his person. He had to enter a building backwards to show that his eyes were always open to watch the entire *kajju* area in order to look after its welfare (Phillip Allahmagani, personal communication). He was not to wear shoes. His hair and nails were not to be cut. In his capacity as ruling elder of the entire Bajju community, he oversaw its wellbeing and gave his blessing to people and to the community. He symbolically represented the wellbeing of the entire community. It was his responsibility to see that any transgression that might cause consequences for the entire community was adequately dealt with. The ruling elder did not go to war. Because of the taboos associated with this position, the Bajju state that he was not a free man in that he had to fulfill the requirements of those taboos.

---

[11] Because Bajju genealogies tend to be short, it is unlikely that telescoping, in which members that should be included were omitted, occurred in the above genealogy.

Figure 2.5. Sanke Kạhwei, Bajju ruling elder at Dibyyi, 1984
(Carol McKinney).

Ruling elders had political and religious authority. During the precolonial era the Hausa established the institution of chief among the Bajju and other ethnic groups in this area. Chiefs (*bạgwam*) dealt with outsiders, such as the Hausa-Fulani and later the British colonial authorities, while the ruling elders dealt with internal matters. Gradually the position and influence of the ruling elders has shifted to their becoming chiefs and advisors to chiefs of villages. The Bajju now have a chieftaincy position for the entire Bajju. It is noteworthy that the first person chosen for this position, His Royal Highness Nuhu Bature, comes from Dibyyi near Zonkwa, the site where Baranzan first settled and where his grave is located.

There is a movement to revive and update the functions of the sections (*kwai*). Leaders of the *kwai* meet to promote various community development projects. For example, during the time I was conducting research (1983–1984), the Bạtạdon met and appointed officers, including a president, vice-president, and secretary.

Functions of the Baranzan narrative

What functions does the Baranzan origins migration narrative have within the Bajju community today? It helps explain why they live where they live, what their economic resource base was (horticulture and hunting), and how they were organized. Baranzan, as their apical ancestor, symbolizes all that is good about the Bajju way of life. In this narrative Baranzan and his family moved from the Jos Plateau down into their current location. Linguistic evidence corroborates this relationship: a number of Plateau languages[12] are in the Proto-Plateau language family as are other languages in southern Kaduna State. Other groups in this area, such as the A̲gorok and A̲tyap, also claim a Plateau origin. It is unknown when various ethnic groups migrated into southern Kaduna State. It is likely that there were successive migrations of extended family groups and villages. Horticulturalists often find that as their land loses its fertility from their slash-and-burn horticulture, they must move and clear new land to farm.

Another possible scenario was that the Bajju originated from people of the emirates further north of them. However, the Hausa speak a Chadic language within the Afro-Asiatic language family while the Bajju speak a Benue-Congo language within the Niger-Congo language family. Because the languages of the Hausa and Bajju are from different language families, the Bajju are not likely related to the Hausa, who live farther north in Kaduna State, but are rather related to ethnic groups on the Jos Plateau.

Their origins narrative begins with Baranzan's migration and describes the relationship of the different sections to each other through kinship ties based on Baranzan, his sons, and their descendants. While some ethnic groups have cosmologies that describe how God created the earth and the creation of each ethnic group, I found no such narrative among the Bajju. They assert that God created the earth and mankind, but they have no story about how God did so.

When we arrived in a Bajju village in December 1968, knowledge of Baranzan was widespread, but today many young Bajju have never heard of Baranzan, nor do they know the history of their own people. In 2010 when a Bajju pastor asked the congregants in a church service if they knew who Baranzan was, the majority had never heard of him.

Summary

The traditional political structure, as presented in this chapter, was a confederacy founded by Baranzan. The presiding elders of each section of the confederacy met yearly at Dibyyi to oversee the wellbeing of the entire ethnic group. They also met to take necessary action in the event of disruptive behavior within the community.

The Bajju society was not one with a centralized hierarchical structure but rather a decentralized one with ruling elders over clans and lineages who exercised authority when necessary. Because of the relationship between the five sections, it had the potential to develop into a hierarchical structure, but by the time of colonialism, it had not done so. This type of political organization was typical of many ethnic groups in west and central

---

[12] There are also Chadic languages on the Plateau. The Mwaghavul speak a Chadic language, and the Ngas language, a language spoken just off the Plateau on the east, is also Chadic (Lewis 2015, where Mwaghavul is referred to as "Maghwavul").

Africa (Vansina 1990). Under the influences of the emirates and colonial rule, the authority of the elders was weakened, with chiefs now serving as important elders within each community. Discussion of Baranzan and the other ruling elders of the Bajju is relevant to this study because it provides the precolonial context of their culture.

3

The Men's Secret Ancestral
Organization and Small-Scale Warfare

Introduction

One evening my research colleague and I arrived at an elderly United Native African pastor's home to discuss the men's secret ancestral organization, the *abvoi*.[1] He began by stating that this topic had "strength" (*cet*). As we settled in for the discussion, the pastor's wives and children sat in adjacent rooms to listen to information that had been kept secret from them for years. Though they were in different rooms from us, they benefited from the open space between the top of the mud walls and the zinc roof, space through which sound readily traveled. They sat very quietly listening; we only became aware of their presence when they laughed at appropriate times. Then the pastor would sternly warn them that they should not be listening, a warning that fell on deaf ears for they wanted to hear the "words with strength." This discussion would never have happened in their precolonial society when this ancestral organization held so much sway over the Bajju.

The *abvoi* was considered to represent the spirits of departed ancestors on earth. Individual members were termed "seeds" or "offspring of the ancestral spirits" (*tswa abvoi*). Another name for this society was *dodo*, a

---

[1] Whereas the *abvoi* is sometimes referred to as a secret society, in Nigeria use of the term "secret society" implies human sacrifice. The *abvoi* among the Bajju did not practice human sacrifice, hence I refer to it as a secret organization.

31

Hausa word that Abraham's *Hausa Dictionary* glosses as "evil spirit" or "goblin" (1962:219). However, the term *dodo* has a wider range of meanings; it is a cover term used in northern Nigeria for masques, masquerades, and more generally the men's secret ancestral organization.

The *ạbvoi* among the Bajju is defunct; young men are no longer initiated into it nor is it celebrated. The Bajju have officially outlawed it within their territory. Occasionally a few old men will meet in one of their houses "to practice *ạbvoi*," where they reminisce about the old days and drink guinea corn beer. These men meet in homes because the *ạbvoi* shrines (*mpfu*) are no longer maintained. Men no longer receive status by belonging to *ạbvoi*, and secrets are told to women and the uninitiated without repercussions, something that previously would have brought a fine or even death within the *mpfu*. According to Kunhiyop, in 1984 only two *ạbvoi* shrines remained in the Bajju area, one at Madakiya and the other at Zonkwa (1984:62). Figure 3.1 shows a Chawai shrine, which is similar to what the Bajju had.

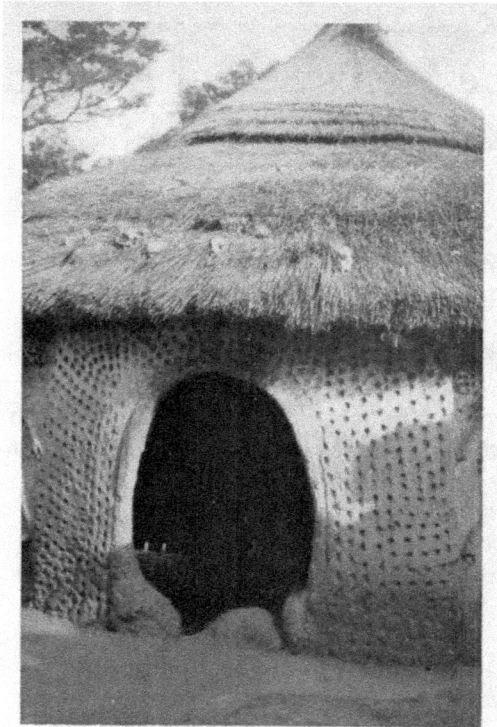

Figure 3.1. Chawai shrine (Meek 1931:154).

Because the *ạbvoi* no longer functions, much of the material presented here is based on the recall of elderly people. However, since it was significant in Bajju pre-Christian religion, its discussion is important for understanding that time period, its opposition to Christianity, and what happened when the Bajju adopted Christianity.

Some of the excessive demands of the *abvoi* contributed to its demise, as those excesses became burdensome on the population. Even before the entry of missionaries into this area, some had ceased to participate in *abvoi*. For example, in 1914, Kirkpatrick, a British colonial administrator, wrote, "It is a favourable sign however that the chiefs of Madakia [Madakiya] and Dan Ata, of their own accord, refuse to take any part in these proceeding [sic] [the *Dodo* cult], which they know to be humbug" (NAK K 2985). By this time other villages had also refused to have the *abvoi* in them.

From a Bajju perspective, the purpose of the *abvoi* was to maintain social control and discipline, particularly to keep women and children under control. Another main function was to oppose stealing, fighting, and drinking unclean water. The *dodo* very commonly killed men, but did not kill women and children. Men killed within the *abvoi* shrine were buried under the floor of the shrine. If a man continued to violate the rules of *abvoi* and told its secrets to women and the uninitiated, he might be killed. The *abvoi* also flogged stubborn people.

The male elders within an area or clan who belonged to the *abvoi* directed events within the community and required women and children to meet their demands. This organization had political, religious, and judicial functions.

The English adjective Bajju most often apply to the *abvoi* is "harsh." This organization maintained an environment of distrust and fear between men and women, including the husband-wife relationship. Isichei noted that Conant, who studied the *dodo* among the Dass on the Jos Plateau, made the point that this organization did not confer the social benefits conventionally ascribed to religion within a functionalist perspective. She quotes Conant as saying, "Dodo religion…is extremely disruptive of any orderly march of events; dodo religion offers little peace of mind…it cuts across ties of friendship and affection" (Conant as quoted in Isichei 1982:24–25). Conant felt that the Dass *dodo* religion was a relevant factor in the persistence of their culture and society (Conant 1960:12). His thinking represents a functionalist perspective, which views most aspects of a society that continue over time as contributing to the persistence of culture and hence having a positive benefit. This was certainly not an insider perspective of Bajju men and women when asked about the *abvoi*.

Origins of *abvoi*

In interviews, each Bajju person I talked with about this organization agreed that the Bajju adopted the *abvoi* comparatively recently; however, they did

not agree on the source of its adoption or exactly when this occurred. One
tradition holds that a slave from a different ethnic group introduced *abvoi* to
the Bajju. Other traditions state that *abvoi* came from Miango, from people
east of them, or from the Bakulu (Bayinkrum, J.), who live north of them.
One source claimed that *abvoi* first came to Adwan and from there it spread
throughout the Bajju area. Most agreed that they borrowed the masquerade
dancer *agyashak* from the Gyong, their southeastern neighbors. Clearly, a
number of ethnic groups adopted a similar men's secret ancestral organization, probably during a relatively similar time period. The Hausa also
had the *dodo* that was similar in function and practices to that adopted by
minority groups in southern Kaduna State.

Leadership

The Bajju called the local *abvoi* leader the elder of the *abvoi*; (*gado abvoi*,
J.; the *magajin dodo*, H.) or alternatively, the chief of *abvoi* (*agwam abvoi*).
This man could be either the ruling elder of the village or another person
whom the ruling elder appointed to *abvoi* leadership. If the ruling elder
was elderly or sickly, and for that reason was unable to organize the *abvoi*
adequately, he could appoint an elder to oversee this work. A man in this
position obtained it either through appointment or inheritance. If there was
no capable person within the household of the *gado abvoi* to replace him following his death, the ruling elder of the village appointed a capable person
from within the clan of the former *gado abvoi*.

The *gado abvoi* had the responsibility to provide for the upkeep of the
abvoi shrine, oversee initiation of male youths into it, produce the sound of
abvoi, provide medical care for those to be treated in this shrine, set and
extract fines for transgressions of *abvoi* rules, and in general was in charge
of anything associated with this society and its influence in the community.

Initiation

Each dry season boys and young men were initiated into the *abvoi*. Their
initiation consisted of three stages: separation, transition, and reincorpo-
ration into Bajju society as adults, a sequence typical of rites of passage
(Turner 1972:338–347). This sequence involved initiates being metaphori-
cally "eaten" by the *abvoi*, who "vomited" them at the end of the initiation
ritual. The Bajju then reincorporated the initiates with their new status as
members of the *abvoi*; they were no longer classified with the women and
children, but with the men.

When the elders and other members of the *abvoi* felt that young men
were ready, they initiated them. Occasionally men decided not to initiate a
young man who was known to be a troublemaker or who talked too much,

until he was more mature. For some this meant waiting even until after marriage. Bajju elders felt that this was for the person's own benefit, because the punishment for divulging *abvoi* secrets could be death. Therefore, they deemed it wise to wait to initiate youths until they felt they could be trusted to keep the *abvoi* secrets. A youth would not know when he was to be taken for initiation; rather the elders would come in the evening and select those they chose to initiate.

Some youths from families of *abvoi* members accompanied their relatives into the *abvoi* shrine while still quite young (for example, seven or eight years old), and others entered when older. Boys in both categories took the *abvoi* oath of secrecy. Chronically ill youths comprised another category of youths who were taken into the shrine while young. Boys taken in while still young were termed *ssuk* meaning "to renovate" or "to make new again."

The elders took the youths in the evening (for example, at 8 or 9 p.m.) for initiation during the month of April or May. When first brought in, the elders instructed the youth to not lift their eyes to look around but rather to lie down on the floor. They then covered the initiates with leaves of the shea tree (*masham*), leaves that symbolized the *abvoi* and that the Bajju used in a number of different situations. Brothers and fathers of initiates made sure that their relatives were thoroughly covered for protection. Youths with no relatives present to look after their interests while undergoing initiation were to be pitied as they were dealt with more severely. The men then beat the initiates while the leader of the shrine (*magaji,* H.) blew the sound of *abvoi* (see below). The men beat troublemakers more severely at this time. The men also took thorns and pricked the initiates while telling the youths that the spirits were doing it. They told the initiates to catch the spirits, and when they were unable to do so, the men beat them again.

While the initiates lay prone on the ground, the men occasionally questioned them by asking who they had "eaten" or committed activities against in the spiritual realm that caused the misfortune, illness, evil, or death of other people. They might accuse a boy of being a witch (*akut*) and ask him a question such as "Aren't you the one responsible for ——'s death?" (see chapter 6 for more details on *nkut*).

During the initiation those outside the shrine heard the cry of *Zabya,* the wife of *abvoi*.[2] An *abvoi* member produced her cry by pulling a stick (for example, the shaft end of an arrow) over a large drum with wet hands. Her sound indicated that the *abvoi* was "swallowing" the initiates. They also heard the sound of *abvoi*, a sound that people heard indistinctly. The *abvoi* sound came from a man speaking into the small dry black *agumkpap* seed (the pod of the *Oncoba spinosa,* L., tree that grows near streams) within the shrine. They pierced this small black apple-sized seed, making two small holes that they covered with spider webs; it served as a resonator. The man

---

[2] Kunhiyop (2005:80) identified Riyam as the wife of *abvoi*.

spoke in a muffled and faraway-sounding voice, and thus his message had to be interpreted by a spokesman, the *madauci ạbvoi,* so that women and uninitiated youths could understand. His voice represented the voice of the deceased ancestors. As he spoke he rebuked disobedient children; he sought to coerce women into complete submission; and he ordered guinea corn beer, cooked meat, and beans from the women who were outside the shrine (Asake 1991:27).

Women and initiates also heard the sound produced by the bull-roarer (*kpạta*), which was constructed either from a piece of palm wood or a piece of iron with a hole pierced in one end. A man inserted a string into the hole and whirled this object around and around. If by accident the iron cut the string and the piece of iron flew off, it could kill the person it hit. When the women outside the shrine heard these sounds, they ran away. Initiates, too, before being told the source of these sounds, were fearful, especially when lying prone covered with leaves and hearing the noises produced in the same room with them.

After these frightening experiences, the elders told the initiates the ạbvoi secrets. They also showed them the large, hard black seed (*ạgumkpap*) with a spider web covering two holes that they blew to produce the ạbvoi sound. They then had the initiates blow the *ạgumkpap* seed. If a youth blew it well the first time, he would likely receive another beating as the men would accuse such a youth of already knowing how they produced the ạbvoi sound, knowledge that was forbidden to uninitiated youths.

They then required youths to drink a small calabash of guinea corn beer with the blood of a cock mixed into it. The blood came from one of the cocks that each initiate was required to pay to join. Next, the men warned the initiates very sternly that under no circumstances were they to reveal the ạbvoi secrets to women and children. The penalty for a breach of that prohibition was death within the ạbvoi shrine, death that they spoke of as being "swallowed" by ạbvoi. The initiates were then required to take an oath of secrecy while jumping over a knife or sword. They swore that under no circumstances would they reveal the ạbvoi secrets.

The initiates spent the rest of the night receiving instruction inside the shrine. One goal of that educational process was to produce youths who were responsible and reliable members of Bajju society. During this time some elders performed wonders. For example, one young man described seeing an older man put fire into his mouth, close his mouth, and then open it again with the fire still visible in it. He also described seeing a dead chicken and being asked what he saw. His answer had to be "*ạbvoi*", and until he gave that answer he was beaten.

In the morning *Zạbya* "vomited" the youths. The elders told the youths to act very weak as the men led them to the stream to be bathed. The ordeal of being swallowed and then vomited by *Zạbya* caused their weakness. The crowd outside heard the ạbvoi sound telling them that the children of ạbvoi were coming out. After their bath, the Bajju poured oil over them, which served as evidence that they had been vomited, then their weakness left them, and they started dancing. The women ululated (*yyuk*) in greeting, thus expressing their excitement and joy because of the new status of the initiates as *ąbvoi* members. Women and children waited for the new initiates at the cleared enclosure (*kątyekon*) that had been prepared for this occasion.

Whereas the initiation described above occurred in a twenty-four-hour period, previously initiation lasted one to two weeks. When youths began going to school, that length of time became untenable.

All the youths initiated together comprised an age set. Those in the same age set have a friendly, familiar relationship with one another. A man feels gladness and joy at seeing one of his age mates, his *cei*. Even as adults, age mates engage in friendly joking and wrestling. Initiates emerged with a sense of unity, belonging, and solidarity with other Bajju.

Following initiation and puberty young men could marry and begin their families. However, as mentioned previously, occasionally the elders allowed a young man to marry before initiation. This was for the youth's benefit.

Though circumcision frequently occurs as part of initiation in many parts of the world, it was not part of the Bajju initiation. The Bajju have a barber circumcise their boys between three and five years of age without any accompanying ritual.

Though initiation through the *ąbvoi* organization occurred in the past, this is no longer the case since the Bajju have officially renounced the *ąbvoi*. While I do not have the exact date when this occurred, I know it occurred after 1984, though in practice the *ąbvoi* organization no longer functioned prior to its being renounced. The functions fulfilled by the *ąbvoi* at initiation, such as learning some of the history of the Bajju, how to relate to the opposite sex, and the facts of life, need to be incorporated in some context for the young. One possibility would be to have classes prior to baptism for the youth, or to have catechism classes for the young prior to confirmation, as occurs in some denominations. What is taught would have to be developed specifically for the Bajju, including religious teaching and other important aspects of adult life. A second possibility would be to have such a class in primary school. Perhaps one could be developed for the boys and another one for the girls.

Celebrations

Ąbvoi celebrations occurred during the dry season when people were free from farming activities. These celebrations also were held for those elders who died and were buried during the preceding rainy season. They centered around the *ąbvoi* shrine and the nearby sacred forested area. Both locations were off limits to women and children. In the sacred forest men dressed in the woven grass masquerade costume of ạkusak, the dancing dodo. In the forest men also wove the small ropes (ntswandyik, literally, 'spirit ropes') that they distributed to women in the village during a mourning period (see figures 3.2 and 3.3). Women extended the length of these ropes, then wore them until the celebration at the end of the mourning period when they gave them to ạbvoi. This mourning period could last as long as four months. During those four months the women went to neighboring villages to beg for grain. People, and especially relatives, would not refuse to give some grain, which was used to make beer for the celebration that was held at the end of the mourning period. During this period women were not allowed to stay in other compounds or villages overnight, unless they had traveled too far to make it home that night. Women were not allowed to pound grain at night. If visitors came at night, the young men were called to pound the grain that was used to make food for them. At the end of this period they constructed an enclosure around the ạbvoi shrine. Women made beer on different days so that the celebration could last for as long as a month with different women providing brewed beer each day.

While wearing these ropes, the ạbvoi forbade women from leaving their current marriages. In this patrilineal patrilocal society, if divorce occurs, it is the women who leave.

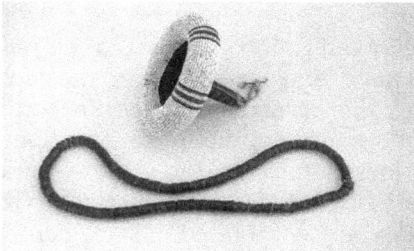

Figures 3.2. and 3.3. Spirit ropes (ntswandyik) (Norris McKinney).

In order to hold ạbvoi celebrations and to continue them, men imposed fines on individuals, particularly on women. These were sometimes for legitimate offenses against societal rules and regulations, but at other times they were for frivolous reasons so that the men could continue celebrating. These fines consisted of goats, chickens, beans, guinea corn beer, and other cooked food.

Masquerades

Masquerades represented the spirits that appeared as part of the ạbvoi cele-brations. Each masquerade was paired with another, its spouse. Ạkusak, the dancing dodo, was the husband of ạgyashak; and Dankpari was the husband of Zạbya. The Bajju borrowed ạgyashak and ạkusak from the Gyong, their southeastern neighbors. As a result these appeared mostly in the southern Bajju area.

A horn blower blew the musical horn made from the bushbuck, the *abyo,* in the morning before the dancing masquerade was to appear that evening (see chapter 5 for further information on horn blowing). In that way he announced that the *Akusak* would dance that evening (see figure 3.4). In the southern Bajju area *Agyashak,* also a dancing *dodo,* appeared together with him. Since *Akusak* wore a woven grass outfit, men sprinkled water on him with shea tree leaves to cool him. The *Akusak* danced with women; he also disciplined them by beating them.

Figure 3.4. Bajju masquerade, the *Akusak,* originally borrowed from the Gyong. This picture was taken at a New Year's Day celebration (Norris McKinney).

Zabya, whose voice sounded at the initiation, led the singing of *abvoi* songs. The name of this masquerade was borrowed from Hausa. The word *zabiya,* H., means "a woman who leads singing." However, among the Bajju it was men who led the singing through *Zabya.* She was never satisfied, but she continued to request beer and other food from the people. She always accompanied her husband *Dankpari,* the furious ancestral spirit. People ran when they heard his angry voice, a voice that sounded like that of a lion's roar. They believed that he killed people who came near him. He ate the residue of guinea corn after beer was brewed from it. In Unguwar Rimi

Dankpari went along the streambed, beginning behind the senior primary school and proceeded towards the village. Although people heard his voice, they did not see him as *Dankpari* did not wear special masquerade clothing, as did Akusak and Agyashak.

Social control

Men exercised social control through the abvoi. Following initiation, youths joined mature men in watching women and uninitiated youths. The initiated reported to the elders any transgressions of abvoi rules committed by women or children. The elders then punished them through the masquerades mentioned above. An abvoi elder would engage initiated youths to accompany women on trips. When they returned, they reported on what had occurred on the trip, including any wrongdoings the women committed. Men used that knowledge to intimidate women, perhaps beat them, and fine them for their offenses. When the masquerades came out, they would tell about those deeds done while the women were away. By having initiates report to them, men perpetuated the myth that the abvoi was everywhere and saw all that everyone did, and thus abvoi was made out to be omniscient and omnipresent. Women and children could not escape their watchfulness, and they would be punished for any transgressions. Consequently, the sound of the abvoi prior to the masquerades coming out in the evening struck fear into women. One woman reported that she would literally start to shake when she heard the abvoi sounds.

Warfare

He who invites war, the war will capture him. (Bajju proverb)

Warfare between ethnic groups in this area involved the abvoi. For example, Bajju kept the skulls of their human victims from other ethnic groups within the abvoi shrine, skulls which they acquired during war. They used them for drinking guinea corn beer. Reasons for warfare included boundary disputes, killing a person in retaliation for his actions, hunting disagreements, disputes over women, and general animosity.

Peace alternated with small-scale warfare. Times of peace occurred during the wet season when people farmed, while small-scale warfare tended to occur during the dry season. Groups involved included the Bajju, the Agorok, the Ayap, Bakontswam/Fantswam (Kafanchan, H.), Attakar, Asholio, and Bakulu, as well as other related ethnic groups. Usual enemies were adjacent neighbors, including Bajju who lived in a different section (*kwai*). Although these groups engaged in warfare, intermarriage also occurred between them. However, the Bajju did not fight with the Gyong because of the reciprocal relationship they had with them in which they accepted each other's exiles who had committed homicide. Table 3.1 lists Bajju sections together with each group's traditional enemy.

Different ethnic groups stereotyped each other in rather uncomplimentary terms. The Bajju considered the Atyap as thieves who engaged in nighttime robbery from the Bajju. The Bajju themselves were viewed as thieves by the Ham (Jaba, H.), their southern neighbors. They also thought that the Bajju were very wicked. But, at the same time, the Ham state concerning the Bajju, "We play with them." The Bajju viewed the Agorok as fearless headhunters of short stature. Conversely, the Agorok considered the Bajju to be of large stature. And the Bajju viewed marriage with Gyong and Ham as unstable, while at the same time they viewed them as friends. These stereotypes are in decline today.

Table 3.1. Bajju sections and their traditional enemies

Bajju section—*kwai*	Traditional enemy—*grendwan*
Bayinhwan	Bada[a] (Ham; Jaba, H.), Bakontswam/ Fantswam (Kafanchan, H.)
Bayintsok and Bayindwan	Batyap (Atyap; Katab, Kataf, H.)
Batadon and Bayindwan	Bagro (Agorok; Kagoro, H.)

[a] The *ba*- prefix in table 3.1 indicates the Bajju name for each ethnic group, with their own name and the Hausa name for them in parentheses. The *ba*- prefix is used for the noun class people are in.

Bajju banded together to defend themselves against a common enemy, for example, the Hausa and Fulani who were from the emirates. The Bajju distinguished between the nomadic cattle-herding Fulani, with whom they maintained friendly relations, and raiders from the Hausa-Fulani emirates. Pastoral Fulani regularly pastured their cattle on Bajju land. Bajju enjoyed friendly relations with some Hausa, such as traders who traveled along a couple of trade routes and who sold them salt, potash, and other commodities that were not available locally, though occasionally they raided these caravans.

While the Bajju and the other groups had various accepted conventions of their small-scale warfare, the Hausa and Fulani from the emirates did not follow those conventions. Rather they would come without warning to ambush people and take slaves. This occurred each dry season. Consequently, there developed a deep animosity towards the emirate warriors.

Bajju blew the large musical horn from the West African hartebeest, the *ajjwa,* to call men to war. Men slept on their left sides so that when the call to war came, they could quickly grab their weapons and be ready to defend themselves. When getting his weapons, a warrior might also drink some beer with medicine in it, medicine he believed would make him invincible to arrows. When a man heard the *ajjwa,* he ran to get his weapons and started acting like a hunter by moving cautiously and stealthily, crouching, hiding behind trees, and so forth; this posturing, termed *dimyak,* applied to activities in warfare and hunting. In this way he prepared himself for action.

Also while eating, people did not engage in conversation; otherwise, if the call for war came, they might not hear it. They would then have to face the enemy unprepared.

Elders did not sanction each outbreak of warfare. When they disapproved of a skirmish, they stood around saying, "*Yi ryok, yi ryok, yi ryok...*" ("You stop, you stop, you stop..."). They did so until they convinced the younger warriors to stop.

War could also break out in the context of a drinking gathering. Brandt described an outbreak as follows:

> For example, a villager from X village would enter Y village with which X was at peace. A subsequent beer-drink might lead to the decapitation of the visitor. After a day or so X village would inquire after the missing man, the circumstances would be revealed, and X would then issue a challenge to Y and a time and place would be fixed for the fight. Such affairs seem always to have taken place in the bush and no attempt seems to have been made by one village to destroy, capture, or despoil the other. (NAK ZarProf 312 9, 1939)

If in interethnic warfare a Bajju killed a man, he did not take the corpse. He took the head of his enemy from another ethnic group. If a Bajju killed a non-Bajju in war, the other Bajju praised him. When Bajju killed an enemy warrior, the first Bajju to put his hand into the mouth of the victim got the head. The warrior first took the head to the home of the *gado* and from there to the *abvoi* shrine. On that day and the next, they celebrated with dancing, feasting, drinking, and horn blowing.

After celebrating, they cleaned out the skull either through placing it in the river for a while or by burying it in the ground where the people of the underground world (*banyet yabyen*) lived. After time allotted for decomposition, they cleaned the skull, then took it to the *abvoi* shrine where it joined other skulls of slain male enemies. The skull served as a drinking cup within the shrine, or it could be brought out during a mourning celebration, the *kanak.* During the mourning celebration, they stuffed skulls with leaves from the locust bean tree.

The Bajju and other neighboring ethnic groups gave praise titles to successful headhunters. Table 3.2 lists praise titles together with their respective enemy ethnic group.

Table 3.2. Bajju praise titles and ethnic groups of victims

Bajju praise title	Ethnic group of slain enemy
Wantsot	Bagro (Agorok; Kagoro, H.); and Bakontswam (Kafanchan, H.)
Wansham	Batyap (Atyap; Katab, Kataf, H.)
Wanshan	Bada (Ham; Jaba, H.)
Wanzuk	Babyruk (Kamantan, H.)

Other ethnic groups in the area had similar praise titles. For example, an Atyap or an Agorok person who killed a Bajju received the praise title *Waliyak*.

When Bajju contemplated initiating warfare, they first consulted a diviner (*abvok*) to inquire whether they would find their victims and do well in their efforts. A diviner would consult his or her stone or cowries to see whether their mission would be successful. The forecast determined whether or not they set out to engage the enemy.

If, in a skirmish, the enemy shot and perhaps killed a Bajju warrior, other warriors upon returning home said nothing concerning this person. To tell his wife that he had been killed in warfare meant that there would be no possibility of his returning home alive. As mentioned earlier, the Bajju believed that, if they remained quiet, some people had the power and ability to come back to life after being slain and that they would then return home and recover.

Bajju had varying success in war. In one instance, they successfully conducted a raid against the Agorok. Temple stated,

> Until the beginning of the nineteenth century they had no Chief, but at that time the Kaje inflicted a severe defeat upon them and extracted an annual tribute of two slaves.... However that may be, the Kaje did not long receive their tribute, but every year subjected the defaulters to a slave raid. (Temple 1922:188)

She continued by stating that the Agorok also slave-raided and collected heads. She noted that no man was fully accredited as a man until he took a human head or obtained that of a monkey, hartebeest, gazelle, or antelope (Temple 1922:188–189).

If warfare became excessive or if it continued into the rainy season when men needed to be out in their fields farming, Bajju had to establish peace. They did so by sending an old, respected woman to the *gado* of the enemy group. Because of the enmity between the two groups, they dared not send a man or he would have been killed; she also risked being mistakenly killed. The peace emissary brought a small calabash of beer and asked for peace. To end warfare, they took a verbal oath (*Ba sswa nak baryat kanu ba,* literally, 'They took an oath with the speech of the mouth').

One effect of the endemic small-scale warfare was that there were no markets in this area prior to colonialism. The Bajju either produced what they needed or purchased it from neighbors or itinerant Hausa traders. They tended to live on top of the rock outcroppings for safety. From their high perch they could see any who came to engage them in warfare.

To do medicine

Currently there is a modern version *abvoi* ritual termed *yya dikan* 'to do medicine'. If someone wants something, they take a hen, guinea corn beer, and medicine. The medicine is put into the beer and onto the hen. The purpose of this ritual is similar to what was done during the time of *abvoi*. Women have to cook one hen for each boy in the house and provide guinea corn beer. They state that they make the way for *abvoi* (*ba tyyi abvoi ryen*). While a few are involved in this ritual, the vast majority of Bajju are Christians and want nothing to do with an updated version of *abvoi*.

Summary

Bajju elders exercised authority through the men's ancestral organization. When young men joined this cult, their status changed from the inferior position of women and children to that of responsible adult men.

The *abvoi* is basically defunct in Bajju society today. The colonial administration and Christian missionaries were opposed to it. This resulted in the *abvoi* being under assault as a way to govern the Bajju. As mentioned before, the Bajju elders have now officially outlawed it. The *abvoi* enforced some of the Bajju unwritten rules; the next chapter deals explicitly with those rules.

4

Bajju Legal System

In any society people have patterned ways in which power, authority, and laws, whether written or oral, are used to coordinate and regulate behavior. Further, there are customary procedures for making decisions, resolving conflict, and maintaining social control. The forms of most political systems are more or less effective in accomplishing the important goals they were set up to handle.

Although it was never written, the Bajju had a legal system that served them well during the precolonial era. Some aspects of this legal system continue into the present even though the Bajju are incorporated within the modern nation state of Nigeria and the wider global community. This system served to cleanse the community of the feared consequences of transgressions, as well as punish the offender and then incorporate him back into society. It included a series of oaths with serious threatened consequences for perjury.

In the Bajju legal system and even today the person's significance is related to society. Kunhiyop asserts:

> Bajju concept of *atsatsak* (good) and *akatuk* (evil) may be understood in relationship of the individual and the society. *Atsatsak* means anything that is good or anything which the society sanctions as good. *Akatuk, asshishik* or *abbyibyi* can mean what is ugly, bad, evil, or sinful. The meaning is determined by the context. For example, *asshishik ayin* means an ugly person. *Asshishik azashiya* means a terrible or an evil

45

thing has come upon us. In the latter case, *asshishik* refers
to death which is an evil or terrible thing.... The conception
of good or evil is viewed through the lens of the community.
(2005:91)

Legal system

Bajju society had a defined set of legal sanctions to deal with those who
broke societal rules. Today there are three ways to resolve conflicts. They
may be resolved through (1) Bajju customary practices, (2) the government
courts, which were established initially during the colonial era, and (3) the
churches. Government courts tend to rely on shari'a law which non-Muslim
Bajju consider inappropriate, so they avoid them if at all possible. Cases
that involve conflicts between ethnic groups rather than internal conflicts
between individual Bajju tend to go to the courts. For example, if Fulani
cattle eat the crops of a Bajju farmer, he might take the problem to court.

The Bajju legal system was and continues to be closely intertwined with
their religion, both traditional and Christian. The ruling elder at Dibyyi,
as the religious and political leader, oversaw the wellbeing of the Bajju
community and gave it his blessing. He dealt with offenses that were not
adequately handled at the village level.

There were a set of fines, penalties, and even death or exile to punish offenders, cleanse the community of ritual danger, and reincorporate
offenders. The penalty depended upon the severity of the transgression. The
Bajju set a fine (*tyyi gbang*) or took other appropriate measures for the following transgressions:

1. Murder
2. Unintentional homicide, manslaughter
3. Adultery within the extended family and clan
4. Incest
5. Theft
6. Revealing the secrets of the men's ancestral organization
7. Pouring guinea corn beer (*nkwwa*) on the ground, an offense against the
   ancestors (*babvoi*)
8. Disrespecting, abusing, or hitting one's parent(s)
9. A woman removing a door or window frame, an action she might take
   if her husband mistreated her
10. Drunkenness that caused trouble
11. Disrespecting senior persons

The elders of all the sections (*kwai*) met for these and any other transgressions that disrupted society. For less serious transgressions the elders
imposed a fine of a pot of beer and/or a red or white cock; a black cock
was unacceptable because black symbolizes impurity or filthiness. Red

represents sin, while white symbolizes purity. For more serious offenses, such as adultery and incest, they imposed a fine of a male goat (*karom*).

Confession (*tun kanu*) and repentance for wrongdoing by the offender were necessary to cleanse the community of the consequences of the trespass. Kunhiyop wrote:

> If a person was suspected of a wrong deed and had refused to confess it even after he has been confronted, he was asked to sit with his bare buttocks on *akukwai/akeket nkpang* (very rough stone). He will sit on it until he can no longer bear the pain and consequently he *tun kanu,* which means that the truth was forced through pain from his mouth. *Tun kanu* simply means that one has completely said the truth and promises never to repeat that wrong deed again. *Sswa batwak* (licking of ashes) means repenting of some evil deed. The person tasted the ashes and spoke thus, *ka bana nwurwang dichuwa ti ba kan tung ajin i, da ma nwurang* (Just as it is detestable and unthinkable to attempt to swallow spit, may the attempt to repeat what I have just done be like the spit I am about to spit). He then spat the ashes out of his mouth. (2005:88–89)

If a person did something wrong, the elders passed judgment that the individual sit on the stones of judgment from sunrise to sunset with no clothes on. People came to see the person who was undergoing this type of judgment. Reasons for this type of judgment included gossip, quarreling, laziness or refusal to work, stealing, or going after other men's wives. When a person confessed his wrongdoing, he paid a fine and was otherwise let go. It was a type of ordeal to encourage a person to admit his wrongdoing. Children could also be threatened—if they were not good, they would have to sit on those stones. Every village had such a place with stones of judgment.

Repercussions

Murder
If an individual deliberately murdered another person, the elders met to impose the death penalty. They carried out this sentence by poisoning at a location near the village of Asakwak.

Homicide
If a person committed homicide unintentionally, the elders imposed exile, usually for one to two years. The Bajju tied a small calabash around the offender's neck and led him into exile. The offender spent this exile among the Gyong on the southeast side or with the Angan on the northwest side, one of two neighboring ethnic groups. If they sentenced him to exile among

the Gyong, they led him from Dibyyi through Asakwak to Gyong. The person farmed for the Gyong while living in exile (NAK 2985, 1914). His hosts gave him food while he completed his sentence. His wife or wives and family did not accompany him. The Gyong or Angan supported this person because of the reciprocal relationship they had with the Bajju, who, when the need arose, supported a Gyong or Angan person who had similarly committed homicide. At the end of the exile period, Bajju elders brought him back. When he returned, they blew horns because of the death that had occurred. When they first brought the exile back, they shaved his head, then sacrificed a horse. The animal was killed, usually through strangling or beating to death, as a means of cleansing the offender and the community of the effects of the transgression. They followed this sacrifice with a cleansing ritual (*ajrang*). They reasoned that if they did not fine the person or kill the animal, the curse that resulted from the transgression could come back upon him, his family and clan, or even upon the entire community. After he returned he was reincorporated into Bajju society. However, the stigma of the offense remained. Many people would not like to drink from the same calabash of beer with such a person; however, there were no prohibitions against eating or drinking with him.

Adultery and incest

If a man committed adultery within the extended family or clan, both the offender and the woman's husband were cleansed. If both men were not treated ritually for the offense, and if one of them became ill and the other man came to greet him, the Bajju believed one of the two men would die suddenly. Or if one of the two men had a cut and some of his blood spilled onto the ground and the other man stepped on it, one of the two men would die. The offender had to pay a fine of beer and either a horse or a ram, though the usual fine was beer and a black ram. He also provided a white fowl. They first gave the offender and the woman's husband the excrement of a black dog mixed with water to drink. The rationale was that a filthy act could only be neutralized by a similar filthy treatment. After drinking this mixture, they slaughtered the ram and removed his testicles. These they hung around the offender's neck or tied around his head and then required him to walk around naked so the people could see him. The rationale was that this person had acted like a male goat, an animal that the Bajju knew would have intercourse indiscriminately, even with its own mother. The goat symbolized promiscuity. Kato added that:

> A long rope is tied round his waist which is held by a man of almost his same age. The offender is asked to lead a long procession from house to house to all the compounds in the agnatic [patrilineal] lineage. When he enters each compound he shouts *karom a ya bayyik* (a billy goat is greeting all of you). Next, the blood of the billy goat which has

been collected in a piece of broken pot (*cicyi*) is taken to the *ǫbvoi* house where it is smeared on the walls of the hut and the sides of its doorways. Some is smeared on the sides of every hut in the offender's compound. The meat of the goat is shared by most elderly members. The priest of the unit will make a speech condemning the act, then beat his staff of office on the floor with the words *kadi kapuwon she kapunwun kadi zibu howok takai a katuk ani ba* 'today is the first and the last. The act must never be repeated again'. (1974:183–184)

Kunhiyop adds:

The ancestors are asked to forgive and forget the act. The offender is asked to provide beer and meat to the elders on behalf of the ancestors. The senior priest drinks his beer and gives some to the offender to reassure him that he has been forgiven. (2005:86)

Following the procession though the community, the elders singed the white fowl. The smoke from this served to ward off evil forces. Following the ruling elder's pronouncement, this act of producing smoke from the fowl, the *ajrang* 'rinsing' or 'cleansing', cleansed the community of the transgression. They then sacrificed the fowl and smeared its blood on the door frames of the woman's hut in order to send the evil spirit away that had caused her to engage in this action. The red blood represented power over sin. Thus it was used to send away evil spirits. The Bajju treated incest and adultery so harshly because they believed that such acts might result in outbreaks of smallpox, plague, other illnesses, famine, or even death within the community. No penalty was assessed against the woman involved, as her status was similar to that of a child.

Temple (1922:194) stated that adultery, like murder, was punishable by death or banishment, adding, "In the case of adultery the injured man could demand the death of both the guilty parties, otherwise they were banished for life, being treated as dogs and fed with scraps out of broken vessels until they were drummed out of the place by old women" (Temple 1922:195).

However, my data contradict this contention. My respondents stated that this was never the case. Further, in the event of adultery, the Bajju punished the man involved, but not the woman as Temple stated. She may be referring to adultery committed outside the extended family or clan. In that case the man might be beaten to death.

From the above description, notice that they had effective means of dealing with transgressions of societal norms. The confederacy was sufficiently centralized that it could take action to maintain law and order within Bajju society.

Today the Christian church is against sacrifice. Their position is that Christ was the final sacrifice for humankind's sins; therefore, other sacrifices are no longer needed. In the case of adultery or incest within the family, the church is not against stripping the man naked such that he feels ashamed of what he has done.

Abusing and disrespecting one's parents

To abuse or disrespect one's parents or seniors was considered very serious. Kunhiyop stated:

> Disrespect to seniors or parents were considered very serious offenses. To strike one's parents or insult them are types of behavior which are sanctioned by parents' powers to curse their children. Withdrawal of a curse is called *sswa batwak* (drinking ashes). In order to cleanse the evil, one not only confessed and asked for forgiveness from his/her parents, he also had to make a special sacrifice. If the apology is accepted, the son is asked to pay bang (a token fine). This always includes a fowl and a goat. White ashes are then brought from a fireplace. The father or mother, depending on who was provoked and offended, stands facing east (the direction of [the] Bajju's origin). After expressing regrets for what was uttered and promising not to repeat it, he or she licks a bit of the ashes and then stamps the rest under his or her right feet [foot], (right feet symbolizes the right attitude or action) with the words, *kadi kapuwon sai kapuwan, akatuk ayuwa njing* (Today is the first and last). The curse is today removed and buried. Licking the ashes symbolizes making cool what was previously hot. (2005:88)

Charms

Diviners made charms. They were made in various ways and treated differently depending on the purpose they were to be used for. The charms had the roots of trees mixed with the fat of some animal, such as the python. A piece of smooth leather was wrapped around and sewed together with strings. After charms were made, they were frequently put into the ground for a week. They were then worn around the waist. Young children wore them around their ankles.

Charms were used for protection, wealth, help in fighting, help in court, and so on. Men often wore charms. One man remembered that his father had several charms that he wore around his waist to protect himself. Each month his father rubbed his charms with fat. He believed that if he had not done so, they would have been made ineffective. He warned others never to touch his charms. He particularly did not want a woman to do so. If she did so, it would have made his charms ineffective. With the coming of Christianity, the use of charms has declined.

Oaths

A further way to maintain law and order was through oaths. An oath is "a promise or affirmation, usually calling on a divine authority to punish the oath taker in case of perjury" (Winick 1977:387). Winick further states that an oath for some people is like a self-curse with almost magical potency. It is a solemn promise in which a person attests that his or her statement is true, or that he or she is determined to keep a promise. Often an oath includes some statement of the possible consequences if the person's statement is found to be untrue or if the person does not keep his or her promise. The Bajju used oaths extensively, and some continue to do so today. Swearing and oath-taking served to discourage people from behavior disruptive of society.

There are two verbs in Jju that relate to oaths: *sshi* and *sswa*. *Sshi* translates as "to swear," while *sswa* translates as "to take an oath" (*sswa nak* 'to take an oath' or literally 'to drink an oath'). They form a continuum, with swearing used for less serious issues and taking an oath for more serious ones. Oaths are sworn on items in frequent use by the one who swears. Previously, no one could make another person take an oath; rather, it was an action that a person took on his or her own initiative. Today taking an oath occurs only within a court context. It is an action that others make an individual take, or a person may choose to do on his or her own in court.

A common expression people use to indicate that what they are saying is true is *karyong ami* 'it is true'. One person stated that the Bajju began to use this expression in the late 1940s or early 1950s. If *karyong* does not work in terms of proving that what one asserts is true, then a person may swear, and finally he or she may use the more serious form of taking an oath.

In some ways Bajju oath-taking parallels that of the Israelites as recorded in the Old Testament. For example, Leviticus 5:4 (New International Version; NIV) states, "If a person thoughtlessly takes an oath to do anything, whether good or evil—in any matter one might carelessly swear about—even though he is unaware of it, in any case when he learns of it he will be guilty."

Oaths were important to a large number of ethnic groups throughout a wide area of Nigeria (Gunn 1956), particularly on the Plateau. Oaths were extremely important for the Bajju. Some oaths continue to be used, including within the customary courts. Some oaths are no longer sworn; however, belief in the efficacy of oaths continues. This includes oaths that one's ancestors swore with the consequences continuing down within the family and clan until today. The consequences of swearing falsely continue until someone repents of the words of an ancestor.

Oaths among the Bajju may be used to affirm that one group owns a parcel of contested land. Because the consequences of swearing an oath falsely are believed to be so destructive, only a person who is certain would swear an oath that the land belongs to him or his group. Boundary disputes between two neighboring ethnic groups or between neighbors are often resolved through oaths.

Bajju oaths may be divided into three categories: men's oaths, women's oaths, and oaths used by both men and women. Each category of oath is considered below, together with the consequences of perjury. The consequences are often associated with the object upon which an oath is sworn.

Men's oaths
Men may swear the following oaths:
1. Oaths related to one's hoe—*sshi ɑnok*. If one swears falsely on the hoe, the hoe may cut his leg. Since farming has typically been a man's primary occupation, a man's hoe knows whether or not what he swore was true or false. Further, if he swore falsely, his use of the hoe will not provide good produce.
2. Oaths related to one's bow—*sswa kɑta*. When swearing, a man holds his bow. If the sworn statement is false, then he may be unable to shoot anything afterwards. Additionally, if one swears falsely, an arrow may strike the oath taker, or he may go insane. A hunter may swear on his bow that his arrow was the first to hit an animal. Even if the man is an excellent hunter, yet swears falsely, the consequence of his oath will be his inability to shoot well.
3. Oaths related to a drum[1]—*sswa byin*. One drum kept at Dibyyi was used for matters affecting all the Bajju. Each village had its own drum kept by the village *gado* that was used to settle more local disputes. The oath sworn *on* the drum is the most serious oath a man can take, and therefore he would not do so without being convinced of the truth of his assertion. The Bajju believe that death is caused by swearing falsely on the drum. The fear of the consequences of swearing falsely is such that most Bajju would not so perjure themselves. It was not unusual for a person to refuse to swear on a drum for fear of the consequences, which would manifest in his family for generations, until someone admits that his relative swore falsely.

This drum oath is indicated in the case of adultery, stealing, and land disputes. When the issue involves the entire ethnic group, this oath

---

[1] Gunn reports that the hill peoples of Lere and Kauru districts in Zaria Emirate and specifically the Kurama similarly kept a drum at the house of the *dodo* (Gunn 1956:56).

takes place at Dibyyi. Today litigants in a court[2] case involving a boundary dispute go from the courtroom to the house of the *gado* to swear. The person who swears wins the court case. In earlier times, they took the drum to the site of the dispute.

As the person swears, he steps over the drum then steps back over it. If, within a three-day period, the person who swore changes his mind, unsure whether what he swore is true or not, he may retract his oath. He then undergoes purification so that he and his family will be safe from the consequences of the oath. After three days, however, the oath stands. If the oath was made falsely, he and his family would suffer later. The type of death associated with this oath involves swelling of the body. The Bajju may attribute illnesses of older people who retain fluid due to heart disease to this cause, though they may also attribute this type of illness to witchcraft (*nkut*)—see chapter 6.

The dire consequences, both individually and socially, of taking an oath on a drum are used to deal with land disagreements, which are frequent reasons for a conflict. Swearing an oath is used to decide who owns land. Land disputes that go to court are usually between communities, especially between members of two different ethnic groups. The consequence of lying about ownership of land can lead to the destruction of an entire lineage or clan (Kunhiyop 2005:87).

The Bajju seek to handle disputes within the Bajju community informally, outside of the courtroom, if possible (Van der valk van Ginnen 1981:18). In land transactions the Bajju usually ask a child or children to witness the agreement. Children, who will outlive the adults, will, therefore, be able to testify to what transpired.

4. Oaths taken in the name of Baranzan, the Bajju founding father—*sswa Baranzan*. This oath is used for matters that affect the entire ethnic group. Recently a group of men who belonged to the Bajju Development Association took an oath on Baranzan when they discussed the issue of who to select for the position of Bajju chief. This oath required that they refrain from sharing their deliberations with people who were not on this committee.

Women's oaths
Women could swear the following oaths:
1. Oaths taken on the black goatskin a woman used to carry her child on her back—*sshi ạbvubvo*. If she swore falsely, the child she carried in the skin may die. Since women no longer carry babies using goatskins,

---

[2] In 1968 Area Courts replaced Native Courts (Yahaya 1980:192).

today a woman may swear on the cloth she uses to carry her infant, or even swear upon her child. See figure 4.1 of an A̲tyap woman carrying her baby in a goatskin. This was very similar to what Bajju women used.

Figure 4.1. A̲tyap woman with baby on her back secured with a goatskin (Meek 1931:20).

2. Oaths related to a woman's headboard—*sswa a̲byyai*. Women carry their head-loads on a headboard. Traditionally they gave birth on them. A headboard can be used as a stool, as when a woman sells her produce in the market—she turns it over and sits on it. Because the headboard is with a woman much of the time, her headboard would know whether or not the oath she swore is true. If what a woman swore is false, anything bad that happened later was interpreted to be the result of taking the oath falsely. Further, when seeking to give birth and having difficulty doing so, she could be asked to enumerate the men she had sexual

intercourse with either before or during the pregnancy. If the cause of the difficulty in childbirth was because of having had intercourse with a man other than her husband—and if she tells the truth—according to tradition, the child will then arrive without further problems. If she swore falsely, she would be unable to deliver her child safely. This practice can still be observed today.

Figure 4.2. Sketch of a Bajju woman with her headboard. (Source: the 1990 Bajju calendar. Used by permission.)

3. To take an oath on a woman's axe—*sshi* or *sswa katssong*. The reason for taking an oath on a woman's axe parallels that for taking an oath on her headboard. Both her headboard and her axe are items she uses frequently. The result of taking this oath by swearing falsely is evident in the oath, "If I have sworn falsely, may my axe cut me."
4. To swear on a woman's pregnancy—*sswa kahwa*. In this oath a woman traditionally asserted that if she swore falsely, may she never see her children.

General Oaths
Either men or women may swear the following oaths:
1. To take an oath on hot oil—*sswa bamyyi*. *Bamyyi* is oil extracted from a tree. A *gado* administered this oath in the event that some grievous offense had been committed by someone unknown. Usually the grievance was major because such a drastic oath would not be used for a small offense. The *gado* asked the one(s) suspected to extract some object (any object) from a pot of hot oil. They believed that an offender's hand would be burned while nothing would happen to an innocent person's hand.

The 1934 *Gazetteers of the Northern Provinces of Nigeria* described this oath as follows:

They have a form of trial by ordeal, or oath by ordeal, which is very uncommon and in which the candidate has to pick a stone from out of a pot of flaming oil. The administerer of this form of ordeal holds an inheritable office and always performs his duties in the same place. Before the ordeal is administered, a fire is lit under the earthenware pot of oil and a hen is produced, its claws being clipped and put in the pot, as well as a feather. When the oil bursts into flames the administerer of the ordeal smears the candidate's hand and forearm with a mixture of the ash and oil which were left over from the last time. The candidate then has to pick out the stone and, when this is done, the pot of flaming oil is immediately turned upside down on the fire underneath it. The fire at once dies and the remains of the oil mix with the ashes and are left there until the next time, when the mixture will be used to smear the arm of the next candidate. After a sufficient space of time the candidate's arm is examined to see if it is burnt. Needless to say, the only part which ever shows any signs of being burnt is in between the bases of the fingers where they join the hand. This is the part of the hand which might not be properly covered when the hand is smeared with the mixture of oil and ash. This form of oath is greatly respected and neighbouring tribes have endeavoured to adopt it, but have not been allowed to do so by Government. (Ames 1934:229–230)

This colonial report continues by stating that Adamu, the fourth emir of Jema'a, introduced this trial to the Bajju from the people of Sanga as a substitute for their swearing on the drum. The reasoning behind this substitution was that the consequence of this ordeal caused only the guilty party to suffer, while swearing falsely on the drum affected the man and his descendants.

2. To take an oath on the ground, dust, or farm dirt—*sswa mbyen*. The Bajju administered this oath on the dirt over a grave during the funeral of a recently deceased person, a person whose death they suspect has been caused by spiritual activities of another person (witchcraft). Most deaths, other than those of the elderly who have fulfilled their functions within life, are attributed to the activities of others, acting within the spiritual realm. For example, when a person is sleeping, his spirit may be elsewhere working to cause the death of another individual. This activity is termed *nkut* by the Bajju.

People who take this oath assert that they are not the cause of the deceased's death through *nkut* activities. Christians asked to take this oath have agreed to do so if they are allowed to swear on the Bible rather than on the earth, and this substitution is acceptable. In taking this oath the person says, "If I am the one responsible for this death, may sickness strike me." The type of sickness is a drying sickness, which causes the stomach to swell. It is an oath against *nkut*.

A man may use this oath as an alternative to swearing on the drum for land disputes. The person takes a small amount of earth from the disputed land. He puts a pinch of it on his tongue. The consequences of this oath are the same as those resulting from swearing on a drum.

3. To swear on the name of an ancestor—*sshi*. A person may say, "*N sshi Shebanyan*" 'I swear on Shebanyan', one's deceased relative. To do so gives legitimacy to one's claim. Although Bajju do not usually think in terms of some specific penalty resulting from this oath, they believe that the ancestors are present and watching over the living.

Retracting oaths

Under certain circumstances a person may find it necessary to repent and retract his or her words to remove a curse. The oath taken for this purpose is termed "to take an oath on ashes" or, literally, "to drink ashes," *sswa batwak*. The person places a small amount of ash into his or her mouth, swears, then spits it out into a small hole in the ground and covers it, thus symbolizing that the bad words that he or she spoke are spit out and buried. After that, the person again puts a small amount of ash into his or her mouth and swallows it, symbolizing a blessing. The Bajju say that God finds the ash that has been spit out and forgives the person. The ashes symbolize coolness of what was formerly hot; Bajju identify anger with heat, while forgiveness and absence of anger are identified with coolness. In addition to taking an oath of repentance after confession of an offense, a person could be fined. This fine could be a black goat or a red cock or hen.

If one's deceased ancestor within a person's clan swore falsely, his descendant may use this means to retract that oath. Doing so stops the negative consequences that have been happening within his family and clan.

Sswa batwak indicates repentance. As such it contrasts in function with the other oaths. The person is not asserting that what he or she said was true; rather the person is asserting that it was false and that he or she is sorry for past words or actions. This oath is used in a number of different situations. For example, if a person said that he or she would never move his house to another site, then decides to move, *sswa batwak* is indicated. Or if a woman is having difficulty giving birth, she may be asked to enumerate the people she "ate" through witchcraft activities (*nkut*) and then to *sswa batwak* 'drink ashes'. Refusal to do so could result in harm to her child. As *sswa batwak* is a general oath of repentance, it is broadly applicable.

Summary of the legal system

When problems arose within the Bajju community, they dealt with them through their legal system, with fines, sacrifices, pots of beer, death for murderers, and exile for those who committed homicide. Following this they went through a cleansing ritual to avoid the feared effects of the transgressions and purified both the offender and the community. Their legal system was augmented by a series of oaths with serious, threatened consequences for perjury.

The churches' response

In the Bible in Matthew 5:34–35 (NIV) Jesus told his disciples "Do not swear at all: either by heaven, for it is God's throne; or by the earth, for it is his footstool; or by Jerusalem, for it is the city of the Great King." Bajju Christians have taken this admonition seriously. After reading this verse, many Christians refuse to take oaths. Hence the assertion *kạryong ạmi* 'it is true', came into widespread use.

Christian churches among the Bajju are often used to resolve conflict within the community. This conforms to Bajju tradition in that the *gado* had both religious and political functions within the community. In some ways pastors now have both functions. Following a church service, a pastor may ask his congregation to stay in order to deal with some problem within the community. People recognize the authority of his office and expect him to do so.

Churches began to have political functions when they were first established by missionaries. Churches punished men for taking a second or subsequent wife, for drinking, for chewing kola nuts, for becoming a horn blower when the circumstances involved the traditional religion, for taking part in the *ạbvoi*, etc. They similarly punished women for being second or subsequent wives. They were not allowed to wear the cloth of the women's group within the church. Although some of these breaches can be viewed as moral issues within the community, the punishments the churches meted out included forbidding a man to attend church for a specified period of time, such as six months. Such men were not allowed to hold positions within the church or to receive communion. These punishments stigmatized people and can be viewed as political in nature.

Further, the fact that the other major religion in northern Nigeria, Islam, does not distinguish between religion and politics forces Christians to do likewise. Not to do so would put Christians at a distinct disadvantage. The concept of a separation of church and state is not applicable in the situation in which the Bajju find themselves, though some missionaries have advocated this separation. The missionaries' perspective reflects their home culture more than that of a Bajju Christian.

5

Hunting and Horns

Bajju men took pride in their hunting abilities. Hunting was a major source of men's prestige and status. In fact, some Bajju leaders selected a picture of a man holding a bow and arrow as the symbol of the Bajju.

Figure 5.1. Bajju hunter.
(Source: the 1990 Bajju calendar. Used by permission.)

As mentioned in chapter 1, the Bajju were known as excellent hunters. As a result of their prowess, there are few wild animals in their area. The Bajju create musical instruments from the horns of the animals they hunt, which they blow on various celebratory occasions.

Horn blowing followed a successful hunt, hence I treat both hunting and musical horns together.

Hunting

Bajju men engaged in communal hunts. One colonial administrator commented on Bajju communal hunts as follows:

> The Kaje are (like the Pitti—but without their horses) renowned for communal drives, which they generally hold themselves in the Bikarantu Kadara territory. It is said that the Kadara [are] require[d] to shut up their goats and even themselves at these times. (NAK ZarProf 607, 1932)

Bajju organized hunting expeditions along kinship lines with the hunting elder, the *gado kapyyi,* in charge. He is viewed as in charge of the animals in the bush. He had to excel as a hunter in his community. It is his responsibility to call a dry-season hunt. A horn blower blew the bushbuck horn, the *abyo,* on the day before the hunt to announce the hunt and tell hunters to prepare for it. That night hunters refrained from sexual intercourse in order to be in a state of purity for the hunt. One elder asserted that hunters refrained from sex for a week before the hunt.

Prior to embarking on a hunting expedition, hunters met at the house of the *gado kapyyi,* who purified them and their bows and arrows in preparation for the hunt. They placed their bows, arrows, and quivers on the ground. Then the *gado* killed a red or white cock and sprinkled its blood over their bows, arrows, and quivers to insure a successful hunt. He should not use a black cock as that would bring bad luck to the hunt. If a hunter inadvertently stepped over a bow, he had to step carefully backwards over it in the same direction as he had come or they believed that he would be unable to kill anything with it. After the *gado* blessed the hunters they took part in a hunt; by following this ritual he declared the hunting season open.

A poison preparer readied *anguma* 'poison' for the arrow tips on the day of the hunt. This person, who was in charge of the hunting medicine, had to have abstained from sexual intercourse the night before in order to be in a state of purity for preparing the poison. He arose early in the morning and greeted no one as he went to collect the poison from the *shing* tree.[1] He first pounded the poison into a powder, then added water to it. He then put the mixture into a cloth and squeezed the poison water through it, water that he collected. He poured this water and the powdered poison into a pot of boiling water on the fire. As the poison preparer poured the powder into

---

[1] Unfortunately, I was unable to obtain the Hausa names for all of the trees mentioned, including the *shing* tree. (The Hausa name would then have facilitated a search for the English and Latin names in a Hausa dictionary.)

the boiling water, he spoke jubilantly, using praise words similar to those used to praise a chief. He told the boiling mixture that he wanted it to have "heat," and that if an arrow tipped with this poison hit an animal, he did not want the animal to go far. Next he went to the river for water, and when he returned, he poured a little out. The water symbolized the blood of an animal after it had been shot.

The poison preparer and the *gado kạpyyi* next placed the poison on the tip and shaft of each arrow. In addition to having poison placed on the arrows, Bajju hunters also took an antidote for the poison with them, which they carried in an animal horn attached with a string around their waists. In the event that an arrow inadvertently hit another hunter, they used this antidote. Prior to setting off, the hunters ate and drank together. The poison preparer did not join the hunters on the hunt.

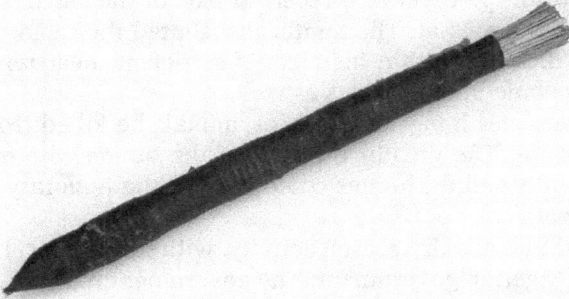

Figure 5.2. Quiver with arrows (Norris McKinney).

If a dispute arose over whose arrow struck an animal first, a hunter could swear an oath on his bow (*sswa kạta*) that his arrow was the first to hit the animal (see chapter 4). This gave him the right to claim the hunter's portion, which is described below.

If the hunting party found no animals, they could build a fire, and when only coals remained, hunters put some medicine on the coals. They believed that if an animal was nearby, it would then appear. When hunting, if a hunter sees something unusual, he is not to look at it; if he does not pay attention to it, then nothing will happen.

If the hunters killed a large animal, such as the roan antelope (*gunki*), leopard (*ccuk*), lion (*zaki*), or African buffalo (*zat*), the hunters blew reed flutes as they approached their home village. This told the women that the hunt had been successful, and they would go out to greet them. The hunters would bring a large animal to the home of the *gado kạpyyi*. There a child from the *gado*'s household would sprinkle medicine (ground hungry rice) on the animal's head and stomach in order to drive away the spirit of the animal, for they believed it had power to harm a hunter for killing it. This action is termed *tun zei*. This medicine was kept in the horn of the hartebeest. They performed this ritual only on animals that were considered very dangerous, such as a lion, leopard, African buffalo, or roan antelope. After doing so, they divided the animal at the *gado*'s house. A smaller animal could be divided anywhere.

Because of the importance of the *gado kapyyi* to the success of the hunting expedition, he received part of the meat of the animal. They gave him the stomach, and at his home they cooked *gbaam,* a type of soup made from it. He could also receive a leg, the kidneys, the chest, or the head. The hunter could receive the head together with a hind and foreleg. He might also give the head to his maternal relatives, his *bazzwak*. By so doing he recognized the special relationship that exists between him and his mother's brother and other men so classified (McKinney 1983). Women received the intestines. The poison preparer also received part of the catch, namely the skin[2] and chest of the animal. The hunter distributed the remainder of the animal to every member within his clan. If sufficient meat remained, he distributed it to people in other clans as well.

A hunter sometimes hung the skulls of animals he killed from a rafter in front of his house. The greater the skill of the hunter, the more skulls he acquired. A really skillful hunter could receive the honorary title of an African buffalo (*zat*).

Hunting continues as a dry-season activity, with some aspects of hunting regulated by the Nigerian government. The government requires licenses to kill some animals, such as elephants, and forbids hunters from killing animals that are endangered. Today hunters have to go increasingly farther away to find game, but the mystique of Bajju hunting remains.

The Bajju celebrate their hunting prowess in a dance called "the dance of the bow" (*song kata*). In this dance, hunters act out a hunting scene, accompanied by drumming and flute or horn blowing. One man pretends to be a lion while another man acts as the hunter, who stalks the lion. The hunters perform this inside a circle formed by the horn-blowing musicians, while others dance and sing outside the circle.

When a skilled hunter dies, the Bajju blow horns for him.

In the next section I discuss horns and flutes in more detail.

Horns and flutes

Tremearne claimed that from some distance away, the sound of Bajju animal horn and flute blowing resembled an organ (Tremearne 1912:250). The

---

[2] Some say that the hunting elder (*gado kapyyi*) received the skin of the animal; others assert that it was the poisoner who received it.

first time we heard animal horns being blown, we wondered what musical instruments could possibly produce such distinctive and wonderful music.

Figure 5.3. Horn blowers (Tremearne 1912:250).

This section describes the place of horn and flute blowing within Bajju society. I will answer questions such as when were they blown? What was the relationship between blowing horns and flutes and traditional religious beliefs and practices? Who could become a horn blower? What happened to a horn blower who was late to a practice?

Figures 5.4. and 5.5. Bajju horn blowers, c. 1974 (Norris McKinney).

Horns *(bǫgba)*

Musical horns are as follows:

1. West African hartebeest (*nnyo*) horn: the *ǫjjwa.*
2. Roan antelope horn: the *ǫhwwak,* the *dikum ccuk* and the *ǫtǫtyi.* The Bajju use three sizes of horns from the roan antelope (*gunki; gwanki,* H.). The smallest of the three from the female roan antelope is termed the *ǫhwwak.* Next in size is the *dikum ccuk.* The largest comes from the male roan antelope, and is termed the *ǫtǫtyi.* These horns are blown only together with other horns; they are not blown singly.
3. Oryx horn: the *ǫgbaryi.* The oryx (*mariri,* H.) horn is a long narrow horn.
4. Cow or West African hartebeest horn: the *ǫgai ǫjjwa.*
5. Reedbuck horn: The reedbuck horn (*k'aji,* H.) is extremely long, as long as a person's arm.
6. Bushbuck horn: the *ǫbyo.*

7. Wooden horn: the *kon ǫgbaryi*. The *kon ǫgbaryi* is a large, long horn carved from wood.
8. Another long horn had a hollow stick plus a gourd (*kǫshyen*) attached to the end of it.

Figure 5.6. Large wooden horn (Norris McKinney).

Horn blowers

The position of horn blower is hereditary within a family. A man inherits this honor together with his father's horn. Although Bajju obtain new horns when hunting, old horns are quite durable and tend to stay within families for generations.

When horn blowers gathered for practice or for an occasion, such as a dance on a moonlit night, and one of the horn blowers did not come or arrived late, the other horn blowers ritually tapped him on his head with their horns or with a drumstick. Then almost all the horn blowers would beat the latecomer with their hands. They might fine him a cock, a goat, or a pot of beer. By this means, the horn was purified.

Occasions for horn blowing

Bajju blew horns for special occasions such as funerals, *ǫbvoi* celebrations, return of exiles, various other celebrations, and dances. One horn, the West African hartebeest horn (*ǫjjwa*), was blown to announce an impending attack from an enemy group, notifying people when they needed to defend themselves. The Bajju likened the *ǫjjwa* to a bugle in the army. It called people together, especially in the event of war or a death. They also blew this horn at night at the mourning celebration, the *kǫnak*, calling people to the celebration. If the deceased had been a good hunter or warrior, a member of his clan blew the *ǫjjwa*.

The *ajjwa* was one of two musical horns that could be blown singly; the other was the bushbuck horn (*abyo*).

Horns are still blown for special events. They are also often blown to show honor to an individual.

Figure 5.7. Musical horns (Carol McKinney).

Bajju blew the bushbuck horn, the *abyo,* early in the morning to call people together to farm. They also blew it to announce a special occasion such as a dance. For example, they could blow it in the morning announcing that the *akusak* masquerade would come out that evening. Another use for the *abyo* was to announce a hunt to the hunters the evening before it was to take place. They did not blow it the day of the hunt, however, as they believed that to do so would spoil the hunt.

When horns are blown together, the *ajjwa* often leads. When all of the animal horns are blown together as at a dance, each horn is blown in turn to form chords. Or the *dikum ccuk* may be blown first, followed by the *atatyi,* and the *ccuk* third.

Dances are held during the dry season when the moon is full. Horn blowing accompanies dancing, singing, and general merriment. The Bajju state that a village without horn blowers did not readily attract wives. Today Bajju blow horns at wedding receptions, though previously, when a woman was captured for marriage, they did not blow horns. Horns are also blown at other celebrations, such as New Year celebrations.

Bajju had a very large drum, with places for the drummer's feet that he would climb up on to play it. This drum has died out due to missionary influence, which condemned horn blowing and drumming as it related to traditional religion. Today the Bajju use a smaller drum that is carried by a shoulder strap. One or two drums are played to accompany horn blowing. The hourglass-shaped drum, the talking drum, is also occasionally played.

Horn blowing and Bajju pre-Christian religion

Bajju blew horns for *ǫbvoi* celebrations, which were associated with their traditional religion. The *ǫbvoi* initiated boys into this society. When they came out the next morning, after they bathed in the river, the Bajju celebrated their new status as members of the *ǫbvoi* by blowing horns. They were now no longer classified with the uninitiated or with women, but rather with men. See chapter 3.

Flutes

Bajju blow hollow reed flutes, the *shrywa*, in similar patterns as they blow animal horns; however, they never blow animal horns and flutes together. In flute blowing one leads, then others gradually join in to form musical chords. Each flute has one tone, so that when blown together each flute player must coordinate his playing carefully with the other flutes. Drumming also accompanies flute blowing.

Bajju blew flutes as they returned home to announce that they had killed a large animal. Today they blow flutes at dances. I recall one performance where the flute players blew their flutes as they performed an elaborate squat dance.

Horn blowing and missionaries

Missionaries who sought to bring Christianity to the Bajju were concerned with aspects of the pre-Christian religion that they saw as antithetical to Christianity. For this reason some missionaries opposed horn blowing. If a man inherited the position of horn blower, the Sudan Interior Mission (SIM) church disciplined him. Such discipline could involve expulsion from the church or suspension for a specified time period (for example, six months) and insisted he cease to be a horn blower. Other missions took a contrasting view. Roman Catholic Fathers invited Bajju to blow their horns to celebrate Christmas. A more careful investigation by missionaries of Bajju horn and flute blowing might have resulted in a more nuanced understanding of the role of these musical instruments among the Bajju and other minority ethnic groups in this area. That investigation could have distinguished between situations where horn blowing was associated with their pre-Christian religion and other situations where religion was not in focus, such as when horns or flutes were blown to call people to farm, to a dance, or to announce a hunt.

Because some missions associated horn blowing with pre-Christian religion, today a different set of musical instruments is used in churches. These include clay pot drums (*bǫkinkyim*) of varying sizes, gourds covered with stringed seeds, and in some churches, such as the Cherubim and Seraphim, a square-type drum. Clay pot drums and gourd rattles are women's musical instruments, which are played only in church. This contrasts with musical instruments, such as drums, flutes, and musical animal horns, which are played only by men in nonchurch contexts.

Figure 5.8. Women playing clay pot drums, 1984 (Carol McKinney).

Figure 5.9. Women playing drums, tambourine, and gourd rattle, 2010 (Carol McKinney).

Summary

This chapter discussed Bajju hunting and musical animal horns and flutes. Both are closely related in that horn blowers blew flutes to welcome hunters home and celebrate the animals they killed. It explains how the Bajju acquired their musical horns. It also discussed the relationship between horn blowing and pre-Christian religion. More conservative missionaries disapproved of horn blowing that was associated with the traditional religion and disciplined those who blew horns and flutes in those contexts. A more nuanced exploration of the role of horn and flute blowing within Bajju society by missionaries would have helped avoid some of the cultural clashes that occurred.

The next chapter discusses witchcraft, an important part of Bajju religion.

6

Witchcraft—*Nkut*

A witch is not like a cricket's leg. (Bajju proverb)

This proverb asserts that while a cricket's legs are noisy, a witch is not like that. Further, the actions of witches are not small and insignificant like the size of crickets' legs. Rather, a witch acts silently, resulting in harm to another. Those actions occur in the spiritual realm, with effects in the physical realm.

Bajju concept of witchcraft

In defining the concept of witchcraft, the Bajju assert that people inherit spiritual power at birth and have an inherent capacity to use that power through psychic acts that cause evil, harm, unexpected occurrences, misfortune, illness, or death in the natural realm. This worldview system was first described by Evans-Pritchard in a groundbreaking work on the Azande in South Sudan, northern DRC, and Central African Republic. His term for this system is "witchcraft," which he defined as "a supposed psychic emanation from witchcraft-substance which is believed to cause injury to health and property" (1937:226). Offiong similarly observes that "witchcraft is the psychic act through which socially disapproved supernatural techniques influence events, and this perception is central to the cosmological ideas of the Ibibio" (1985:153). The Bajju term for this system is *nkut*.

Use of spiritual power is a psychic act; it involves no rites, spells, sorcery, magic, or medicine. It explains phenomena such as breaches of social

69

relations, unusual attitudes or actions, antisocial behavior, unexpected occurrences, misfortune, evil, sickness, barrenness, and death. It attempts to answer questions of why misfortune happens to specific people at particular times and places, with the result that social relations are fractured on the basis of "socially relevant causes" (Evans-Pritchard 1937:73).

The Bajju believe God is inherently good, so no evil comes from him. Therefore they explain evil through *nkut* beliefs. Kluckhohn (1967:83–84) describes witchcraft from the psychological perspective, as an outlet for hostility between people, because it displaces evil from one person to someone else.

The explanation of the use of a person's psychic acts related to specific events does not invalidate immediate physical cause and effect, but rather complements them by dealing with the question of *why* things happen to specific people at particular times and places. The Bajju recognize that a person may be injured or die in a motorcycle or automobile accident, which is the immediate physical cause. But they are also concerned about the *ultimate* cause, i.e., who used his or her spiritual power against an individual and thereby caused his or her injury or death. To many, the ultimate cause is more important than the immediate physical cause. Basically, the belief is that actions do not happen by chance, but rather have both immediate and spiritual causes.

While the capacity for *nkut* is innate rather than learned, one who specializes in the use of this power to deliberately harm others is a witch (*akut*, sing.; *bakut*, pl.). Kato reported a Bajju oral tradition that explains the origins of witchcraft: After God created man, he sent two messages. The first was that man would not die, and the second was that man would die. A hare carried the first message while a tortoise carried the second. Since the hare rested on the way, the tortoise delivered God's second message first. According to the oral tradition, the hare's sleep was purposeful rather than accidental. Consequently, no death is natural. Some deaths (*dikwu Kaza*) are because of God's judgment upon an individual for a person's evil actions. But all others, including death from most diseases, are caused by *nkut*— *dikwu nkut* 'death by witchcraft' (Kato 1974:157–158). Witches can send snakes, animals, flies, or lightning with secret messages to cause harm to someone.

Today some assert that while most people are born with witchcraft substance, certain people are born without *nkut* but acquire it later. Women and children, especially if they are weak-minded and have desires for worldly things or pleasure, are among those who may acquire *nkut* rather than being born with it (Phillip Allahmagani, personal communication, 2010). This contrasts with the traditional belief that, although not all make use of it, all are born with this inherent capacity.

When a person suffers misfortune, responsibility is usually ascribed to someone other than that person. But generally only people in one's patrilineage and clan are accused of witchcraft (Kato 1973:219–222). This perception causes division within a biological family or clan. Women and children are usually exempt from accusation. Since wives come from other lineages, their witchcraft is not considered effective while they are in their husband's family; husbands, on the other hand, may resort to witchcraft as one means of preventing their wives from leaving them. With regard to children, the *nkut* of children is too young to do harm—witchcraft becomes harmful only when a person reaches maturity.

Typically, the Bajju phrase their explanation of *nkut* in terms of "if... then." For example, if multiple children within a family die, then someone within the extended family is practicing *nkut* against them. If more than one in a series of husbands dies, then the wife is practicing *nkut* against them. If one contracts smallpox, then that person was seeking to practice *nkut* against others but the *nkut* reverted to attack him or her instead. If multiple youths die in motorcycle and automobile accidents, then someone is practicing *nkut* against them. If one farmer's crops are better than another's, then that farmer is practicing *nkut* against the other farmer, causing his crops to fail. If a first wife's children all live and the second wife's children all die, then the first wife is practicing *nkut* against the children of the second wife in order to protect her own children. In all cases of death by witchcraft, the Bajju say about the victims, "the spirit eats them" (*tswa ya banyet*).

The Bajju assert that people are born with two sets of eyes. The first set allows them to see visually; the second set allows them to see in the spiritual realm. Those who practice *nkut* are believed to use their second set of eyes. Parents tell their children to close their second set of eyes, their *nkut* eyes, both to protect them from harm and to keep them from harming others. During epidemics children were told to close their eyes in order not to catch a disease by looking at an ill person. The Bajju do not look at someone intently when talking with him or her; however, a witch will stare at people at random. (For more on the importance of one's eyes in the Bajju worldview, see chapter 10 on expressions of respect.) It was also the case that if people perceived spiritually that a witch was coming, children were told to run away and hide inside their houses.

The Bajju perceive a close relationship between the practice of *nkut* and dreams. A person may be told in a dream that someone wants to kill him or her. Or in a dream one may become ill through someone's *nkut* and feel bound. One man dreamed that someone was stepping on his chest so that he could not breathe; when he awoke he thought he could see the footprint on his chest.

More recently a certain amount of flexibility exists as to who is blamed for someone else's misfortune. Some who have moved to urban centers believe that *nkut* exists in Bajju villages more than in cities. Another variation is that people in one denomination practice *nkut* against those in another denomination.

Protective *nkut*

Bajju distinguish two types of *nkut*: good *nkut* (*ạtsatsak nkut*), which involves protective discernment and/or power in the spiritual realm, and evil *nkut* (*ạbibyyi nkut* or *ạkạtuk nkut*), which uses *nkut* power for evil. People who use evil *nkut* are referred to as "witches with eyes" (*bạkut ạtacci*).

Just as *nkut* may cause death, it may also protect through discernment of possible psychic emanations against one's family. Some elders within a community are believed to possess protective *nkut*. This enables them to protect members of their community, lineage, and household. Persons with this ability are able to discern those who might intend evil through *nkut* activities against others.

One night a man while drunk went to the compound where his sister lived. Her husband met him and refused to allow him to enter the compound because he believed that he came for evil purposes. He stated, "I know why you have come. You have come to do harm to my wife, but I won't let you. Go to your own house, which is over there." So the man stumbled home. A couple of months later the brother-in-law's daughter died. His sister's husband said, "Aha, didn't I tell you that he had come for an evil purpose, but I wouldn't let him enter my house. So he carried out his evil purpose within his own house." From his perspective his use of protective *nkut* enabled him to perceive the evil intent of his brother-in-law and thus protect his family.

This account illustrates protective *nkut* and evil *nkut,* the latter of which people may not necessarily be aware. In this sense *nkut* has an unintentional and capricious aspect to it.

Assumptions and functions of *nkut*

The basic assumptions that undergird witchcraft are that in a perfect world life should be free of evil, sickness, death, misfortune, and barrenness. These occurrences are not random; each must have a specific cause or agent. Human beings who experience illnesses, misfortune, and death are usually seen as helpless victims of psychic acts, spirits, or powers. Therefore when these things occur they must be explained. *Nkut* fills this function. Once the cause of possible *nkut* activity is identified, then it is necessary to take action against that agent and to exact revenge. However, the person identified as the one responsible may state, "I was not aware of this." Bajju believe an individual's spirit may have been off working elsewhere during sleep without the person being aware of it.

A corollary to the unnatural, unintentional nature of *nkut* is that interpersonal relations may be managed through *nkut* accusations. Those accused of practicing *nkut* may have been angry, may not have acted in a socially acceptable manner, may be inattentive when spoken to, and in general do not relate well with others. *Nkut* beliefs help avoid direct confrontations, giving society an indirect route to deal with interpersonal difficulties.

Nkut also serves as a leveling mechanism. For example, if one person does well financially, but his neighbor's children continue to die, then he might be accused of becoming wealthy by causing their deaths through practicing *nkut* against them. To avoid *nkut* accusations, development projects need to help all members of a community to rise together rather than allowing specific individuals to do well while the majority of the population continues to live in poverty.

This conceptual system allows people to avoid responsibility for their own problems. Someone else can always be accused of causing their problems. It involves scapegoating or blaming another for one's problems.

In a society where people did not know the germ theories of disease, which teaches that specific illnesses are caused by bacteria, viruses, retroviruses, and parasites, this conceptual system provides answers concerning why specific people become ill, suffer misfortune, or die. It answers basic worldview questions of causality, questions of why there is evil in the world, why specific people become ill when others around them remain well, why locusts eat one person's millet field while they do not eat their neighbor's millet in the adjoining field, and so on. While the presence of Western medicine has helped to provide explanations for some illnesses, there are still areas where *nkut* continues to be the explanation people give as the cause of a specific problem.

It is interesting that Western-type education, which is now prevalent in the Bajju area, has not eradicated *nkut* beliefs. In fact, it has hardly touched this explanatory system. Missionaries began schools in this area, but since they did not study the local belief system or learn any of the local languages, they did not offer teachings about *nkut*. Some Roman Catholic missionaries did become aware of it, taught that *nkut* beliefs were superstition, and that people should not believe them.

While missionaries did teach about the power of Satan and some cast out evil spirits which can enter people and animals (for example, pigs, see Matthew 8:28–34), many Protestant missionaries failed to know that local Christians adhered to the *nkut* explanatory system. Today, to the Bajju, *nkut* explains some things while Christianity and Western medicine explain others.

Some aspects of the *nkut* explanatory system have changed. Christians today sometimes assert that the spirit of Satan or an evil spirit enters an individual, thus causing him or her to practice *nkut* against another individual. When exploring the role of evil spirits in the Bible, nowhere does it say that when an evil spirit enters an individual that it allows or makes a person's spirit leave his or her body to meet with other spirits in the spiritual realm and thus cause someone else's physical problems. The possessed person can become ill, irrational, have fits, etc., because of it, but that particular illness does not extend to others.

Nkut, magic, and sorcery

In many societies in Africa there are separate words for sorcery and psychic emanations. In others these two concepts are expressed by one word. In Jju there are two words to express these different concepts, one for performing sorcery and conjuring, while *nkut* refers to psychic emanations and the conceptual system on which they are based. *Akacci* refers to the world beyond, the spiritual realm in which *nkut* operates. One who is accused of using his or her spiritual power to harm others is termed a witch (*akut*). Among the Bajju, if sorcery or miracles occur, the phrase *nkyang mamaki* is used, which literally translates as "things of wonder."

It is important to distinguish the use of psychic emanations or witchcraft from magic and sorcery. Magic is an attempt to mechanistically control supernatural forces that involves ritual procedures, which if done correctly, are supposed to bring about a predictable result. Sorcery is use of magic with the intent of harming another person. By contrast, *nkut* involves no rituals or magical procedures. The psychic emanations of an individual operate while the person is asleep mostly without the individual willing it. However, the way people speak about this phenomenon often contrasts with their definition of it. At gatherings people may be told to "cool" their *nkut* as though it is volitional. This has led some scholars to speak of "voluntary witchcraft" versus "involuntary witchcraft."

Up to this point this chapter has described many areas of Bajju life that *nkut* impinges upon. It is important to put *nkut* into its larger cultural context in order to understand how such accusations come about. Below I cite an example the Bajju attributed to *nkut.*

Nkut deaths

To the Bajju no human death, other than the deaths of elderly people, is due to natural causes. As Mbiti states:

> There are always physical causes and circumstances surrounding every death. These include sickness, disease, old age, accident, lightning, earthquake, flood, drowning, animal attack, and many others. But African peoples believe that a particular person will only die from one of these physical causes because some human or other agent has brought it about by means of a curse, witchcraft, magic and so on. These are what we may call mystical causes of death. (1975:112)

Bajju believe that those who have not fulfilled their appropriate roles in society are reincarnated. Their belief in reincarnation is a rather loose one in which a man may be reborn as a man, bird, animal, or even a woman. Reincarnation beliefs are not tied to merit, as in Hinduism, but rather to whether or not a person has fulfilled his or her appropriate functions in life.

In one example of *nkut* an expatriate man was driving in Kaduna when his car struck a young Bajju man and killed him. When the police questioned the driver, he stated that he saw a cat in front of his car; he had not seen a man. The fact that an expatriate stated that he saw a cat, and that the Bajju tend to ascribe honesty to expatriates, confirmed to the Bajju that *nkut* was involved. They believe that the spirit of an individual with evil *nkut* can enter into the body of a person and transform him or her into an animal. Hence this cat had the spirit of the young man in it.

Because this death was attributed to *nkut*, the Bajju next needed to find out whose spiritual power was involved. They did this by asking each person who attended the funeral to swear on the ground of the grave that he or she was not responsible for this death. This ceremony of swearing is done only if the Bajju suspect that someone is responsible for a particular death. It is known as "to swear on the ground" (*sswa mbyen*) (see chapter 4). Each person swears, "I am not responsible for this death. I am sorry for any words or actions I may have spoken or taken that caused it." As mentioned in chapter 4, many Christians prefer to swear on the Bible, which is acceptable. In this instance the deceased's father refused to swear because he believed that this custom was nonsense. Consequently, people accused him of having killed his own son by his *nkut* activity.

Normally all who attend a funeral will swear that they are not responsible for a specific death. The Bajju believe that if a person swears falsely, then the consequences will show up for that person or for his or her family members later. Then the Bajju would know whether or not someone had sworn falsely.

The deceased's sister wanted to escape having something similar happen to her, so she returned to the Bajju home area for a month. When she returned to Kaduna, she visited her brother's grave. As she left the gravesite, she too was hit by a car and killed. Her father was again accused of causing the death of his daughter. By this time the father was so overcome with grief that he was reduced to talking nonsense. To most Bajju this was further evidence that he was responsible for both deaths. Though this man could have asserted that he was not responsible, now no matter what he said, some Bajju would still have believed that he was responsible.

Nkut and meat

In preparation for a wedding the groom's parents purchased a cow and killed it to serve at the wedding reception. After the wedding and reception, as the groom's uncle was traveling to his home in the back of a pickup truck, he fell from the back of the truck and died.

Bajju explained this sudden death by *nkut* beliefs. When they killed the cow for the wedding reception, they were actually killing the uncle whose spirit was in the cow. Those who ate the beef ate the uncle, so they were thereby responsible for his death. This reflects the close connection between meat and *nkut*.

Identifying those who practice *nkut*

The Bajju say they can recognize witches (*bakut*) by their words and behavior. Socially unacceptable characteristics disrupt the flow of normal interaction. Indications that a person is involved in *nkut* activities include the following:

1. Someone who stares at people at random. A person does not look intently at someone while talking with that person, but a witch will do so.
2. A person who displays characteristics the opposite of friendliness, goodwill, generosity, civility, and qualities that maintain social harmony. The Bajju esteem these characteristics highly. Persons who do not display these qualities are apt to be accused of *nkut* because their spirits may be off working elsewhere while only their bodies are present.
3. Someone within the household who makes life difficult and disturbs others.
4. Persons who live alone. One man who lived alone would physically touch and feel the people who came to greet him; therefore he was accused of being a witch.
5. A person whose children continue to die. For example, a former diviner was accused of using her *nkut* to kill the children of her co-wife. Once all her co-wife's children died, then her children also began to die. Therefore she was accused of causing the deaths of her own children too. In order to keep a child from dying, Bajju may give that child the name *Bakut* or *Nkut,* so that no further *nkut* would harm the child and he would not die. These names are prayers that those who practice *nkut* will leave this child alone. Formerly, if one's children continued to die, a diviner counseled a person to move to another environment to escape the *nkut* being practiced in the area.
6. A person who is disabled. The fifth child of a Christian pastor and his wife was severely disabled. He could neither talk nor walk. He moved by scooting, and he recognized few people who were always in his everyday environment. His mother gave birth to two other children after him, each of whom died. People reasoned that the disabled young man must have been the one responsible for the deaths of his two siblings. In this situation the disabled person was accused of using *nkut,* though more usually it is the parents who would be accused.

7. Elderly people of either gender who have edema in their feet, ankles, and legs due to heart problems. Swelling of the body is indicative of *nkut* since it is not a natural condition.[1]
8. Women who are widowed, remarried, and widowed again are especially suspected of *nkut*.
9. A person who is groggy for whatever reason, as when he or she is first waking up from sleep. That person is not yet in complete command of his or her faculties, indicating that the person's spirit has not completely reentered his or her body. The spirit of the person may have been off working elsewhere, engaging in *nkut* activities.
10. A person who does not participate normally in conversations. It is as though that person's spirit is not there, only his body is present; his spirit is off working elsewhere. This includes students who stare out the window and daydream instead of paying attention to their teacher in class.
11. Maternal relatives may be accused of *nkut* if harm comes to a woman's children while she is visiting them. However, usually it is patrilineal relatives who are seen as responsible.
12. If someone has something extraordinary happen to him, he may be accused of being a witch.
13. If a person has riches and others around him die, he may be accused of practicing *nkut*. He may be getting his riches from those around him.
14. While it was people within the patrilineage who were accused of *nkut*, today it may be those in another denomination or those in the home area as opposed to those who live in urban areas.
15. People who died from smallpox.

One man always kept his compound clean and always bathed in the same place. Hence people said that he was a witch. Anything that is unusual and out of the ordinary can bring a witchcraft accusation.

Some assert that people's spirits may go out at night and become mosquitoes. When people are asleep, they bite them and vomit into them when they draw out blood. They thereby cause illness and death. The solution is to have people sleep together so they can avoid having this happen to them. Use of mosquito nets is a more effective solution.

There is the belief that a witch may strangle a person in the spiritual realm, though not physically. The spirit does this and then returns to the person physically. There is a whole set of beliefs about what can happen in the spiritual realm, which result in problems in the physical world. Witches who operate in the spiritual realm are termed *bakut atacci*.

There are certain kinds of snakes, especially specific ones found around the river, which people are forbidden to kill. The reason is that the spirit

---

[1] Besides having heart problems, another medical cause of swelling of one's joints is rheumatoid arthritis. It can cause retention of fluid in the affected joint(s). While rheumatoid arthritis usually attacks the joints, it can also go into the soft tissue, including one's heart.

of someone who is sleeping or who has a fever may be in that snake. If it is killed, the person will then quickly be in agony and die.

In another example, two children of a young Christian couple died. Members of the household urged the young wife to leave her husband and return to her father's house because they believed that her husband was responsible for their deaths through his *nkut* activities. So she left and went home. While there she had a dream in which one of the recently deceased Christian ancestors appeared to her. He urged her to return to her husband and told her that if she did not do so, when she died she would not find God. Consequently, she returned to her husband.

Actions to deal with *nkut*

When a person was accused of being a witch, the elders were called. They came and cautioned all the people to desist from witchcraft activities. They did not blame a person directly. However, if the elders really suspected a certain person of being responsible, they warned that specific person that if something happened to another person, then he would be held responsible. It may take a long time before something happened; however, the one warned will still be seen as responsible. In the case of a sudden death, especially of a young man, people are warned to cool their witchcraft so that others do not die from witchcraft.

If a person was called by the elders to defend him- or herself against a witchcraft accusation, the decision to impose a fine was not taken unless the person accepted responsibility for what had happened. He would only be warned. However, if he did accept responsibility, then a penalty was imposed.

As mentioned under "*nkut* deaths" above, in the case of evil *nkut*, Bajju requested that people at the funeral swear on the ground of the gravesite that they are not responsible for this death. A second way to address *nkut* is for the Bajju elders to warn people to refrain from engaging in *nkut*. The fact that there are a lot of young men dying in motorcycle and automobile accidents is seen as evidence that there is a lot of *nkut* being practiced. Hence some feel that pastors should warn people to desist from their *nkut* activities. Or if there is an epidemic, Bajju first pray to God to intervene for them, then they warn people to desist from engaging in *nkut* activities.

Occasionally a person accused of *nkut* has been beaten and forced to leave the village, hoping this would stop the problems that person has been accused of. The Bajju reason that if a person has performed witchcraft once, he or she may do it again. In the past, if someone was accused of causing the death of a person, that person had to stay with the corpse overnight in order to revive the corpse.

Some women accused of witchcraft have been beaten, sometimes severely, and then sent back to their fathers' compounds. This happens particularly to elderly women. Since swelling of the feet and ankles is seen as unnatural, as mentioned above, this is indicative that a person is a witch.

When someone dies and a particular person is suspected of being the one who caused the death, he will be asked to repent through the *sswa mbyen* ritual, as that ritual deals with a single death. However, if two or more young people die, then the ruling elder beats a stick on the ground to assert that this should not happen again (*zzu shan*). The elder states, "anyone responsible for this act, that person will have...happen to you." *Zzu shan* is considered very effective.

Concerning witchcraft in African traditional religion, Turaki writes:

> Witchcraft and sorcery are the two most dreaded social practices, and fear of them is pervasive in modern Africa. They are usually accompanied by selfish ambition, fear and tyranny, and they spread panic and death. The deaths of young people, mysterious deaths, accidents and incurable diseases are usually attributed to witchcraft and sorcery. There are many reported cases of old people being beaten to death after having been accused of being witches or sorcerers. It has also been reported that some urban residents sneak away without bidding farewell to relations and kinsfolk after a visit to their birthplace or village for fear of witchcraft and sorcery. (2006:102)

Taboos related to *nkut*

There are a number of taboos (see chapter 10) related to *nkut,* including the following:
1. As mentioned earlier in this chapter, people are not to kill spirit snakes in which the spirit of a sleeping person or person with a fever may have entered. If a person kills such a snake, the person whose spirit is in it will quickly be in agony and die.
2. People must be careful concerning the source of meat they eat. The Bajju tell their children to bring home any meat they are given at another compound and not to eat it. Their mother will then throw it away. It may be meat obtained through *nkut* activities. The belief is that if a child were to eat that meat, it is as if the child had received a loan he or she would have to repay later. This usually meant giving another person to the other world, killing another person with their *nkut*.
3. Women and children were not to eat eggs, chicken, birds in general, hyena, monkey, monitor lizard, and food prepared for the men's *ǫbvoi* organization. If a woman ate eggs, it meant that she would also "eat"

(practice *nkut* against) her own children thus causing their illnesses and death. Further, it is as if she would eat her own eggs from her womb and thus would not be able to have children.

Illness and *nkut*

No illness was believed to be from natural causes. Hence, when someone became ill, people would consult a diviner, an *abvok,* who investigated both the immediate and ultimate causes of the problem. Illnesses are dealt with in the following chapter.

Nkut and Christianity

Kunhiyop asserts that the Bajju have no concept of individuals being born with original sin (2005:84). From a Bajju perspective to even talk about evil would likely result in evil occurring. Belief in *nkut* is the closest they come to the biblical concept of original sin. Hence *nkut* is used to explain evil. People harm each other through their spiritual power.

The concept of salvation in many African societies is that

> A man's well-being consists, rather, in keeping in harmony with the cosmic totality. When things go well with him he knows he is at peace, and of a piece, with the scheme of things, and there can be no greater good than that. If things go wrong then somewhere he has fallen out of step. He feels lost. The totality has become hostile and, if he has a run of bad luck he falls a prey to acute insecurity and anxiety. (Taylor 1963:74–75)

Thus both sin and salvation are centered on the human condition. Salvation involves people doing well in their lives. If things are not going well, then they may pray at the grave of an ancestor, asking forgiveness for some past sin and praying that things go well in the future. They may also offer a sacrifice to cleanse the community of a sin that has occurred. They might also go to a diviner who identifies who caused their problem.

Some Christians assert that an evil spirit or demon enters an individual to explain why that person's spirit leaves his or her body, meeting with other spirits in the spiritual realm, and then causes evil to another person. As mentioned earlier in this chapter, from a biblical standpoint, while people may become demon possessed, there are no examples of peoples' spirits leaving their bodies to meet with other spirits in the spiritual realm and thus cause harm to others through psychic means. However, Bajju Christians do not seem to question the whole explanatory system of *nkut*. Rather they are incorporating it into their Christianity.

Christianity has not dealt well with this explanatory system. Bajju Christians are now faced with explaining from a Christian perspective what this system deals with. Normally they do so by drawing on their experience of life, without denying the existence of *nkut*. Part of the problem is that there is no ultimate evil being in their spirit world. In the Bible evil is explained through the actions of Satan—the devil, a fallen angel who rebelled against God—and through the actions of evil forces. Ephesians 6:12 (NIV) states, "For our struggle is not against flesh and blood, but against the rulers, against the authorities, against the powers of this dark world and against the spiritual forces of evil in the heavenly realms." The devil is spoken of as a liar, a deceiver, the prince of this world who stands condemned, the accuser, an ancient serpent who leads the whole world astray (see Revelation 12:9). He and his fallen rebellious angels are identified as the perpetuators of evil in this world.

Summary of *nkut*

Belief in *nkut* enables Bajju to address the question of why there is evil in the world. This conceptual system relates directly to their beliefs about God. God is good and gives only good things to people, such as his blessings, good crops, children, health, and answers to prayer. God is not responsible for things that are evil other than those which come because of his judgment and punishment for wrongdoing (for example, for sexual sins including adultery and incest, murder, stealing, sins against parents, and revealing *ạbvoi* secrets (Kunhiyop 2005:85)). Specific incurable diseases are identified as the result of God's judgment. Further, though there are various categories of spirits, most of which are evil, there is not one ultimate evil being, such as Satan, who is present within the Christian tradition. Therefore it is necessary to have some other explanation for why evil exists. Basically, *nkut* fills this function. People harm each other through their psychic acts. Death separates loved ones; therefore Bajju consider it to be evil. The Bible agrees when it terms death the last enemy to be destroyed (1 Corinthians 15:26). From a Christian point of view, Christ's death paid for humans' sins, and vengeance belongs to God (Romans 12:19); there is no need for retaliation against a person identified as a witch. Today people accused of being a witch may take their accuser to court. The judge then dismisses the case, since it is not possible to prove witchcraft accusations.

7

Illness and Medicine

Local medical systems intertwine with religion for people worldwide; this is true for the Bajju who divide illnesses into two categories: illnesses of God and illnesses of man. In the pre-Christian era, there were no medicines for illnesses of God, because they resulted from God's judgment and punishment for a person's wrongdoing. In the past, Bajju herbalists and diviners provided medicine for illnesses of man.

Illnesses of God

Illnesses of God result from a person's own activities. They are unnatural deaths, which include accidents, epilepsy, leprosy, severe diarrhea, smallpox, suicide, and HIV and AIDS.

Accidents

This category includes deaths due to hunting accidents, drownings, falls from trees, violent deaths, and road accidents. These are due to *nkut*. As one friend stated, "We know that there is lots of *nkut* being practiced, otherwise why do our young men continue to die in motorcycle and automobile accidents?"

Epilepsy

Bajju attributed epilepsy to the *gajimale,* the spirits that live in clear pools of water. The Bajju term for epilepsy is *rong ncen,* literally, "fire of the river," which explains this etiology. When a person suffers an epileptic seizure, according to Bajju belief, he is engaging in sexual intercourse with a *gajimale* spirit.

Leprosy

At the early stage, leprosy is euphemistically termed *atanyrang,* a term that refers to ringworm, in a patient's presence; it is often characterized by a white place on the skin, a spot termed ringworm (*dibyit atanyrang*). The Bajju treated leprosy in its early stage with *dikwai,* a vine that grows by the river that produces its fruit every year. The later stage of leprosy characterized by the disease entering a person's fingers is termed *gbap* and was considered an illness of God for which no treatment was available.

Severe diarrhea

While no longer placed in the unnatural disease category, severe diarrhea in the past was attributed to a person having sought to practice *nkut* against someone else, but it turned and attacked that person instead. Severe diarrhea is termed "a thief's stomach" (*kahwa atang*). Cholera is an example of severe diarrhea that results from drinking unclean water containing the bacterium *vibrio cholerea,* or food contaminated by feces with this bacterium in it. It results in vomiting and severe diarrhea, which leads to dehydration and even death. A couple of other causes of severe diarrhea are bacillary dysentery and amoebic dysentery. A person needs medical care when he or she develops any form of severe diarrhea because today medicine is available to treat these diseases.

Smallpox

As mentioned in chapter 6, Bajju believed that smallpox resulted because a person tried to practice *nkut* against someone, but it turned and attacked that individual instead. Hence a diviner asked the patient to count the number of persons he or she had "eaten" or caused to die through *nkut.* If the person refused to do so or did not name all the persons he or she practiced *nkut* against, then Bajju would claim his or her illness and subsequent death was due to their own activities. However, if the person gave the names of recently deceased persons he or she had "eaten," then the diviner gave medicine.

    In one amusing incident, a young man with smallpox was so anxious to recover that he listed everyone he could think of who had died, including some who had died before his birth. According to Bajju reasoning, he could not possibly be responsible for the deaths of those who died before he was born.

Because smallpox was attributed to witchcraft, when an individual contracted smallpox, another person, who had been accused of being a witch, had to stay with the patient. The Bajju also had persons who had recovered from smallpox stay with the patient to attend to his or her needs.

The Bajju practiced variolation, a form of vaccination. They squeezed a small amount of fluid from the smallpox sores and gave it to others who had not had the illness. If a person so vaccinated became ill, this was evidence that he had "eaten" others through his *nkut* activities. Worldwide vaccination campaigns have rid the world of this dreaded disease.

Suicide

Bajju believe that suicide is a dishonorable death. Sometimes when a person is unable to handle the pressures of life, he might hang himself from a tree.

Discussion of unnatural deaths

A person's status within the community did not change Bajju perception of the cause of his or her death. Thus, even if a *gado,* a respected elder, died from smallpox, he still received a dishonorable burial.

Illnesses of man

By illnesses of man Bajju speak of those illnesses that are brought about by someone else's *nkut* or spiritual activities towards the patient. The exception to this is the deaths of elderly people, who have fulfilled their functions in society and who die natural deaths. The verb Bajju use to describe their having arrived at this point in life is *kop,* which translates literally as "to ripen." It is the same verb that is used for fruit ripening. Hence since elderly people have ripened, it is their time to die.

Mourning for those who died natural deaths was cause for celebration of their lives. If a person had married, had children and perhaps grandchildren, became a respected elder, and lived a long, productive life, then they celebrated that life and death. An elderly man entered the underground world termed *ayabyen,* and from there his spirit would oversee the activities of the living. Rarely would an elderly respected woman enter the underground world. She would more likely be believed to be reincarnated. The feasting and dancing following the death of a respected elder was termed *kanak bapfo* 'mourning/crying with dancing'.

Ascertaining the cause of misfortune, illness, and death

Because there are various causes of misfortune, illness, and death, Bajju ascertained the cause of specific episodes by consulting a diviner. Diviners had spiritual vision, and as such they were deemed able to see into the spiritual realm to discover the cause of a problem.

When a patient and his family first went to a diviner, the diviner would ask, "Are you aware of this illness?" By this question the diviner wanted to know if the person was the cause of his or her own problem by having engaged in *nkut* activities. The majority of illnesses of man are caused by someone else's *nkut* activities.

In addition to diviners dealing with causes of illnesses and deaths, they also served as advisors to ward off natural disasters, such as droughts and locust invasions. They counseled people on the advisability of undertaking warfare or hunting. And they helped people with problems such as barrenness.

Diviners used stones or cowries[1] to discern the cause of a particular illness. A diviner would put his or her hands on the stones and ask them if medicine existed for a particular illness. If the stones agreed, he or she was able to pick the stones up; otherwise, they would be too heavy. A second means was to throw small cowries and see which way they fell. If many were on their backs, they agreed. Otherwise he or she was not able to treat the illness. The exact formula of their agreement depended on the person who performed this ritual.

In addition to diviners, there are also herbalists among the Bajju. Herbalists are frequently male, while diviners were both male and female, though most were female. Both diviners and herbalists gave medicine for illnesses of man. Herbalists deal with herbal remedies for various categories of illnesses. Some specialize in one area or condition and become known for their specialization. One man was good at dealing with snakebite; another was good at helping with complications in childbirth, etc. The Bajju assert that herbalists are good at treating hepatitis with various medicines made from the bark and leaves of specific plants. They claim that their medicine for hepatitis is as good as or better than that found in Western medicine, and they may well be right, because Western medicine does not deal well with it, though today Western medicine does have vaccinations to prevent both hepatitis A and hepatitis B.

---

[1] A cowry is a marine mollusk shell. Cowries were used as money in the precolonial era in the north of Nigeria.

Ascertaining the cause of the sickness or death of a young child

A diviner divined the cause of a sickness or death of an infant or young child through a ceremony termed "to cover the child," *kup kạwon.* If the child died, the mother together with her husband and an elderly woman went to the diviner to find out what caused the child's death and whether or not the child would be reincarnated. The ritual had slight variations if the child in question had not died but was very ill and the mother desired to find out why.

A former diviner provided the following description of *kup kạwon.* People who came for this ritual brought hungry rice (*tson; acca,* H.), guinea corn beer (*nkwwa; burkutu,* H.), salt (*ntwak*), a hen (*nyon*), beniseed (*cwrang*), and two shillings (twenty *kobo*). First, a person went to the river to blow a flute in order to entice the spirit of the child to come because the spirits of children are believed to live in river water. The diviner and her assistant assembled the equipment needed for the ritual, which included a large basket, a small basket, a small drinking calabash (*ạwa*), and some leaves of the locust bean tree (*kạron*). Then the ritual began.

The mother of the child sat holding the hen in her hands. The diviner took some hungry rice and poured it out. Then she mixed some beer, beniseed, salt, and medicine in the small calabash. The diviner put some hungry rice into the small basket together with some beniseed. Next she set the calabash on top of the small basket that held the hungry rice. She covered both with the larger basket. The diviner set these behind the chair where the mother sat. The diviner set some locust bean leaves on top of the head of the woman as well as on each of her shoulders. The diviner then took a small amount of the beer into her mouth and sprayed it onto the mother. The diviner next beat some leaves of the locust bean tree on the basket.

In order to induce the spirit of the child to come, a diviner on occasion went into a trance that might be induced by beating rhythmically on the calabash or gourd; a reed rattle (*zinzom*) might also be played. As soon as she heard these sounds, she might be aroused, and a trance was induced. Then the spirit of the child was believed to enter the basket and speak to the diviner. She would interpret the child's words for the mother and the others present. After the child indicated his or her presence, the diviner again sprayed the mother with beer. A conversation ensued between the diviner and the spirit of the ill or deceased child. The diviner welcomed the child's spirit. After exchanging greetings, the diviner asked specific questions, such as "Why did you come? What caused your illness or death?" The spirit told the nature of the problem, then the diviner gave a name for the next child that would be born to the couple.

After the spirit of the child finished his or her conversation with the diviner and the others present, the diviner gave the mother the small calabash with beer and medicine in it to drink. The diviner next took the hen from the mother's hands. If the child had died, she placed the hen on top of the mother's head. If the child had not died but was very ill, the diviner placed the hen on the floor in front of the mother's feet. The mother drank the mixture of guinea corn beer and medicine while the hen was on top of her head. The hen flew off her head on its own accord; no one was to take the hen down. When the hen was leaving, the diviner told those around to catch the hen. They gave the hen to the person in the diviner's household who first welcomed the guests who came for this ritual. However, if the child was alive, the diviner requested that no one catch the hen. After the hen left, the diviner beat the basket three times, then opened the basket. She took out a small amount of beniseed and gave it to the mother or to her child if her child was very ill.

The diviner I interviewed stated that she routinely washed her face with a certain type of medicine, which enabled her to see things in the spiritual realm and hear voices that most people were not able to. In the above ritual of *kup kạwon,* the diviner claimed that the child occasionally told her to give back the things that the mother and her husband had brought. When that occurred, she was unable to continue the ritual and would tell the parents that the child refused to speak. She also stated that when a child did speak, she did not tell the parents everything that the child told her.

In addition to the parents' request, the diviner would ask others present if they needed help. Before giving the parents a new name for their next child, the diviner helped others who needed her assistance. They would give her hungry rice that she then added to what was already in the basket. The child's spirit then diagnosed their problems too through the diviner.

This diviner asserted that by this ritual she helped the mother get her child back. She asserted that her ability to hear the spirit of the child and to discern the cause of illnesses was an ability given to her by God. She repeated several times that the basket did not lie.

I asked her why she no longer practiced divination. She replied that she had gotten tired because people would come to her at any hour of the day or night to request her aid. She also said that her brother, a pastor, had asked her to stop. After doing so, she became very ill. The people around her told her that her illness was the result of stopping practicing divination. However, her brother took her to a mission dispensary where they gave her medicine that helped her recover.

I also discussed this ritual with a woman who had gone through it when her child died. The memory of her deceased child was still painful. I asked her who had spoken to her from the basket, and she replied that it was the small spirits (*nạtenyrang*—see further chapter 8, "Small spirits"). This contrasts with the perspective of the diviner who stated that the voice she heard was that of the child.

Infanticide

The first mention of infanticide as practiced in Southern Zaria comes from Tremearne, a British political officer stationed at Jema'a in the early 1900s. He wrote concerning the Agorok practice as follows:

> If a child be an idiot, or unable to move about, it may be thrown into the water, "but not killed," so they say, though it comes to very much the same thing as far as the ordinary person can see. This usually happens when the child is between the ages of one and four, but in some cases it may be given a much longer time in the hope that it will recover and become a normal being. "It is evidently a snake, and not a human being," so I was told, "and if, after you have thrown him into the water, you go away, and then come back silently and hide yourself, you will see the child lengthen out until it becomes a snake." (Tremearne 1912:239)

Tremearne also stated that the parents could request someone from another ethnic group, such as a Fulani, to place the child by the river. Although the above quotation was specifically about the Agorok, he states that this custom was prevalent in the groups throughout the Jema'a area. He mentioned that if an Asholio woman gave birth to such a child, she may nurse it even for an extended time. However, if the child did not improve, she left the child with the father. She would not return to that husband as long as that child lived for fear that the evil influence of that child would prevent her from having a normal child.

An early description by SIM missionaries of the Agorok states similarly, "...little deformed and handicapped children were thrown into the hollow trunk of a large baobab tree and left to die" (Ames n.d.).

Bajju shared this practice of infanticide. A child who did not thrive was termed a *dison*. Children in this category had the mental level of idiots or were children who were unable to crawl, walk, or speak. If, after a reasonable length of time, the child did not improve, the parents decided it was a *dison*. Their reasoning was that such a child was not human, but rather a spirit from the river (*kyang ncen* 'thing of the river') or water spirit. Because such a child was not human, the rational course of action was to return the child to the place where he or she belonged, namely the river. The father or another relative would place the child beside the river and the child would fall in of his or her own accord. If the parents felt that they could not do this, they gave the child, together with some money, to a Fulani. He would place the child near the water's edge, then place a calabash nearby. When the child reached for the calabash, he or she fell into the water and drown.

There were situations that were ambiguous as to whether or not a child was a *dison*. In those situations the parents went to a diviner who helped them know the appropriate course of action. Those situations included a child who was born deformed, a child born with erupted teeth, or a child with an unusual birthmark. In contrast, a child born with the amniotic sac (*ạtro*) around it was said to have dignity and therefore would grow up to be a chief. Such a child was not given a special name.

One baby boy was born with a birthmark on his neck. Since this was not normal, his mother wondered whether or not he was a *dison*. So this young mother went to the diviner to ask about her infant. The diviner said that this mark indicated that this young baby was destined to do something great, hence she should take him home and care for him, which she did. His life was saved through the wise counsel of that diviner.

Bajju Christians have resisted this custom. Some of them receive advice from friends, relatives, or neighbors to drown a child who does not thrive, but they refuse to do so. Thus with the advent of Christianity, this custom is dying out. I found no mention in the archival records of attempts on the part of the British colonial administration to stop this practice, though it might have occurred.

Difficulty in childbirth

If a woman had sexual relations with many men and then had difficulty giving birth, she may be asked to count the people she slept with. Following that, she was asked to repent. The woman placed ashes on her tongue and then spat them out, which was part of the *sswa bạtwak* ritual described in chapter 4. As mentioned there, the woman again took a small amount of ash into her mouth and swallowed it; that ash represents a blessing. God then finds the ashes that she spat out and forgives her evil actions. After she finished counting the last man's name, they believe that the baby would be born immediately.

Another possible way of assisting was for her to use hungry rice. The hungry rice consists of small grains, indicating many men. These she threw to indicate that she had had sexual relations with many.

They might also ask the woman to count the people she had practiced *nkut* against. If she enumerated all the people against whom she had practiced *nkut,* then they believed that she would be able to deliver her child safely. If complications persisted, that was evidence that she had not confessed all the people against whom she had practiced *nkut.*

Euthanasia

If a woman had aged sufficiently but she had not died, her situation needed to be looked into. Her longevity could be due to something in her earlier life. For example, if an elderly, physically infirmed woman who was perhaps unable to see or walk anymore had earlier in her life given food to her parents, they may have blessed her with a long life. Hence, she would not die even if she had aged sufficiently to do so. Then she might ask for hungry rice (*tson; acca,* H.); her relatives would come to feed her hungry rice that had poison (*kasop*) mixed into it. Those relatives would first ask her if she wanted it, and if she agreed, then they gave it to her. However, if she disagreed, they would let her live. After they fed her poisoned hungry rice, her family would begin dancing. They would then say, "God heard the mourning, and she died" (*Kaza a hok kanak ka, a ku*).

Usually this form of euthanasia was not practiced for elderly, infirmed men. However, it was not unusual for elderly, infirmed women to request it. In gathering data with an interview schedule, my research assistant became interested in the question of euthanasia. When he encountered an elderly man or woman, he asked whether or not there was poison in the hungry rice that was given to an elderly, infirmed woman. In his informal survey, he found that most elderly women replied that poison had not been added, while elderly men replied that it had been. One elderly pastor assured me that it was poisoned; however, he stated that men withheld this information from women. While this form of euthanasia was traditionally practiced, since the advent of Christianity it is no longer done.

Illnesses and remedies

Table 7.1 summarizes some causes of Bajju illnesses, symptoms, and typical remedial actions that formed part of their traditional medical system. This table is incomplete because there are local remedies for most, but not all, illnesses. Also, in each village an herbalist and diviner had medicines and procedures he or she would not reveal to others, so that there was no standard remedial action for an illness. The terms "illness" or "sickness" refer to those afflictions "...which have named socio-culturally relevant causes and require culturally defined and socially mediated responses" (Glick 1967:39). Illnesses contrast with ailments, which are relatively minor and transient afflictions.

Table 7.1. Illnesses (*nhyu*), symptoms, causes, and traditional remedial actions

Illnesses	Symptoms	Ultimate cause	Local remedial action
Blindness, a blind person (*atutwan ayin*)	Loss of sight, cataracts	Having seen the *gajimale,* a serpent that lives under mountains or in the water	

Diarrhea (*dikwang, kḁhwa ḁtang*)	Diarrhea, dehydration	Formerly considered to be caused by *nkut*	Drink ashes (*bḁtwak*) or potash (*kḁmanda*) mixed with water
Epilepsy (*rong ncen*)	Convulsions	Caused by having intercourse with a water spirit (*gḁjimale*)	Pour water on the person when convulsing
Evil spirit encounter (*ḁkḁtuk wun*)	A person speaks nonsense because his intelligence is stirred up	Meeting an evil spirit	Prayer by a Christian
Fever (*bḁsoza*)	Elevated temperature	Offending the small spirits (*nḁtenyrang*)	Remove bark from the *dikok* tree (Latin: *Bombax buonopozense*, English: red-flowered kapok tree) at the site where the sun strikes it in the morning and in the evening. Combine the bark with three stalks of ground millet to make a porridge, which the person drinks twice daily. If the fever persists, bathe the patient in water.
Leprosy (*gbap*)	Leprosy has entered a patient's fingers	Called an evil sickness, formerly considered to be caused by *nkut* activities	See ringworm[2]

Meningitis (*amampfwa*)	Fever, stiff neck, vomiting, rash, loss of consciousness		Porridge prepared from the pounded roots of the *ccuk* and/or the *abvat* vine.[3] Today they take the patient to the hospital where the doctor is likely to prescribe a needed drug.[4]
Ringworm (*atanyang*)	Discoloration and thickness of places on the skin; the early stage of leprosy		(1) The leaves of the mandim vine (*cowitch*, species of velvet bean, *Mucuna pruriensis*) mixed with water. The patient drinks some of this mixture and bathes in it. (2) Place a hot knife on the site of the leprosy (a Fulani remedy).
Scorpion sting (*nyang top ayin*)	Pain and swelling at the site of the bite, fever, incision at the site of the sting		Mix chicken excrement with water and give to the patient to drink

---

[2] Since leprosy is a bacterial disease, there is medication for it within the Western medical system. This medication must be taken for an extended period of time.

[3] I was unable to find the English translation for this vine. I was also unable to find the English translation for the *jjun* tree.

[4] It is important to get the patient to medical care as soon as possible, since it is a matter of time for the medicine to take effect. The longer one waits to take the patient to medical care, the more likely the patient will die.

Sickle cell anemia (*hyyu bạtwak*)	Insufficient blood, pale skin color, blood cells form sickle shapes that block blood vessels		Lick powdered medicine morning, noon, and evening; the patient is not to step on grass. If he does so, the treatment has to begin again
Snakebite (*ryik bvvok ạyin*)[5]	Pain and swelling at the site of the bite, incision from the fangs, fever		Drink medicine and place the medicine on the site of the bite. Shave a small area on the head, and make a cut to allow the poison in the blood to exit. Give the patient a raw egg to eat to induce vomiting.

Common medicines

Two common medicines used for a variety of illnesses are potash (*kạmanda*) and ashes (*bạtwak* or *bạatwak ạbyeng*). Potash is put into soup and drunk. It is known as the medicine of blood. It might be given to a mother after childbirth to cause the remaining blood to come out of her uterus. It might also be used for intestinal problems, including both diarrhea and constipation. The word *ntwak* translates as "salt," consequently the word *bạtwak ạbyeng* is related etymologically to salt. *Bạtwak ạbyeng* is made from the ashes of stalks of roasted millet. The bran is thrown away, and water is poured through the powder that remains, leaving a smooth paste. This is then put on the fire to allow the rest of the water to evaporate. The remaining powder is *bạtwak ạbyeng*. This medicine may be drunk with water or mixed with millet porridge (*ạhyu*). It is used to counter intestinal upsets due to having eaten bad food, too much meat, or other causes.

---

[5] To prevent snakebite, an individual could eat raw leaves from the *jjun* tree each day for seven days. Then if a snake saw the person, it would be unable to open its mouth. Individuals must not eat too much of this medicine as it could cause death. It was also ingested by a woman to abort a fetus. Roots of the *kạntrik* tree were also used to prevent snakebite.

Summary

The Bajju divided illnesses and deaths into two categories: illnesses of God and illnesses of man. This chapter presented remedies for various illnesses. Today there are at least two hospitals in their area: the government hospital at Kafanchan and Saint Louis Catholic Hospital at Zonkwa. Further, missionaries and local Christians have set up dispensaries that deal with the physical illnesses people have. Each SIM mission station was supposed to have a dispensary. Today the local churches have taken over these dispensaries. Hospitals and dispensaries practice Western-type medicine though many people continue to believe and follow older Bajju illness etiologies and remedies. Medical facilities are widely used and appreciated by the local population. Diviners no longer practice their craft, so people no longer go to diviners, though herbalists continue to provide their services to those who request help from them.

The next chapter addresses traditional concepts of God and the spirit world.

8

God and the Spirit World

The Bajju spirit world consists of God, the living dead, and various categories of spirits. A person's continued prosperity, including conception of progeny and long life, depends upon the blessings of God and the living dead. This chapter explores the Bajju concept of God and the spirit world.

God

God (*Kaza*[1]) presides over the world. He is the creator of both mankind and the universe; however, Bajju have no narrative about how God created the universe and the things in it. At a location near Kamarum, a village within the Bajju area, there are a few round indentations on top of the dome-shaped mountain where Bajju elders went to pray to God for rain. The Bajju claim that the power present at this location is that of God. When the Bajju elders used to go to that location, they cut the grass around those indentations, offered a sacrifice to God, and prayed for rain. They believed that rain would come even before they reached home. There the strength of God is greater than that of any other spirit. There are similar locations at Asakwak, Kudan, Azaru, and Cenccuk.

---

[1] *Kaza* is pronounced *[kadza]*; however, because there is no contrast between [z] and [dz] in Jju, and [z] and [dz] tend to fluctuate, in the alphabet this sound is represented as "z."

For both the Bajju and the nearby Ham, God is associated with natural phenomena: rain for the Bajju, and the sun for the Ham.[2] The word *Kaza* also indicates the direction north, high, and up.[3] The Ham term *Nom* refers both to God and the sun. The Bajju have a cognate term *nom,* which translates as "sun" or "day," but Bajju never use it to refer to God. Other expressions commonly used to refer to the Supreme Being are "the God who is chief" or the "Chief God," *Agwam Kaza;* or the "Lord God," "the Chief of heaven," *Agwam Tazwa;* and "God in heaven," *Kaza Tazwa.*

Kaza is used frequently in daily life expressions. In order to understand the semantic domain of the word *Kaza,* I elicited the following expressions that relate to him:

"God is" or "God exists," *Kaza an shyi,* gives comfort and assurance that God is ultimately in control of all things on earth and that he will act on a person's behalf.[4] This frequently used phrase affirms God's protection, blessing, and presence with us. When all else fails, there is always God.

"God saves me," *Kaza an tun,* indicates that God is the one responsible for saving somebody from misfortune. It may be used if a person got his hand stuck, but then he was able to free it.

"God is sufficient," *Kaza a maai,* implies that God is sufficient to right the wrongs done to a person. He is almighty. If a person has been wronged but does not desire to take vengeance or has given up trying to do so, he

---

[2] The word for God is composed of the noun class prefix *ka-,* and the noun stem *za,* which means "rain." However, Bajju do not usually think of God as the "one of the rain" or the "one who gives rain."

[3] One day our language assistant asked my husband, Norris, what his name meant. As he began to translate his name meaning "king of the north," he realized that a literal translation would come out in Jju as "the Lord God." Norris got as far as "chief" or "king" and then evaded the question by saying, "How is the weather?" He could not translate his name because the collation of words in Jju meant something quite different from the English words.

[4] One day as my husband, Norris, a Bajju friend, and I drove north towards Kaduna on a rough, unpaved washboard road from the village of Unguwar Rimi where we lived, two tires blew out at the same time. We stopped, changed one tire with the spare tire, and began working on taking the other tire off in order to patch the inner tube. Soon an army truck stopped to help us, and one soldier enthusiastically used the tire iron to help get the tire off the rim so that we could patch the inner tube. He quickly had the tire changed and put back on our car. He had worked quickly and vigorously. We thanked him and proceeded on our journey. Fifty kilometers (31 miles) later the tire the soldier changed went flat. We pumped it up with air again, then proceeded on our journey. Fifty kilometers farther the same thing happened, and so on until we got to the city to have it attended to properly. It turned out that the soldier's vigorous work resulted in the initial hole being patched, but it also put six new holes in the inner tube; hence it went flat every fifty kilometers. However, each time we pumped that tire up, our Bajju friend said, "God exists, we go!" *Kaza an, shyi, zi cong!* From his perspective there was no problem that God is not aware of and that is not under his control, even tire problems!

may assert *Kaza a maai.* An example is, if a child is beaten by someone larger against whom he has no chance of retaliation, he may use this expression. Likewise, the question "Who is sufficient?" *Yamaai* implies that God is sufficient. This phrase may be given as a boy's name to imply God's sufficiency.

"May God make it happen" or "God allowed it to happen," *Kaza a yya,* is a prayer used to affirm that God is able to cause whatever is in question to come to pass. A pregnant woman may use this to pray that God will cause her delivery to be safe. Or someone could use it when traveling as a prayer that God will allow him to arrive safely. Another related expression is "May God allow you to arrive well," *Kaza a yya yi nwwa bu kankreng.*

"God will see," *Kaza a ba ryi,* implies that God will see and protect. It may be used to express sympathy to a woman whose newborn child has died. A boy born after other siblings have died may be given the name *Kaza,* a shortened form of this expression, as a prayer that God will protect this child.

"May God raise us" or "May God awaken us," *Kaza za shyek,* is a common response to the evening parting phrase "Until tomorrow," *Se kantson.* It asserts the desire that God will raise us from sleep the next day.

The expression "You will meet with God," *A ni mon bu Kaza,* is used to assert that God will deal with a person who wronged another person. This indicates the Bajju concept that God will judge deeds committed in this world and that he is the final judge in the afterlife.

The idiom "God protects us from crying," *Kaza za cam nkun,* indicates that God helps in situations where people are helpless.

The common expression "God is in heaven" or "God is up in the sky," *Kaza a shyi an tazwa,* affirms the existence of God. The Bajju live in an awareness of his presence.

"May God let it be," *Kaza a yya,* is a prayer often used at the end of meetings. It asserts that only God is able to bring to pass what has been decided upon.

"God preserves and protects," *Kaza an tun* is used when God delivers a person from danger, an accident, or some misfortune.

The above expressions give some idea of the Bajju concept of God, including his nature and work. He is the creator of man and the universe. He is the one to whom final appeal is made. In the event of illness when all other remedies have been tried but to no avail, one can always appeal to God. God is just and man's final judge; consequently God may be asked to punish someone who wrongs another person. He is all present, all knowing, eternal, and good. God gives only good things such as children, good hunting and crops, wealth, health, and blessings; thus death, illness, natural disasters, misfortunes, and evil cannot originate with God, other than those that a person deserves as punishment for his or her offenses. For example, if a man swears falsely on the drum, the death that results comes from God.

Prior to the coming of Christianity, the Bajju had knowledge of God, but they did not worship him directly.

As a result of the attributes of God, coupled with God's association with the sky, Bajju did not look up too much when walking, in order to show respect or a high regard for him. God's association with the sky is expressed in the common phrase "God of heaven" or "God who is up in the sky," *Kaza tazwa.*

According to one United Native African church pastor, Christianity made God known to them. He stated that prior to the introduction of Christianity, Bajju knew that God existed, but they did not know him. Christianity did not teach about a different God, but rather it expanded their knowledge of him. Further, they knew that there is an afterlife. Since they bury people in the ground; the afterlife (*ayabyen*) was associated with the ground. Only good people were believed to go to *ayabyen*, while bad people were rejected. After a person died and was buried, people tended to walk carefully and softly on the ground in order not to disturb the recently buried person. Christians assert that they knew there was an afterlife, but they did not know God would be there. Those who do not go to *ayabyen* were believed to be reincarnated on the third day after their burial.

The mother of God

Elderly Bajju speak of the mother of God, whereas younger Bajju are unaware of this concept. However, elderly speakers refer to her either as *ana Kaza,* "the mother of God" or *ana Agwam Kaza,* "the mother of the Chief God."

The Bajju concept of the mother of God parallels that of the Mwaghavul concept of God, *Naan,* who is feminine. The Mwaghavul, or Sura (H.), are a Plateau people, and the Bajju originally migrated from the Plateau. Under the impact of Christianity the Mwaghavul now conceive of God as masculine (Datok 1983:84–85; Isichei 1982:28). Similarly, the concept of a mother of God among the Bajju declined. Although I do not know the cause of this decline, it seems likely that it relates to the impact of Christianity. Only in Catholicism are prayers addressed to "Mary, the mother of God."

Serious matters were referred to the mother of God. A person might have said, "You will meet with the mother of God," *A ni mon bu ana Kaza.* In discussing this phrase with various people, the general consensus was that it relates to the high esteem with which a mother is held. One person suggested that it parallels the expression "You will win over your mother," *A ni ya ana nwan,* (literally, "You will eat/win over your mother"). The shortened form of this abusive phrase is "Your mother," *ana nwan.*

Small spirits

Small invisible spirits, known as *nątenyrang* (*kątenyrang,* sing.), inhabit villages in the bush away from people or live among people in the Bajju territory. Some assert that the *nątenyrang* are people who have been reincarnated as spirits. They are thought to be either black or white. If black, they have an evil nature, and they are short in stature with big heads (Kunhiyop 1988:12), and if white, they have a good nature and bring good fortune and goodness. These spirits have their own chief, known as *ągwam kątenyrang.* Their villages resemble those of the Bajju, complete with round huts, paths, and roads. They are known to surround their compounds with thornbushes; consequently, one way that Bajju recognize that a site was inhabited by *nątenyrang* is by the presence of thornbushes.

The *nątenyrang* can inflict illness upon people for offending them (see chapter 7). In order to determine the cause of illnesses, people consulted diviners who determined whether or not the *nątenyrang* were responsible for specific illnesses. The illnesses attributed to *nątenyrang* included severe fevers, mental illnesses, and convulsions from epilepsy. Since the *nątenyrang* are small, they beat people where they can reach, namely on the legs. The Bajju attribute illnesses associated with a person's legs, such as wounds and paralysis, to the *nątenyrang.* Barrenness may also be ascribed to the *nątenyrang.*

Such illnesses do not go away readily without taking medicine or placating the spirits that might be offended by people being there. People could take money or cooked beans to them and leave these in the bush for them to pick up and eat. If a Bajju perceived that the *nątenyrang* were near, as by seeing their footprints or broken pieces of their pottery, then that person could make a smoky fire from a special kind of sticks or leaves that produces a scent to drive them away.

Most people lack the capacity to see *nątenyrang* and their villages because these spirits are invisible. Some people with spiritual vision, such as diviners (*bąbvok*), could see them. However, for most people to see *nątenyrang* implies that sickness results.

When humans move into an area, *nątenyrang* may move to other sites, as they do not like noise or light. After they abandon their villages for other sites, anyone is able to see the ruins of their villages. Evidence of their abandoned villages are small round mud walls, pot shards, and thornbushes. The mud walls of such abandoned *nątenyrang* houses are valued as medicine. People come to Kajju from as far away as Zaria in order to obtain this type of medicine. It can be mixed with water and herbs and then rubbed on a person's affected legs as well as drunk.

Figure 8.1. Abandoned
ruins of a *kạtenyrang*
house (Carol McKinney).

Figure 8.2. Ancient granary at
Nok (Carol McKinney).

According to Kato, the Ham associated abandoned furnace hearths used
for iron smelting by prehistoric people of the area with the houses of the
spirits (1974:37). The same is probably true for the Bajju. One Bajju man led
me to a site near Zaria that he thought might have been a former *nạtenyrang*
village (see figure 8.1). The small, round, broken-down walls of the houses
were surrounded by thornbushes; however, nearby we found a slag heap
indicating that people who formerly occupied the area had smelted iron on
this site. Alternatively, these obviously human-constructed ruins may be
what are left from the weathered granaries of prehistoric people (see figure
8.2). The pictured ancient granary was left by prehistoric people who lived
in the village of Nok, likely from people of the Nok Cultural Complex. It is
so well preserved because it is located in a small cave.

Because white *nạtenyrang* are believed to be good, people may appeal
to them for good fortune, children, and so on. They are harmless to people who pass through their areas. When white people first came to the
Bajju area, the local people identified them as the *nạtenyrang*. By contrast,
black *nạtenyrang* bring evil, including pestilence and drought. Although
nạtenyrang have a tendency to do evil things, not all of their activities are
evil. Some simply want to live their own lives, free from interference by
humans; however, humans may interfere with their lives by inadvertently

stepping on them, their houses, their clothes, their villages, and their children.

Because of the actions of *ŋatenyrang,* people avoided specific activities. The Bajju used to tell their children not to go out during the hottest part of the day when the sun is very bright because *ŋatenyrang* might bring delicious food, such as cooked beans, to tempt them. If a child saw the food, he might eat it and then become very thirsty. If a diviner ascertained that the *ŋatenyrang* caused a specific child's illness, she might ask the child what food he received from the *ŋatenyrang.*

If people suspect that these spirits are nearby, they can put a stick in the fire. When they hear it burning, the *ŋatenyrang run* away. Another way to appease them is to give them money and put it into the bush for them.

Some areas within Bajju-land are known as sites where the *ŋatenyrang* reside. One woman told of hearing the *ŋatenyrang* speaking at night at a hill near Adwan, a hill called *Tsom Byyai.* She said that while she was walking, carrying a headload of oranges, she heard something fall around her feet. Her first thought was that she had dropped an orange, but when she looked, she saw a stone that she was sure the *ŋatenyrang* had thrown at her. Since their actions occur primarily at night, she was not afraid to go there during the day. Generally, *ŋatenyrang* are more active at night so people are often afraid to go out then. One old man told me of lying in his bed at night and hearing the *ŋatenyrang* pass by outside his house.

Water spirits

Water spirits, the *baconcong (aconcong,* sing.), are also known as the *gajimale.* They live in clear, still water as well as in the bush, in trees, in a forest, or in caves. A water spirit may come out of the water to seduce its victim by transforming itself into a beautiful woman and appear thus to a man, or as a handsome man who appears to a woman, or as a snake. While *gajimale* can transform themselves, one can identify them because they cannot transform their toes, which are like those of horse hooves (Kunhiyop 1988:14). The *gajimale* are also thought to be serpents that live under mountains.[5] Various water spirits are known to come out around noon and again around 6 p.m.

When a Bajju person crossed the Atacap River by the spectacular Matsirga Waterfall near Kafanchan in the southeastern Bajju area, they sought to avoid the mist that arose from it. Water spirits and the spirits of unborn children who live under the water are associated with the mist and water in general. If the mist touches a person, it is believed that illness or death may follow because of contact with these spirits.

---

[5] The Kuteb of Nigeria also believe in a giant dragon or snake that lives under mountains. When a mud slide occurs, they believe it was caused by the dragon or snake moving (Rob Koops, personal communication, 1984).

A person may keep a *gajimale* in his or her room or in some other convenient place. Kunhiyop reports that while he was growing up in a Bajju village, a woman named Lamit was believed to keep one in a tree beside the main road (1988:14). They called the tree Lamit's tree, *kạradwan Lamit* (Kunhiyop 1993:70). The reason people keep them is in order to employ their services to be successful in business or in farming. To receive their aid, a person must give his or her children to the *gajimale* through *nkut* activities or through telling others' secrets to them. To give one's children to the *gajimale* means that the children of that individual continue to die while the person becomes rich. It is believed that telling others' secrets to the *gajimale* may help one become rich but will cause others' children to become ill and die through *nkut* activities.

The *gajimale* cause illnesses, as can the *nạtenyrang*. For example, as mentioned in chapter 7, Bajju term epilepsy *rong ncen* (literally, "fire of the river") and attribute it to having sex with the *gajimale*. (See above under "Small spirits" for another possible spiritual cause of epilepsy.) Because this illness is associated with the *gajimale,* death from epilepsy is an abnormal death; so a person who dies from it is not given an honorable burial within the compound. Some people consider epilepsy grounds for divorce. The *gajimale* may also cause blindness. One elderly man attributed his increasing blindness to having seen the *gajimale*.[6] They can also cause accidents; a bulldozer operator blamed the *gajimale* for an accident in which the bulldozer was destroyed.

If a person is sent out on an errand, such as to obtain live coals for making a fire from another compound, and happens to go by the river, that person may feel something psychologically on his or her head. People are instructed to run away when they have this feeling, and in the future they would not want to go that way without having someone accompany them.

If a rainbow appears, it indicates that the *gajimale* have appeared. Therefore it will not rain again.

Bajju are not alone in believing that spirits live in rivers. Datok describes similar beliefs among the Mwaghavul.

> They believe that there are certain beings living in waters of the streams, and who have supernatural powers, such that can affect human beings. At times good things or special abilities are derived from the 'river people' (*Nyem dung*), e.g. some may dance very well or may farm more than usual, etc. Some of these are said to be borrowed glories from the river people. (1983:86)

---

[6] The physical cause is the presence of cataracts, which grow when peoples' eyes age. The lens on the eye becomes opaque. In many countries eye doctors take the lens off and insert a new lens so that people can see clearly again. If a cataract is not removed, the person can become blind in that eye.

He continues by stating that river spirits may catch people who offend them, but that they never catch honest or straightforward people. Mwaghavul[7] and Bajju beliefs coincide in that people may enter into a relationship with these spirits, who provide them with abilities they would not possess otherwise. These include the ability to become rich, to farm well, and to prosper. But there is a price extracted for collaboration with water spirits. Given the Bajju belief in the *gajimale,* their assertion that death by drowning is a shameful death is understandable. Infants born deformed or abnormal may also be viewed as water spirits, and thus must be returned to the river where they belong (see chapter 7 on infanticide, *dison*).

Tall spirits

The *baninyet* (*aninyet,* sing.) are very tall spirits who reach high into the sky. An *aninyet* is so tall that an adult cannot see its head. These spirits appear late at night or early in the morning, as between 3 to 6 a.m. when some people set out on journeys. Some assert that if a person sees one and admits it to others, that person will die. One source stated that the *baninyet* are a type of *natenyrang,* though others put them in a class by themselves. *Baninyet* may speak to people when they meet them.

Others say that they are not harmful to humans, but only frighten them (Kunhiyop 1988:14; 1993:71). Kunhiyop asserts that if a person goes to the dwelling of an *aninyet,* that spirit will not hurt him or her. He also states that the *baninyet* have their dwellings among human beings.

One Christian Bajju man reported seeing an *aninyet* early one morning. When he saw it, he closed his eyes and prayed; when he opened them again, the spirit had vanished, thus proving to him that the power of the Holy Spirit was stronger than that of the *aninyet.*

Ancestral spirits, the living dead

The largest and most important category of spirits is the spirits of the departed. The Bajju term ancestral spirits the *banyeyabyen,* or *abvoi,* sing., *babvoi,* pl.; they occupy a central position within Bajju daily life. They are viewed as still living, hence many speak of them as the living dead. The Bajju believe spirits inhabit an underground ancestral spirit world, *ayabyen.* After the introduction of the *abvoi* organization, the two categories of spirits, *banyet yabyen* and *babvoi,* tended to merge. Elderly male ancestors comprise

---

[7] The relationship between these two ethnic groups may not be as close as one might posit based on the fact that at one point in time both resided on the Plateau. This is because the Bajju speak a Benue-Congo language, while the Mwaghavul speak a Chadic language within the Afro-Asiatic language family. So they did not come from the same protoculture. However, living in close proximity could have resulted in their influencing each other.

most of the *ạbvoi*; however, though rarely, respected elderly women could also become ancestral spirits within a family. Spirits of deceased infants, children, women, and men who had no progeny did not become *ạbvoi,* but they were reincarnated.

Ancestral spirits had to be cared for, so that they in turn would care and provide for the living. This care included offering sacrifices to them at their gravesites, praying to them, invoking them in times of danger, and putting food out for them to eat. In addition, a Bajju may swear by an ancestor as it provides legitimacy to what is sworn.

The ancestors provide protection, blessings, and forgiveness for when they were wronged during the ancestor's lifetime. They are present to watch over the household and give abundant harvests and fertility to the land and people. They ward off evil and provide for people's needs. To the Bajju the ancestral spirits are real, as real as any living person. The belief in and respect for ancestral spirits is an extension of their respect for and submission to the Bajju elders.

At the burial ceremony and again at the mourning celebration, the Bajju send greetings to others who have died who are related through their recently deceased relative. They used to sing, "Where, where, where ... have you gone" (*Ke, ke, ke* ...) and give the names of people that the departed should greet.

Before death some elderly persons provide guidance concerning their wishes after their death. They remind their families that they will still be living and watching over them. One elderly grandfather stated that after he died he did not want anyone within his family to become a chief, and to this day no one from that family has. In the early days Bajju viewed chiefs as wicked persons who collected taxes and related to outsiders; they were not among the respected elders in Bajju communities.

After the death of an elder, his family continued to bring food into his room because his spirit was believed to come back to eat the food. They placed this food on a high shelf in his room. Early each morning for one week to one month the children of the household were to eat some of this food from which the spirit of the deceased had also eaten.

Ancestral spirits survive death and take a lively interest in the activities of the living. Anything that concerns people within their extended families also concerns the ancestral spirits. They are concerned about the continuation of the family, lineage, and clan.

While serving the function of guardians of their families, ancestral spirits are viewed by some as intermediaries between the living and God. They are viewed as being closer to God than the living, so some pray to God through the ancestors.

These spirits may be either good or evil. Evil ones are feared and dreaded, while good ones are harmless. Ancestral spirits may also be offended; and if this occurs, they must be appeased. If a person offended a parent during his or her lifetime and if he or she did not ask forgiveness from that parent before the parent's death, following death that spirit may still be troubled. If a person perceives that this is the case, then he or she must seek forgiveness by praying to that ancestor at the gravesite.

Ancestral spirits may appear to people in dreams and visions and thereby provide continued guidance for the living concerning their wishes. Dreams work differently for different people. One man kept seeing his deceased father in dreams. When his nephew came home soon after those dreams, he said that he knew something good was going to happen. Whenever he saw his father in a dream, it indicated to him that something good would occur soon.

If somebody encounters an ancestral spirit in a face-to-face situation and not in a dream, it is considered a bad omen. It usually means that that person will die, especially if it occurs when that person is ill.

Kunhiyop writes,

> The *banyeyabyen* can be wronged and be appeased. If, for example, a son who offended a deceased father during his lifetime and did not seek for forgiveness, he may later be required to seek forgiveness when he realizes that the spirit of his departed father is still troubled. He would, therefore, take wine [likely guinea corn beer] to the grave of his deceased father. The elders would take the wine, and forgiveness would be sought from the spirit of the ancestor. (1993:71–72)

If a household head feels that things are not going well for his family, he may decide to offer a sacrifice to an ancestor in order to do what he can to cleanse the atmosphere. If there is constant quarreling between members of his household, he may seek to forestall possible negative consequences by this sacrifice, confession, and prayer. He may also decide to do so if he or a member of his household has constant bad dreams (Kunhiyop 1993:94).

Bajju respect the graves of their deceased ancestors. Consequently, those graves are either within the courtyard of the compound or under the floor of the house of the deceased. It is not unusual to go into a compound and see a grave either in a room or in the courtyard. Graves remain places to show respect to one's ancestors.

Today each compound tends to have an area nearby set aside as a burial site for their deceased ancestors. By having their own private cemeteries, people do not have to move quite so much. Previously people moved when there were too many burials in a compound (see chapter 9, under "Death"). The use of commercial fertilizer also makes moving less necessary than previously occurred. In the past, with their slash-and-burn horticulture, people moved when the soil became exhausted. This is no longer necessary.

Intrinsic to beliefs and practices concerning ancestral spirits is the belief that each person has a spirit as well as a physical body. These Bajju beliefs are similar to those of related ethnic groups such as the Irigwe, A̲tyap, A̲gorok, and others. The Bajju also share with these groups belief in reincarnation. Sangree states with respect to the Irigwe, "Every human being is the reincarnation of the soul of someone who lived before, and at the same time a new and unique person" (Sangree 1974:47). The same applies to the Bajju who view life as a circle beginning as a spirit, then birth as an individual, marriage resulting in children, death, followed by rebirth.

Spirit possession cult

The spirit possession cult among the Bajju, the *bvori*, likely spread to the Bajju from the Hausa and Fulani as evidenced by the use of the Hausa loan term *bori*. This term probably originated in northern Benin Republic from the village of Bori where this cult continues to be practiced. Various scholars have described the Hausa Bori cult, including Tremearne (1912) and Besmer (1983). Sargent (1982:77–82) described a similar cult among the Bariba in northern Benin. Within this cult people go into altered states of consciousness. Bourguignon (1973) studied altered states of consciousness in general, and Lewis (1971) theorized that women and others of low socioeconomic status join spirit possession cults in order to enhance their social status. Berger related the role of women in spirit possession cults as a religious alternative for them in societies where they were excluded from the men's ancestral cult activities (Berger 1976:167).

Like so much of Bajju indigenous religion, *bvori* is no longer practiced among the Bajju. Christian forms of religious worship and Western medical care have largely replaced local practices. Hence much of the description that follows is based on the recall of elderly people, including one interview I conducted with a woman who was formerly possessed by *bvori* spirits.

Though Bajju probably acquired *bvori* from the Hausa and Fulani, it was never as developed as the *bori* cult in Hausa society. It existed as a peripheral religious cult among the Bajju for a much shorter period of time. The Bajju *bvori* practice was decentralized with each practitioner acting independently.

Bajju women were among the main participants of *bvori*, though some men also became practitioners. Kato argues that these activities helped to compensate women for their low status within the Bajju society (Kato 1974:188). *Bvori* activities frequently took place near the river. There, different types of music were played until a *bvori* practitioner went into a trance. The music that caused the trance became the person's signature song. Thereafter that music would be played to induce a trance. The Bajju felt that a *ka̲tenyrang*[8] (see above under "Small spirits") entered a woman

---

[8] Among Christians the word *ka̲tenyrang* is used to refer to Satan.

and spoke through her. When possessed, she might fall to the ground or even into a fire. When in the trance the person would request sacrifices and offerings in order to bring her out of the trance. The Bajju felt that one who was a witch (*ạkut*) could be possessed; hence there was a relationship between spirit possession trance and *nkut*. A person possessed by a spirit had spiritual insight. Alternatively, if a person walked through an area where the *nạtenyrang* lived, she could become possessed.

The former *bvori* practitioner I interviewed told of being extremely sensitive to the spirits. She had special knowledge that enabled her to know things through spiritual insight. She knew when people were ill or had died even before being told. The spirits would speak through her as they conveyed their messages. People came to consult with her about their problems and bring their pennies for payment. She would go into a trance to ascertain the type of medicine(s) that would heal their sicknesses.

A *bvori* practitioner functioned very similarly to a diviner (*ạbvok*), including being possessed by spirits. These functions included consultations for healing, barrenness, causes of deaths or illnesses, and general misfortune. A *bvori* practitioner had esoteric knowledge not available to most people within the society.

Summary

This chapter focused on the Bajju traditional religious beliefs, beginning with their beliefs about God. It then discussed each of the various categories of spirits that comprised the spirits they believed in. Spirits can take any form. Lastly, it examined the *bvori* spirit possession cult and showed how it related to other Bajju beliefs such as *nkut*.

With the coming of Christianity, many of the spirits discussed above have been identified with demons, which come to possess people. Early missionaries cast demons out of specific people. While I heard of this occurring, I never witnessed it.

The pre-Christian concept of God correlates well with the Christian concept of God. Some view Christianity as allowing them to know God, the same God they already believed in. The traditional word for God, *Kạza*, is used in the Bajju Christian Scriptures. While the Hausa Bible uses *Allah*, and that name for God is used in Hausa Christian church services, the Bajju translation of the Christian New Testament uses the Bajju word for God.

Satan is termed *kạtenyrang*. Hence there is a continuation of this belief with another important term within the Christian Bible.

The following chapter discusses the life cycle that each person passes through. All of life is lived with an awareness of God and the spirit world discussed in this chapter.

9

The Life Cycle: Birth, Marriage, and Death

Marriage is the most important activity of man's existence. (Kunhiyop 1982:22)
Relatives cannot be washed (separated). (Bajju proverb)

A life cycle refers to the stages of life and the roles a person passes through during a normal lifetime. In this discussion of the Bajju life cycle, birth is discussed first, then marriage, and finally death. Initiation, which is also part of the life cycle, is covered in chapter 3.

Bajju view life as a circle that moves from birth to puberty, to marriage, to parenthood, to old age and death, followed by rebirth through reincarnation. Alternatively, elderly people may gain entry into the company of the ancestors. They recognize this cycle in a number of ways. For example, a new infant may receive a name such as Abrak meaning "he has returned," referring to the reincarnation of an ancestor.

Birth

Being married and having children is necessary to continue the patrilineage. A man desires to have descendants; if a person dies childless, he is forgotten. If a young woman is unable to conceive and bear a child, she may be sent back to her father's house[1] or her husband may take another wife. Thus, having children is extremely important for everyone.

When a young woman discovered she was pregnant with her first child and she had reached the third month of her pregnancy, it was a time for a celebration. Women prepared beniseed with hungry rice and mixed it with water. They also put some leaves in the fire. When the leaves were burned, the women added the ash to the other mixture. The new mother was then bathed in it. It was first put on her forehead, then her right shoulder, followed by her left shoulder, and then on her knees. After the medicine had been put on each part of her body, it was brushed off. After that, she drank some of the medicine. This ritual could be performed for one woman or several young women at a time. Then they gave some beniseed paste to lots of people in the house who had come to watch the ritual, though they were not given the beniseed paste with medicine in it, such as they gave the young mother(s). During this ritual they put a small pot on the fire in the morning with unground guinea corn, which was cooked until the afternoon. While her pregnancy was celebrated at the home of an elderly woman, her husband went hunting in the bush. If he was successful, people rejoiced because he demonstrated that he would be a good provider for his family. At six months this ritual was repeated. If it was the dry season, her husband again went hunting in the morning. That evening they drank guinea corn beer quickly, then dispersed. Not every house performed this ritual.

Many young women give birth alone or with the help of a midwife. When they give birth alone, people speak of young mothers having tough courage. Today many women opt to give birth in a hospital where conditions are more sanitary, thus contributing to the health of both the mother and infant. A young woman either gives birth at her husband's compound or, today, at a hospital. Following the birth of a woman's first child, she returns to her parents' compound for the next three to four months. This return is termed "to go warm oneself by the fire," *nat wai rong*. There the mother recovers from the birth in the comforts of her natal home, and her baby grows and becomes healthy and fat. At the end of this time, her husband comes to bring his wife and child home, bringing gifts for his in-laws. If he has not finished paying the bridewealth, he must do so at this time, otherwise the baby belongs to his wife's parents. It is a time of joyful reunion of the new father with his family.

Bajju tend to value baby boys more than baby girls because boys remain in their father's households while girls marry outside the household, and thus they are considered as external property. For this reason boys often

---

[1] When we asked Rev. Karick, a Christian pastor in an ECWA church, whether or not Christians would send a barren woman home, he asserted to us that even Christians do this because having children is extremely important to the Bajju in order to continue the patrilineage.

receive a better education than girls do. Male children are considered the foundation of the home.

If a child of either sex dies suddenly, the belief is that he or she will come back through reincarnation. The oldest man in the clan will be the one to bury the child. Just before burying the child, the man takes a razor and makes a cut anywhere on the child's body, together with an incantation wishing the child to return soon. From then on everyone will be watching expectantly for that child to return, possibly within the same family, and they will expect that the child will have the scar where the dead child's body was cut.

Naming ceremony

A naming ceremony for an infant[2] was held four days after he or she was born. People gathered for the celebration, and the infant was brought out of the house and placed on a winnowing tray. Then two women lifted the tray with the infant on it and moved to all the thatched rooms in the house, pulling out a single grass stalk from the roof of each room. Then they came back to where they started from. The master of the compound was then called to come bless the child. He put some pounded beniseed into the infant's mouth, then spoke words of blessing. The child on the tray was then ceremonially swung to the east by the two women. For a female child they said, "This represents the tribes you might marry" (*nwap nyreng*), and for a male child, "this represents the tribes of war" (*nwap nzwang* 'tribes of wars'). They did this pointing to each of the four compass directions. They showed an infant boy a shield and spear whereas they showed a girl a winnowing tray and a headboard (*abyyai*). By so doing they were wishing the child success in all that he or she did. The father usually gave the infant his or her name, but the mother or an elderly woman in the household could also select the name for the new infant. The people who gathered ate beniseed on this occasion.

Bajju names are meaningful, often based on what is happening at the time of a woman's pregnancy or at the time of the infant's birth. It is sometimes possible to arrive at approximate ages of people based on what event occurred when they were named. In precolonial times a number of boys were named Tagwai around the time a Bajju killed the Hausa warrior Tagwai with a poisoned arrow near Asakwak.

---

[2] In Jju an infant girl is termed a *baby* and an infant boy is a *bamboi*. Their use of *bamboi* and *baby* makes clear the sex of the infant. Here I use the English term "baby" to refer to a baby girl and a baby boy.

The following are a few Bajju names together with their meanings:

Boys' names

Name	English meaning of name	Reason why a name is given
A̱brak	He has returned; he has been reincarnated	A name given to a boy who is born soon after a relative has died.
A̱ra̱ntong	Shooting star	A name given to one born at the time of sighting a shooting star. Such a child is believed to be a reincarnated person.
Cat	Wanted, Loved, Desired	A name given to a desired son.
Da̱mbvvo	Would that they knew	If people have harmed others, then the child might be given this name.
Ka̱rik, Ka̱rick	Division in the household	A name given to a son born into a troubled household.
Ka̱yit	A child born outside the house, as on the farm or in the bush	A name given when a woman gives birth outside.
Ka̱za	God. This is a shortened form of "God sees them," Ka̱za a̱ ba ryi.	If someone has been practicing *nkut* against a woman, but she conceived and bore a son, then the son might receive this name.
Nkut	Spiritual power or ability to harm another in the spiritual realm	The child so named is at the mercy of others with this ability concerning whether he lives or dies.
Tungzwang	A child born when people were gathered for war	People were gathered for war.
Tyyimbvwak	To hold in one's hands	A name given to a small infant.

Girls' names

Name	English meaning of name	Reason why a name is given
Anang	A gift	The baby girl is seen as a gift from God.
Bvvokabying	She has delivered again	A name given to an infant girl born prematurely or with low birthweight.
Cincong	Little	A name given to a low-birthweight girl.
Dikwu	Death; Epidemic	If lots of people are dying around the time of the birth of a child, she may be called "Death." Since she is already "dead," death will leave her alone and thus she will live. Alternatively, if a woman's children continue to die, the next infant might receive this name to cause death to depart from the infant so she would then live.
Kasham	Beautiful	A name frequently given by Christian parents to a daughter.
Zataat, Ashya	You have reached us; She has found us	If a woman had not conceived for a long time then did so, the child might be given this name.
Zigwai[3]	We are thankful; We are happy	A name often given by Christian parents to a daughter.

Marriage

At an African Christian Fellowship panel on marriage, one single young woman was selected to represent those who were single. This woman dismissed singleness with the comment, "We know that we will all get

---

[3] The 'i' in Zigwai is now being spelled as Zigwai.

married!" Her attitude represents the importance of marriage for Africans (comment given at an African Christian Fellowship conference near Columbus, Texas, n.d.).

For every Bajju person, marriage is an obligation. It brings completeness, status, respect, and responsibility. Until a Bajju person marries, irrespective of age, he or she is categorized as a child. It is the duty of all Bajju men and women to marry, to have children, and to live a full life. One of the principal purposes of marriage is to have children to continue the family, the patrilineage, and the clan. Marriage and procreation insure that people have descendants. If a person is not married, the Bajju say "You have no home if you are not married." Homosexuality is not looked at favorably, as it does not fulfill the essential role of having children to continue the patrilineage.

A Bajju proverb states "Blessed are those who have people" (*Banyet byyi banyet ahwok shasham,* Kunhiyop 1988:17). In general Bajju prefer to have large families. I encountered this perception of blessedness while living among the Bajju. Though my husband and I have four children, a couple of Bajju women informed me that we have a small family. When I asked how many children they considered to be a minimum so that I have done my part, they responded that I should have at least five children!

Prior to marriage a woman is known as a girl (*kaneyang*) irrespective of her age. In Bajju society young women married early, and widows were eligible to be inherited as a wife a month after their husbands' deaths. Today ideally young men and women marry once they have completed their education.[4]

In the past a young man who did not farm would not readily get a wife, as farming and hunting were the main occupations of men. A young woman's parents would not want a lazy man to marry their daughter. Such a man would be chastised by a masquerade from the men's secret ancestral organization.

For a man to be an elder he must have married, had children, and demonstrated that he could handle his family well. In the past this involved being married polygynously and handling his polygamous family capably.

Exogamy

Kato (1974:116–118) listed the following categories within which a Bajju man could not marry: (1) a woman from a lineage that another of his close kinsmen had already married into (persons already in the relationship of

---

[4] When our daughter Susan was a senior in high school at approximately seventeen years old, one elderly Bajju woman asked me why she was not married. I responded that she had not yet completed her education. This was an acceptable answer within this Bajju context. In fact Susan eventually completed university and medical school. The day after she graduated from medical school, she married. Thus she fulfilled the Bajju ideal!

in-law to the people of the man's lineage); (2) a woman of his own lineage or his *yaryi* group (see below); (3) a woman from the lineage of his mother or from other families closely related to his mother; (4) a woman from his father's mother's family; (5) a woman from the household of his father's sister's husband or his close relatives; or (6) two women from the same lineage. A woman could not marry into reciprocal kin categories. Thus people did not marry people who were related by blood or marriage. This includes marriage forbidden between cousins or between people who belong to the same clan.

The Bajju did not intermarry with the Chawai, Irigwe, and Atakad. This prohibition relates to the Baranzan founding charter. All of these groups were viewed as being too closely related to the Bajju by kinship ties in the past. According to the Bajju founding charter, the Chawai and Atakad were descendants of brothers of Baranzan. This prohibition is breaking down today.

Clans and marriage

Bajju practiced clan (*sot*) exogamy. To marry within one's clan was considered incest. However, if a clan increased in population to the extent that intermarriage was desirable, the elders met to divide the clan into intermarrying units. The Bajju state "they divide themselves" (*ba ya trya*) to describe the ritual of separation into intermarrying units. Prior to the separation, the clan elders must agree that the population was large enough to warrant its division. Further, Bajju elders desired that the two halves have some natural boundary between them such as a stream, forest, or swamp.

At this ceremony the ruling elder provided an animal, such as a goat, that was all one color. The color symbolized the oneness of the group. They killed this animal and divided it into two, symbolizing that though it was one, it was now separated into two as the Bajju thereby separated themselves into intermarrying units. The blood of this animal was believed to drive away evil. They smeared some of the blood of the animal on the doorway of the ruling elder's house in order to protect him from evil that might have resulted from the creation of two groups. They also poured some of the blood on the path that separated the two units, and poured the rest of the blood on slightly damp grass so that when lit its smoke would rise into the sky to ward off evil (Kato 1974:63–68).

At the ceremony the elders announced that from that day onwards intermarriage was allowed. Prior to that declaration these units were considered "one blood," and thus intermarriage within it was incest. Even after the declaration, these two units recognized their close kinship relationship. Each half was termed a *yaryi*. A man could obtain a wife from the other *yaryi* either without paying bridewealth (*ryi*) or with very little bridewealth. Ideally a marriage between members of groups with a *yaryi* relationship should not end in divorce.

The practice of fission of exogamous units, such as described above, continues today, though without some of the elements of the ritual described above, namely without animal sacrifice. This ritual, which relates to the formation of intermarrying units, explains the formation of new clans within the Bajju area.

If two people married, and afterwards discovered that they came from the same clan within which intermarriage was forbidden, the ruling elder performed a similar ritual to that described above in order to dissolve the union and to protect its members from harm. This ritual, known as *hyyuk,* "to wipe off," involved slaughtering a goat and smearing its blood on the walls of the houses of the two parties in the marriage to ward off danger believed to result from marriage within an exogamous unit. The marriage was thereby annulled. If a child had resulted from their union, that child was allowed to live.

The practice of women marrying only outside their village is no longer practiced. As long as the prospective spouses are from different clans or different *yaryi* groups within the village or from different villages, it is acceptable for them to marry.

Marital alliances

Bajju men stated, "We do not marry wives from villages where we marry sisters." The question then arises concerning the difference in marriages between wives and sisters. In the past Bajju maintained marital alliances between specific villages. If the need arose, villages with such alliances would help each other during warfare. Villages without such alliances did not cooperate in the same way. Bajju men from one village would marry the sisters of men from a village with a marital alliance with their village, and vice versa. These first wives were the "sisters." Contrastively, second and subsequent wives came from other villages; they are the "wives" in the above saying. Marriages to these wives were termed secondary marriages. The reason for not taking a second wife from a village with a marital alliance was that they did not marry women who were already in an in-law relationship.

This system of marital alliances between specific villages did not exclude the possibility of a man obtaining a first wife from some other village. It did mean that men could more easily obtain wives from villages with established reciprocal marital alliances. Villages with marital alliances were usually geographically close to one another. Waters-Bayer relates that a marriage alliance existed between Dihwan and Beibyet to ensure peace between these villages during the time of warfare (1982:5).

Just as there were villages with marital alliances, there were also villages between which marriage was forbidden. These villages had a relationship of enmity or rivalry between them, and they were known as *arendwan.*

This term refers to enmity or rivalry between brothers. It also applies to the relationship between two men, one of whom had taken the other man's wife in marriage.

The Bajju were not the only ethnic group in Southern Zaria and on the Plateau with this marital relationship. Smith translated the cognate term *nendwang* in Agorok as "a thing of trouble" or a "wife abduction" group. He contrasted this term with *niendi,* which he described as the relationship between two groups that contracted first marriages (Smith 1975:7). He stated that groups identified as *nendwang* and *niendi* were opposing groups in a moiety structure. He felt that this moiety structure formed historically through groups that arrived by successive migrations.

> There [at Kagoro] the immigrants were distinguished from the original settlers as Kpashan. Since the Tacherak of Dussai were included among the original settlers as *Ankwei* the tribes therefore came to have a moiety organisation, in fact as well as in form, when the Kpashan arrivals increased in number. Thus the moiety organisation has a historical origin and development. (1975:7)

Muller also spoke of a moiety structure for the Rukuba, a related Plateau ethnic group. He described their moiety structure as follows,

> Taken as a whole, the Rukuba population is divided into two exogamous moieties. All the girls born in one moiety have to be married in the other. Both moieties are, however, not named. Briefly, a moiety is comprised of a certain number of discrete units, a little more than twenty for each moiety, which stand as partners to any like unit of the opposite moiety in marrying each other's unmarried women in primary marriage... they take wives from each other in secondary marriage.... (Muller 1976:740)

In many aspects of their marital patterns, the Bajju had many similarities to the Agorok and Rukuba. The Rukuba may have had a moiety system, though Muller points out that this is an analytical construct rather than a named category within their language. When examining Bajju marital patterns, I sought a cognate term for the Agorok term *niendi,* a term Smith used to characterize the relationship between two groups that had a marital alliance. Thus far I have failed to find a Jju cognate for this term or to identify anything that I would describe as a moiety structure among the Bajju.

Looking at similarities among the Bajju and Agorok, both arrived in their respective areas through successive, often small-scale migrations. Further, Bajju share with the Agorok and Rukuba the existence of villages with marital alliances. These alliances were not always symmetrical. For example, the Bajju villages of Dibyyi, Kanshwa, and Jjei could contract first marriages with the "sisters" of Azunkwa, but Dibyyi and Jjei could not contract first marriages with each other. Men from Azunkwa obtained women for first marriages from Jjei and Dibyyi.

The Agorok shared this asymmetrical relationship between groups that Smith characterized as *niendi* and those he termed *nendwang* (Smith 1975:65). The Bajju system of marital alliances between villages was far more complicated than a moiety system would suggest. Muller recognized a similar complexity among the Rukuba when he stated:

> However, on the ground, the situation looks more compli-
> cated. Wife-taking units are not always easily sorted out. For
> the purpose of this study the most inclusive relevant unit
> on the ground is what I call a village. A village is not neces-
> sarily composed of one wife-taking unit but it may include
> members of both moieties. (1976:741)

Spouse selection

In the past a family selected a spouse for their child. They did so because they believed that though their child may love a potential spouse, love may be blind to potential problems while parents are not.[5]

If a man came to a compound soon after a woman gave birth to a baby girl, he could give the family a ring, string of beads, or some other token gift as a sign of the betrothal of this child to his son. The gift was to help the girl's family remember the person who gave it. Alternatively, if the father of a boy heard of the birth of a baby girl, he could send two hens and one cock through an intermediary to the father of the infant to betroth her to his son. The baby was then termed a reserved bride, *hung kaneyang*. The son is likewise a reserved groom, *hung kaseyang*.

Parents sought spouses for their children from families that were hard-working and that had sufficient food for a year. They avoided potential spouses from families that had histories of illness such as epilepsy, leprosy, or sickle cell anemia, were lazy, or from families known to be thieves. If a child had a significant physical problem, they sought someone with a similar problem for their child.

Today young Bajju men and women tend to select their own spouses, after which their relatives proceed with marital negotiations. Further, today Bajju young men and women usually marry Christian spouses, whether

---

[5] One Bajju man, who stayed with us for a week in Dallas, told of his marriage. His mother had selected his spouse when he was young. On the day before his marriage, she told him that he was going to be married on the next day. His marriage has worked out so well that he is convinced that parental selection of one's spouse is the way to go. He proceeded to tell our children that they needed to listen to their parents when it came time for them to marry, as love is blind but parents are not!

those persons are Bajju or from some other minority ethnic groups, such as the Ham, Longuda, and Mada. If a Bajju man marries a woman from another ethnic group, their children are Bajju because of patrilineal descent. However, if a Bajju woman married a non-Bajju man, their children belong to the patrilineage and ethnic group of their father.

First marriage

Prior to the first marriage, the primary marriage, the groom could be asked to do bride service, which was usually in the form of helping the bride's family with farming, beginning with farming hungry rice, the first crop planted. However, elderly Bajju stress that bride service was never as important or mandatory for them as it was among the Atyap. Sanke (1976:33) stated that bride service was not seen as part of the bridewealth. Rather it was a sign of appreciation and respect for the girl's parents. Sometimes the young groom would bring some of his friends, who joined him in his bride service.

The family of the groom and that of the bride would negotiate the bridewealth. The bride and groom might or might not have been aware of the arrangements in advance. When the time came to set the date for the marriage, the groom's father gave four chickens to the intermediary, often the father's brother, to indicate that he should complete the marital arrangements and set the date. The intermediary brought a goat for the future mother-in-law (*bvon ǫna*). Handleless hoes were given from the groom's family to that of the future in-laws as part of the bridewealth. Some of these hoes were quite old, while others were new. The hoes indicated that the family she was marrying into were not lazy farmers. Sanke stated, "A girl who married without a hoe included in her bridewealth was not given high honour in the marriage, and she did not give great respect to the husband until the hoe was sent." (1976:32)

Hoes, five hundred cowries (twenty-five kobo; Sanke 1976), four chickens, two pots of wine,[6] and a goat were used as currency in the precolonial time period, and all were part of the bridewealth. It was given by the groom's family to the bride's family.

When the date of the marriage was to be set, four pots of wine were taken to the parents of the girl. The parents and the boy's kinfolk drank the wine to wish her a good, happy marriage. The date for the marriage was then set, though they were very careful not to tell the young bride. Sanke stated, "Often the bridewealth was kept with her middle man. This was to avoid the girl running away" (1976:33).

Bridewealth establishes the legitimacy of a marriage and the legitimacy of any children born to the union in the eyes of the community. Sanke stated,

---

[6] "Wine" usually indicates guinea corn beer, though it could also be palm wine.

A man who had not given the bridewealth had no legal right over the wife and the children born to him. The parents of the wife had the right to call her back with the children until the husband had paid all the required items. Normally the wife was not called home until she had had a child or two with the husband. The parents could decide to give her to another man if the first husband failed to bring the required items, and the children born to the man were claimed by the wife's kin …. If the wife marries another man and the first husband pays all the bridewealth, he could claim the children. (1976:34–35)

Today a bride's parents often request payment according to the level of education their daughter has attained in school. This payment is based on what the parents have spent on their daughter's education, as education is seen as an economic asset. The payment for a bride includes a mother's gift, which is compensation to the mother for her care of her daughter. This replaces payment of a hoe. The amount is not fixed but is subject to bargaining. A family may also demand a high bridewealth if the groom has a good job and is doing well financially.

Today during the actual marriage ceremony, the bride's father does not attend. Her mother attends as do her other relatives. Since her father has received the bridewealth, he has been compensated for her loss to the family.

Marriage by capture

In Bajju society marriage occurred by "capture." The families, particularly the fathers through an intermediary such as uncles of the bride and groom, completed the marital arrangements. After the goat was paid to the future mother-in-law, they set a day to capture the bride. She was not informed of these arrangements, and often neither was her mother. The arrangements were kept secret. The day before her capture, her parents would feed her well, an act of kindness on their part towards their beloved daughter. Her family would send her on an errand, such as to fetch water or to go to another village. The groom and his friends would hide, often beside the road where she would pass. When she appeared, they captured her. Often there was a brief skirmish in which the bride and her friends resisted the capture; and in some instances she succeeded in escaping from her captors. If she did so, she knew enough not to return home because her father was in on the capture plans. Rather she ran to the home of some other relative; however, she knew that eventually she had to go live with her new husband. If the young men failed in their efforts to capture the bride according to the arrangements, from then on they were free to capture her anywhere. If she escaped, something that was rather uncommon, her parents were responsible for feeding the groom and his friends until their daughter could be found and turned over to them.

Once captured, the bride cried and cried. The young men did not take her directly to the groom's house, but rather they took her to the house of the intermediary who gave the money for the bridewealth. Friends of the groom stayed with them that evening, then left the couple together for the night. The next morning the wife of the intermediary brought cooked beans early in the morning, for example, around 4 or 5 a.m., to the groom. If she found the groom still asleep, he had to pay a fine of a goat or a chicken. The couple remained there for four days. At the end of the four days, the bride's family came with some cooked beans. At this point she realized that her family was giving her in marriage to the groom and his family. She no longer had the option of running away to her people. On the evening of the fourth day, she went to live at the groom's home.

A Bajju bride is sad because of leaving the home in which she was raised. Even if a bride is quite happy to be married, tradition dictates that she must not show it during the marriage ceremony and the reception afterwards. Frequently marriage receptions last all night; this means that for hours the bride must maintain a sad countenance. If she cries, it is seen as so much the better. To appear sad is an indication of her sadness and distress at leaving her natal home and joining another family.

For approximately the first two months of marriage the bride works closely with her mother-in-law in food preparation and its distribution to family members. When her mother-in-law feels that she has learned sufficiently how things are done in that household, she sets out cooking utensils for the new bride; this practice is termed *rong ndong,* "fire, fire." From that day onwards the bride cooks independently for her husband.

When the bride became pregnant, her family came. They again brought cooked beans and put them into a large water pot, a *sup.* They gave her a bitter leaf paste, *ditun kawha,* which they put into her mouth. This implied an end of the traditional marriage ritual.

Today a modified form of marriage by capture called *cong,* meaning "to walk," is practiced, in which the girl is escorted by her friends from her parents' home to that of her husband. On one occasion I encountered a group of young women escorting a weeping young bride to her new home. Everyone else in the group was talking happily, but not the young bride who was walking in their midst crying. As noted above, brides are not to show their happiness at the marriage. This occurs even when the couple has selected each other as spouses and is quite happy to get married.

Today marriages are usually performed in church, with the bride wearing a white wedding gown, and bridesmaids wearing matching outfits. Outwardly the marriage ceremony is similar to Western weddings. However, the bride's father does not attend the wedding. He remains home, while his daughter walks down the aisle of the church by herself after her bridesmaids have done so.

Wedding receptions tend to have lots of food prepared for the guests. The celebration usually lasts through the night and sometimes continues for two to three days. Gifts to the newly married couple are usually monetary. The master of ceremonies goes around the circle of guests collecting money. He shouts out the amount that each person gives. Sometimes there is a competition between guests, with one person stating that he will give, say, 100 naira, provided that someone else matches it. Since the groom's family has expended a great deal of money for the marriage and reception, the money collected at the reception benefits the groom and his family. They are not left in abject poverty because of the wedding expenses. Often a number of people in his family have contributed towards the wedding expenses, including the bridewealth.

Elopement

Elopement was known as a "horse trot," *tyong tsaab.* A prestigious man could attract a woman to elope with him. Elopement also occurred when the bride's parents opposed the marriage, but the couple decided to marry anyway. After the elopement the couple completed the marital formalities, including payment of the bridewealth and reconciliation with their respective families.

Second and subsequent marriages

Since Bajju valued large families, a man could have multiple wives. The acquisition of multiple wives enhanced a man's and his household's social prestige. The work of the household could continue when one wife was ill or confined following childbirth, a period when the wife was to refrain from cooking or farm work for seven days. Men with more than one wife enjoyed various benefits: (1) food preparation continued for the household during the times of a woman's menses when she was forbidden to cook or have sexual intercourse; (2) a man could engage in sexual relations with his other wives, when he was forbidden to do so with one wife during the approximately two to two-and-one-half-year period when a woman nursed her child; and (3) the number of offspring increased, thus enabling a man to farm a larger area.

Second and subsequent marriages, termed secondary marriages, occurred after the persons have already married. Types of second and subsequent marriages are as follows:

1. Wife capture. This involved forceful capture of a woman without her consent. This could occur during warfare or when a woman was outside her household for some reason. Wife capture was not limited to unmarried women. Fear of wife capture meant that when a man went out with his wives to farm, they walked in front of him and he went fully armed walking behind them in order to protect them from capture by other men.

2. Widow inheritance. Widow inheritance is called "keeping the woman," *sak ambyring*. It is not viewed as a new marriage, but rather it is a continuation of the first marriage. It involves no further bridewealth than the money already paid by her deceased husband. Any children born to such a union belong to the biological father, not to the deceased husband. If she chose not to be inherited, she must leave her children with her deceased husband's family as the children belong to the patrilineage. A brother, son, or other close male relative may inherit the widow(s) of a deceased man within the extended family. While a son may not inherit his own mother, he could inherit other wives of his father upon his father's death. However, inheritance of one's father's wives was very rare. Typically when this occurred it was viewed as an unhappy marriage, and it often ended in divorce. A father or uncle could never inherit his daughter-in-law. If a man died, his brother inherited her. Today women often do not want to be inherited and brothers hardly help with her children.

Widow inheritance occurred one month following the death of one's spouse. During that month the woman mourned her deceased husband. She was termed a "widow," *akwwuk*. At the beginning of this mourning period people shaved her head. She did not speak to her brothers-in-law as she did not know which one would inherit her. The Bajju would interpret her speaking to a man as an invitation to be inherited by that man. At the end of the mourning period, the brother interested in inheriting her sent her a tobacco wrap (a twisted piece of tobacco). She would ask who sent it. If she accepted the tobacco wrap from a brother of her deceased husband, she became that man's legal wife; however, if she rejected it, then another man within the extended family could send her his tobacco wrap with the goal of taking her as his wife. When I talked with one woman about her own experience, she knew how long it had been since she was inherited.

However, if there were no men in the line of the deceased to inherit her, she was permitted to marry elsewhere. Sanke found that eighty-five percent of his sample were against it, while fifteen percent still favored it. He found that old men and some women accepted it (1976:65). Today many no longer favor this marital practice.

The goal of widow inheritance is to keep the family together, including keeping the mother together with her children. It is believed that if a woman left the extended family and married elsewhere, she would take the blessing of that family with her, something that the family strongly objected to. It is a duty to keep the family together.

Because of the possibility of being inherited by a woman's husband's brother, a joking relationship exists between the woman and her husband's brothers.

Polyandrous polygynous marriage

The Bajju practiced a form of marriage that has been called polyandrous polygynous marriage (Peter 1980). In this marital pattern a woman might be married to one man and have a child by him, then marry another man, or be captured by another man. It was her marital guardian who arranged another marriage for her, but she could return to her first husband at any time provided that the bridewealth had not been returned and that she had had a child by that man. When a child had been born to a union, the bridewealth was rarely returned. Meanwhile her first husband may have married another wife. In essence both were married to two spouses. She was married to her first husband as well as to her second husband, and he was married to his first wife as well as to his second. Thus she had two husbands, so she was married polyandrously, and he had two wives, so he was married polygynously. The wife only lived with one husband at a time, but years later when her second husband died, she could return to her first husband. Hence they had a polyandrous polygynous marriage. Rarely would a man return the bridewealth, so there had been no divorce of the first marriage. In fact, prior to colonialism there was basically no divorce. The British imposed the Hausa practice termed *iddah* in which a woman could not marry another husband for a three months' period in order to ascertain whether or not she was pregnant by her first husband.

Wife stealing was commonly practiced. There were villages where a man could steal another man's wife, and other villages where this did not occur. Taking another man's wife was termed *bang ạbyring*. Sanke states:

> It was common for a woman to be sought in marriage by a man when she was already married to another. In this case the intending husband paid visits to the woman secretly at night in her husband's house or the woman might be waylaid and captured in the bush without her consent. There were clearly defined villages and clans where one could capture another man's wife. (1976:61)

The two villages with a marital alliance were ones that could get wives from a third village. Because they often sought the same girls as wives for their sons, these two villages were rivals. This rivalry was expressed through stealing each other's wives. A woman captured could decide either to stay with the second man or to return to her first husband. In the latter situation she would let her close kin know her desire, and she would then look for a way to return to her first husband.

Bajju men also captured wives from other ethnic groups such as the Agorok, Fantsuam, Kanikom, and Ham people. Thus wife capture occurred both within the Bajju ethnic group as well as with other ethnic groups.

Sangree described a very similar situation among the Irigwe on the Jos Plateau in which women regularly went from husband to husband, a practice that seemed expected at that time (2008). He also related that this practice led to women being greatly distressed if they were forced by their marital guardians to marry other husbands. He described witnessing a case of severe separation depression (1982) that a woman experienced by being forced by her marital guardian into another marriage or by being captured by another man. The outward evidence of this woman's distress was a cry similar to that a child would give when in great distress. A woman in her distress would cry, not respond to normal social interaction, and become rigid. This was interpreted as a spirit possessing her, and in general she acted completely out of the ordinary. One result was that they would plan a spirit possession dance for her soon after the initial incident.

I have not seen instances where this occurred, but it is not hard to imagine that it occurred. The closest evidence I have for this type of situation among the Bajju came from a discussion I had with three elderly women. I asked them the difference between now and before Christianity came to their area. Their response was that they could trust their husbands now because their husbands were not out looking for other wives and because new marriages were not being contracted for them. It was a relief to them that their spouses were faithful to them.

Under colonialism, administrators frowned on these practices of wife stealing. For example, they ruled that should a man contract a marriage for a married woman, he would be jailed (NAK 1024). They reasoned that some marital guardians were greedy and would contract marriages for married women in order to obtain further bridewealth. Because of the colonial decree and missionary disapproval of this marital pattern, it is largely no longer practiced by the Bajju. So while the Bajju and other related ethnic groups practiced polyandrous polygynous marriages, this is no longer the case. While living among the Bajju I heard of only one instance where a man stole another man's wife. The person who told me strongly disapproved of this marriage.

Some scholars have written that since women from the Jos Plateau could marry more than one man, they must have had the high status of a "liberated woman" (Peter 1980:375). This position is inaccurate; in fact, this practice reflects the fact that women had very low status. It was a woman's marital guardian, whether her father, brother, uncle, or other close male relative, who arranged for her to be married to another man. If a woman had had a choice about whom she married, she might have been considered a liberated woman. Then Peter's assumption might have been true; however, a woman had little to no say in the process. The severe separation anxiety that Sangree (1982) wrote about indicates the difficulty women experienced when forced to move from husband to husband.

Relationships between spouses in marriage

According to Kato, the husband "owned" his wife (Kato 1974:142). Because of this relationship, a woman could not travel outside of her village without his approval.

Within a polygynous family the seniority of a wife depends upon the order of marriage, with the first wife occupying the senior position. She has the responsibility of telling the other wives what to do, and they often refer to her as "Mama." The rivalry and jealousy between co-wives is expressed by the term *ǫhwwuk*, which is translated as "co-wife," "rival," and "jealousy." Jealousy is usually expressed in a controlled way. When a wife is grinding grain for the evening meal, she sings her complaints against her co-wife. The next day her co-wife while grinding grain sings her response to the other's complaints. Children often go from compound to compound, listen to these complaints, and thus know the latest gossip in the village.

In a polygamous family the husband often has a favorite wife; she is "the loved one," *ǫpyya*. Further, there is often a wife in disfavor, a disfavor expressed by the term *ǫrak*, "the rejected one."

Each wife cooks for her husband in turn, except during the time of her menses. Ideally, the husband spends an equal number of nights sleeping in the house of each wife.

On occasion a husband might have mistreated his wife. In response she might remove a frame from a door or window. If she did so, she was required to pay a fine. The fine was usually beer or a male goat.

Bachelors, spinsters, and widows

Some people do not marry, whether from early death, illness, or for some other reason. A bachelor or spinster who does not marry is termed an "empty person," *ǫkpatyok*. This word also translates as a "worthless person." This term may also be applied to a widow who does not remarry. From a Bajju perspective, such people are lonely and incomplete. They do not have spouses to do such activities as cooking, clearing fields, planting seeds, weeding the crops, harvesting their fields, chopping firewood, carrying water, or caring for them when ill.

If a man does not marry and have children, Bajju describe him as one whose name is lost (*diyrek nu bryik*) (Kunhiyop 1988:16). Such a person will not have descendants to remember him. When he dies they cut his chest so that he will not be reincarnated.

Barrenness

Bajju attach great importance to having children. Perhaps the greatest tragedy that can befall a person, whether male or female, is to be barren. Consequently, this is an area that causes great anxiety. If a man is infertile, he may ask his brother to have sexual relations with his wife in order to have a child. Under ordinary circumstances such behavior would be considered adultery and subject to supernatural sanctions. However, having a child is so important that in this case it is exempt from being classified as adultery.

Children are a gift from God because of his goodness. Consequently, some simply pray, asking God for children. They assert that God will see, hear, and give children in response. Previously, others sought the reason for their barrenness through consulting a diviner. A diviner might ascertain that a person offended a small spirit (see chapter 8 under "Small spirits"). The cure for that problem was to leave some offering, whether food or money or both, for the spirit. Another means of countering the problem of barrenness was through the *ǫbvoi,* because they could give a woman medicine mixed with beer to drink to cure her barrenness.

Breaches in social relations could also cause barrenness—for example, if a child struck his parent(s), when he matured he might be barren. At the time such an incident occurred, the parent(s) might curse the child, saying that he or she would not have a child. However, the more common curse given to such a child was that he or she would be useless; he would not farm or do anything useful. If a barren person's parents were still alive, they would hold a family conference to talk the matter over and forgive one another. If the parents were deceased, the person, together with the elders, would take a pot of beer to the deceased's grave. They would discuss the problem and ask the deceased for forgiveness. After that, they would pour some beer out as a libation, then drink the rest of it with the goal that the ancestor would remove any obstacles to conception.

Divorce

Divorce involves return of the bridewealth. Without return of the bridewealth, a divorce is not final even if there has been a divorce decree granted by a customary court. When a man decided to divorce his wife, he tied a millet stalk to her leg, then sent her back to her father's compound. It is not hard to picture her returning while crying loudly for all to know of her distress. If a couple has had a child, return of the bridewealth is rare and usually a man would not request it. Since this is a patrilineal society, in the event of divorce the child remains with his or her father. If a child is still nursing, the mother may take him or her with her; however, at some point in the future, the child must be returned to the father.

The changing status of women

Women in Bajju society were unequivocally subordinate to men. As one Bajju man stated, "A man is the absolute head of the house!" In society women's status was on the level of a minor, equivalent to that of children, including uninitiated boys. Boys, even ages ten or eleven who had been initiated into the *ạbvoi*, enjoyed a higher status than women. Various Bajju expressions about women reflect this inferior status:

Ạrembyring ạ shyak bu kạbawon ka.	'A woman is not different from a child.'
Ạrembyring ạ yet ạrembyring.	'A woman is a woman.'
Ạrembyring ạ yet kyang ạtạsa.	'A woman is a thing from outside [of one's household, from another lineage].'
Ạrembyring ạ yet kyang ạbang ạyin.	'A woman belongs to another person's house.'

While male children are known as "the foundation of the household" (*dityin kạryi*), female children are called "children of the outside" (*nạwon ạtạsa*) because they marry into other patrilineages. Consequently, parents prefer to have more boys than girls. This was brought home to us when one young father asked us to drive his wife home from the hospital after she had given birth to their first child. I enthusiastically asked whether she had had a boy or girl. He responded, "I didn't ask!" indicating his disappointment over having a baby daughter.

The status of women increases as they marry and bear children. Various statuses of women are presented in table 9.1.

Table 9.1. Types of status of females

Status of females	Characteristics of females in this status
Girl—*kaneyang*	An unmarried female of any age
Girl woman—*kaneyang*	A married woman without children
Woman, wife—*ambyring*	A married woman with children
Barren woman—*anankwo ambyring*	A woman who is unable to bear children. It is an insecure status as the woman has not produced children to continue her husband's patrilineage. She may be sent home to her father's household.
Widow—*akwwuk*	A status that applies to a woman for one month following the death of her husband. After that she either remarries, is inherited, or is known as the wife of her deceased husband.
Honorary man	A status accorded to a respected elderly woman who has fulfilled her roles well within society, including bearing children. This rarely occurs.

There is asymmetry of statuses of males and females that are reflected in male ownership of land and houses. A woman cannot own land or houses nor inherit them upon the death of her spouse or father. Rather it is the male children or other male relatives of her husband or his father who inherit his land and houses following his death. Widows may be left destitute upon the deaths of their husbands. Early Christian missionaries were concerned over the status of widows. Consequently SIM set up a widows' school that taught widows various ways to make a living to enable them to provide for themselves.

Women and the *abvoi*

One of the primary functions of the *abvoi* (*dodo,* H.) was to keep women and children in submission, as mentioned in chapter 3. Ames similarly described its function as follows, "They [the Bajju] also possess a *dodo* cult which is admittedly only for the purpose of terrorising their womenfolk" (Ames 1934:192). When women heard the sound of the *abvoi,* it instilled fear in them.

One function of the *abvoi* was to help men keep their wives from leaving them. As mentioned above, when separation and divorce occur, it is the women who leave their marriages rather than the men as this is a patrilineal patrilocal society. Various means to accomplish this goal are the following:

1.   Members of the *abvoi* would come at night and place a large stone or log on top of a woman's house, it remained there for one year. This warned

a woman not to leave her husband. A woman with a large stone or log also had to abide by certain restrictions including the following:

a.   She was not to pound grain at night.

b.   She was not to carry a naked light at night.

c.   She was not to have her hair cut.

d.   She had to provide food and beer for the *abvoi;* but she was forbidden from eating or even tasting the meat or beans that she cooked for the men's *abvoi* organization.

Since this warning could be used for other infractions of the *abvoi* besides desiring to leave her husband, men watched her behavior to determine that it had improved. At the end of this period she went through a cleansing ritual in which her hair was cut and the stone or log was removed from on top of the house.

2.   A member of the *abvoi* placed leaves of the shea tree (*masham*) around the household as a sign that a woman was not to leave her husband. This practice was similar to that of placing a large stone or log, mentioned above.

3.   Men from the *abvoi* gave women small ropes made from raffia leaves (*dikwot*) with a round mushroom-shaped lumbar ornament (*ntswandyik*) to wear during a mourning period (see figure 9.1). These were given out at the beginning of the dry season and worn for four to five months. While they wore these ornaments, they were neither to marry nor to leave their current husbands. When a woman returned the small rope to the leaders of the *abvoi* towards the end of the dry season, the men in the *abvoi* could choose to accept it or reject it from a woman who was disobedient to her husband. They rejected it by refusing to accept her pot of beer. As beer drinking was part of the *abvoi,* the likelihood of their refusing beer was not very high. Other restrictions placed on women during the time they wore these small ropes with the lumbar ornament include the following:

a.   A woman was not to speak to men other than her husband.

b.   A woman was not to beat a child at night. To do so would mean that she was beating the heads of the children of the underground world (*ayabyen*).

c.   She was not to go to her parents' house other than to beg for grain to make guinea corn beer.

d.   She was to wear the *tswandyik* for one rainy season.

e.   During the time she wore it, she had to beg for grain and beans for the *abvoi.*

f.   She had to pound grain early, as in the afternoon, but not at night.

g.   She had to go to the river early as for bathing or fetching water. She was not to go at night.

h.   She was not to contract another marriage during this time.

Figure 9.1. Bajju women wearing mushroom-shaped lumbar ornaments (*ntswandyik*) (Tremearne 1912:76).

Further, women were forbidden to go out when the *ǫbvoi* came out. If caught, the masquerade would likely beat women who had transgressed any of these prohibitions. Women were forbidden to take grain out of the granary, as the grain represents the blessing of the household. If a woman entered the household granary and later left her husband to marry another man, they believed that she might take the blessing of the household with her.

Women were occasionally beaten and mistreated by their husbands. Men divorced their wives if they were stubborn, barren, opposed to their husband's taking other wives, or had only daughters.[7] Given these restrictions, Bajju women's motives for converting to Christianity were partially to be free from internal Bajju oppression. Women now have a say in what happens to them.

Marriage and Christianity

Christianity includes women in religious practices, whereas women were excluded from the activities of the *ǫbvoi*. Most women were constantly assessed fines for infractions, fines that required them to brew beer and prepare beans, meat, and other food for the *ǫbvoi*. As reported

---

[7] We now know that the sex of a child is determined by the husband's sperm, so hopefully women will no longer be blamed for not having sons. The sex of an infant is determined by the father, not by the mother.

in chapter 3, one elderly woman with whom I spoke told of the fear that the sound of the *ạbvoi* produced in her. When she heard it, she literally started to shake, fearing that she would be beaten. Women currently participate actively in Christian churches. Many attend church on a daily basis. Most denominations have women's organizations, the *zumunta mata* (H.), which are well attended. Churches often hold large women's meetings, usually during the dry season, that bring together women from a number of villages.

There is a woman's branch of the Bajju cultural organization. These women are known as "the daughters-in-law of Baranzan," *Bạkạmbvon Baranzan,* the founder of the Bajju. During my research time I attended one such meeting at Tsoryang. Women from nearby villages walked to the meeting in groups while others from more distant villages arrived by minivans or trucks, singing as they traveled. As each group emerged from the vehicle, they danced to their seats. They brought with them clay pot drums (*bạkinkyim*) and gourd rattles to accompany their singing.

Christianity also brought with it increased economic opportunities. SIM missionaries, for example, introduced economically profitable trees, such as fruit trees. Within Bajju society the question arose concerning ownership of citrus trees. Men argued that since they planted the seedlings, they should own them. Women argued that since they carried the produce to market and since the trees were planted in the area adjacent to the houses where they farmed their beans (the *kạdak*), they owned the trees. According to Kato, the women won this argument (1974:209–210).

At times men complain that their wives have more money than they do. This may well be true. Men and women each have their own money. With the cessation of warfare and the introduction of a market economy, both men and women have benefited economically.

Men sometimes complain that whereas formerly their wives were not allowed to drink beer, now some women have drinking problems, though the same can be said of some men and children.

Under Christianity married women no longer live with the constant fear that their husbands will turn their misdeeds into the *ạbvoi* for punishment. Further, men who formerly sought to acquire more wives are no longer out looking for them.

In 1978 Smith investigated the Ạgorok marital situation. He found that because economic and educational factors led to the migration of young men to urban areas in Nigeria, there was a disproportionately large number of young women in rural areas. Because of Christian marital regulations, these young women could not easily find husbands. Consequently, there had been a rise in the illegitimacy rate among the Ạgorok (Smith 1980:274). He summarized the situation as follows:

> Christian prohibitions of polygyny, divorce, and widow-inheritance are a perfect recipe for structural havoc in Kadara, Kagoro, and other secondary marriage societies grounded on principles of patriliny, polygyny, and virilocality. (1980:277)

His suggestions to remedy this situation were, first, that more females should migrate to urban centers, thereby bringing about a balance of the sex ratio. Second, he suggested that more A̲gorok people join one of the Christian denominations that accept polygynous marriages. Third, he noted that some A̲gorok have withdrawn to more isolated locations on top of Kagoro Rock where they are free to practice whatever marriage patterns they choose. He states, "It is just possible that others resistant to Christian teaching could follow and try to re-establish a pagan community atop the Rock" (Smith 1980:277). That is not likely to happen as A̲gorok evangelists frequently evangelize those who reside on top of Kagoro Rock, and Christianity has entered almost all areas among them.

Smith's suggestion that people return to a "pagan" community simply does not take into account current realities. The status of women has risen too greatly for women to agree to a return to their former religious and marital practices with accompanying its lower status. Women value the trust relationship that exists between them and their spouses that has occurred through the demise of the a̲bvoi and the introduction of Christianity.

One possible solution to the problems of male emigration to urban areas would be the introduction of increased economic opportunities in the Bajju home area, something that Smith did not mention. Some of their agricultural produce, such as citrus, grains, and hogs, could be processed closer to their source of production. This in turn could provide needed employment so that men would stay in the home area. Ahuwan concurs with this suggestion when he states, "If industries are opened in our home towns only a few will be going to Kaduna and many from Kaduna will return home to their father land" (Ahuwan n.d.:7).

A second problem with Smith's suggestion of a return to a "pagan" community is that it does not take into account current values of the people. Both Christianity and education are highly valued. Young men and women readily take whatever opportunities they find available for further education. Consequently, increasing numbers of young women are joining the men in urban settings, seeking educational advancement and employment opportunities. The Christian church is now so embedded within the culture of southern Kaduna State that any social change to remedy marital or other problems cannot easily bypass the church. Problems exist among the Bajju similar to those Smith found among the A̲gorok, even though Bajju men may easily practice polygyny while continuing to worship within Christian churches. There are sufficient churches of the African-initiated variety, such as the Cherubim and Seraphim and First African Church Mission Inc., in

Bajju villages that allow their members, including their leaders, to have polygynous marriages. Further, most of the more mainline churches, such as Evangelical Churches Winning All (ECWA), Roman Catholic, Anglican, and Baptist, allow polygynists to attend, though they restrict leadership roles and privileges to monogamously married men.

Death

Death marks the transition of a person from one social status to another, from that of a living member of the community to that of an ancestral spirit, an *abvoi,* a person known as a living dead (see chapter 8). Funeral rites for elders consisted of those that took place soon after a person died and was buried on the one hand, and those that took place the following dry season on the other. After death, various restrictions were placed upon the living in order to protect them from death or other misfortunes. The time soon after a death was a dangerous time for the living.

The burials of children, young people, and men who have not had offspring are short. These burials are termed *kanak bassi* or *kanak akun* 'crying with tears'. Soon after such deaths, Bajju men may or may not blow horns for perhaps an hour. Some of these people are believed to be reincarnated. The exception is men who do not marry, whom the Bajju do not want to be reincarnated. Three days after the death, there is a cleansing ritual. The ruling elder talks with the Bajju, rebukes them, and tells them that if they know of any person who wants to practice witchcraft against others, they should stop. This fits in with their belief that no death is normal, but most are caused by witchcraft.

When an elderly person dies, Bajju state that witches "will eat tough meat tonight." This statement reflects the belief that those who practice *nkut* meet together in a meat market in the spiritual realm where meat is bought and sold; the meat is the flesh of the recently deceased. The Bajju also believe those who practice *nkut* may eat the soul of a person in the spiritual realm, thereby causing that person's physical death.

More elaborate funeral rites were reserved for the elderly. Their funerals are termed *kanak bapfo,* "crying with dancing." At their funerals people celebrated their long lives with horn blowing accompanied by dancing to honor the deceased. This celebration occurred during the dry season possibly many months following the death. They did not have this celebration for every elderly man who died, though they certainly had it for important men such as the elder in charge of the *abvoi.* During the *kanak* women rubbed henna on their legs from their knees down. It indicated thankfulness for the life of the man who had died. Bajju men did not put henna on their legs, though the Irigwe men at Miango did. At the *kanak* the man's widow cried. The *kanak apfo* lasted from one to three days. At the end of it, they performed the purification ritual (*ajrang*) in order to protect them from death returning.

When an elderly man became so ill that death would soon occur, another elderly man would attend him. Women and children were not allowed to see him. The *gado kapyyi* examined the body of an elder, then announced the death. If the deceased was a *gado,* the *gado* next in line for that position announced the death, stating that the deceased man was now an ancestral spirit, an *abvoi.* In the announcement by a mature person, an elderly person or the *gado* who attended him announced the death by singing a special death song called *dikwu bvwa zaki* 'A lion has died' or 'A lion has fallen'. While singing this song he played the two-stringed guitar (*zinzom*).

The corpse was then washed. Men washed the body of a man, and women that of a woman. Those who washed the corpse washed themselves in the same water they used to wash the corpse in order to avoid death from the same manner as that of the deceased.

Next they slaughtered the "goat of the ancestors," *bvon abvoi,* which is seen as a sacrifice to the ancestors so that they admit the deceased into their community (Kato 1973:221). Several goats could be slaughtered, depending on the number of relatives and others expected at the burial. They collected the goat's blood, then sprinkled it on the ground, the meeting place between the living and ancestral spirits. From the skin of a goat, they cut the "skin for the hand," *kpa bvak.* This small piece of goatskin with a hole was placed on the thumb of the corpse to symbolize that the deceased had well-to-do relatives. Next they broke the limbs of the deceased to prevent the deceased from returning right after being buried so that he did not bother the living (Kato 1973:221). Prior to burial, the daughter-in-law, the wife of the deceased's eldest son, fed her deceased father-in-law his last meal. This meal was a special white pasty food, termed "paste of the stomach" *ditun kawha,* which she would put in his mouth. She then ran out of the house screaming. It was a fearful thing for her to come into contact with a corpse. Kato stated that since women were not to see a corpse and since in this case it is ritually prescribed that she did so, she had to leave screaming or else she could become mad or die (Kato 1973:221). Formerly the body was laid on a mat, and later a white cloth, provided by the family for burial. Today, a coffin is used for burial, although many elderly people do not want to be buried in a coffin, as their spirits would not be strong enough to open it to leave their bodies. Kunhiyop described the preparation for burial as follows:

> The muscles of the deceased were then broken[8] in order to make them easy for wrapping before burial. Kato explains that "flexing the muscles prevents the deceased returning immediately after burial to disturb the living" (1973:219). [Prior to burial they placed the hand of the deceased on

[8] The muscles were flexed and the bones were broken, not the muscles as in Kunhiyop's quote.

his or her cheek, such as occurs while sleeping.] Before the
corpse was taken out of the room and lowered into the grave,
men formed a wall in order to prevent children and women
from seeing the corpse lest evil befall them. The corpse was
wrapped in a new mat of plaited palm-leaves and men carried it to the grave, shouting, blowing and drumming, while
the women and children remain indoors. [When they carried the corpse into the room, the head went first. When
men carried the body out, the feet went first.] The chief
priest wished the spirit of the dead and the bereaved family
well, and the body was lowered into a grave shaped like a
prayer board, either close to the porch of the house if the
deceased had children, otherwise outside under the shel-
ter of the wall. ... A round stone covered the cavity. They
believed that the souls of the dead can enter the womb of a
living woman and be re-born. (2005:77)

The *gado* selected the spot for burial and began digging. Then under the
direction of the elders, younger men took the hoe and finished digging the
grave. Gunn described the shape of Bajju graves (1956:114). They had a
vertical shaft three to four feet [1 to 1.2 meters] in diameter; the neck of the
grave was two feet [0.6 of a meter] across, then a tunnel which extended
both east and west from the hole for the body. The grave was six to eight
feet [1.8 to 2.4 meters] deep. Two people lowered the body into the grave
with the feet and legs going first into the grave. These two put herbs from
a tree into their ears and nostrils so that the person's spirit would not enter
their bodies and cause their deaths. They buried men facing east, the direction of the origin of the Bajju (Kato 1973:221), while they buried women
facing west. Women who marry Bajju men may come from any group, not
necessarily the Bajju. Further, women come from outside the lineages of
their husbands. This was ritually symbolized by the direction a woman
faced in burial. A second reason advanced for this practice of women facing
west in burial was that the status of women was not up to that of men. The
top of the head of both men and women faces north.

After they placed the corpse into the grave, they covered it with logs
from the palm tree or a round stone, and then covered that with mud and
soft earth. The burial was often in the floor of the hut where the person
lived or in the courtyard of the compound of the deceased. It is not unusual
to see cemented graves in either place. Figure 9.2 shows a traditional A̱tyap
grave, which was very similar to that of the Bajju.

Death, other than that which results from God's punishment of a person, is not considered natural. The cause of death was key to how and
where a body was buried and the rites that occurred. Few deaths are viewed
as natural; rather, people needed to know whether it was an illness of God

or of man caused by *nkut*. The cause of death determined whether a person was given an honorable or a dishonorable burial.

Deaths from God's punishment or from one's own witchcraft, which turned and attacked the person himself, are those that resulted from small-pox, severe diarrhea, and tragic or violent deaths (drowning, suicides, falls from a tree, etc.) (see chapter 7). These people are known as having *tsswa assi* 'spirit eyes'. As mentioned in chapter 6 on witchcraft, people are thought to be born with two sets of eyes, those with which they see physically and those with which they see in the spiritual realm. The burials for those who died because of the use of their spirit eyes were in shallow, rectangular-shaped graves as opposed to the more usual oblong-shaped graves (Kunhiyop 1988:26). People drag the corpse of a person who died a shameful death to a shallow, rectangular hole in an area outside the compound, similar to the rectangular grave made for a dog. There were no burial mats or ceremony associated with this burial. It is termed *jjying*, meaning "to throw away." Bajju stifled their grief for people who died such deaths. The practice of burying such people outside the household continues today for those who die from shameful causes or who are considered to be witches (*bakut*).

If a person died from smallpox, the Bajju belief was that only witches came down with this disease. Because the Bajju believed that the patient was a witch, he or she would not be able to give a satisfactory defense for his or her actions that resulted in the smallpox. When the patient died, he or she died a dishonourable death and thus was given a dishonourable burial.

Most deaths are a result of witchcraft from another person having eaten a person's spirit. These deaths are from illnesses of man. The Bajju sought to find out who caused the death by their witchcraft activities. There were various means to obtain this knowledge. First, at the burial each person was asked to swear on the dirt over the grave that they were not responsible for this death (see chapter 6). The person who refused to swear or who did not swear truthfully was then accused of having caused the death. Second, people went to a diviner, who through ritual identified the person who caused a particular death.

Family members, usually the daughters of the deceased, were responsible for providing the burial mats or cloth used to wrap the corpse. They flexed the limbs of the deceased before wrapping the corpse in woven grass mats. Later they used white cloth to wrap the corpse in. According to Kato, this wrapping was to prevent the deceased from returning immediately after burial to disturb the living.

If the deceased was a baby or small child, or any child who dies suddenly, he or she was believed to definitely come back through reincarnation. While uttering an incantation the *gado* made a small mark with a knife on the child's body. Since the Bajju believed in reincarnation, the mark would enable the living to know when the child returned. When that happened, it would still have the mark on it. (See under "Birth" above.)

The Bajju did not want some persons to be reborn, such as an unmarried man whose chest was cut. Another means of preventing a person from being reborn was to break eggs into the eyes of the corpse. If a person died with his eyes open, they felt the need to keep him from returning. This custom ties in with the Bajju concept of individuals having two sets of eyes, one set used for witchcraft and the other to see with visually. If the person was a good person, they desired that he or she return through reincarnation, but they preferred that an evil person not return.

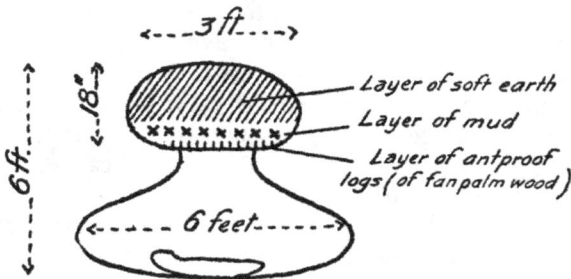

Figure 9.2. Diagram of an Atyap grave (Meek 1931:74).

The Bajju buried their dead in their compounds. When there were too many graves, they moved their compound. Today, people are buried just outside their compounds in private cemeteries associated with each compound. This allows people to continue to live in their compounds without having to move because there are too many burials within a compound. Graves are now rectangular in shape in order to receive a coffin. However, some elderly people continue to request that they be buried wrapped in mats or cloth.

On the third day after the burial elders examined the dirt on the top of the grave, looking for footprints of the deceased. Specifically they looked for the position of the deceased's footprint so that they could tell which direction the deceased went. After that, they cemented the top of the grave.

At the *kanak* celebration horn blowing was accompanied by dancing. The life of a respected elderly person, who had fulfilled his functions in life, was celebrated. His functions in life include being married, having children, providing well for his family, leading an honorable life, and being an elder. It also includes not being an alcoholic. A person who did not lead an honorable life, had stayed single, did not have children, etc., was not celebrated; rather, they cut his chest so that he would not be reincarnated.

Cremation is neither practiced nor understood. On one occasion an Indian doctor, who died in an automobile accident, was cremated alongside the Atacap River near Unguwar Rimi, according to a common practice among Hindus. The Bajju reaction was that the people who cremated him did not do what was right. They questioned how that person could enter the afterlife if he had no body.

Obligations of the living

As mentioned at the beginning of chapter 8, the deceased becomes part of the living dead. This term indicates that although a person is physically dead, his spirit continues to live (Mbiti 1970:32). The deceased's spirit is watching the rites performed in his honor. The living must help the deceased enter the afterlife. To do so, they warmed the spirit of the deceased through burning chaff (*sinsso*) and observed various restrictions.

Formerly, when young men used to plait their hair, all the men in the age group of the deceased had their plaits shaved off as a sign of mourning. A widow had to abide by a number of restrictions for the one-month mourning period following the death of her husband. As mentioned previously, she could not talk to the brothers of the deceased because she did not know who among them would inherit her, and therefore in order to be circumspect, she was not to talk to any of them. Her hair was left unshaven, and in some sections of the Bajju area it was wrapped with raffia leaves. She did not work and her food was brought to her.

Other restrictions placed on a widow were to observe silence, isolate herself from the rest of the household, refrain from taking part in any domestic activities, and refrain from sexual intercourse. She was not to put on any make-up, and was not allowed to have water touch her body, other than a small amount to wipe her face (Kato 1973:222).

During the one-month mourning she was called *akwwuk* 'widow'. After the month of mourning, she was known as the wife of the deceased, not as *akwwuk*. Then she went through a purification ritual at which time her hair was shaved and wrapped in raffia leaves, and she bathed. Both marked the end of her status as *akwwuk*. Men then blew horns because of the death that occurred (*ba tyak dikwu*, meaning they blew because of the death that occurred). Then everyone shared food and beer together. After her purification, she could be inherited by one of the brothers who made her an offer or by another close male relative of the deceased.

The practice of widow inheritance is a means of keeping the blessing of that household within the family. The resulting marriage was seen as a continuation of the previous marriage, hence there was no further marriage ceremony or bridewealth paid. It is practiced by non-Christians as well as by Christians because it keeps the family together. It is termed *sak ambyring* 'to keep the woman'.

Many are believed to be reincarnated after death, either as another person or an animal or bird. A shooting star is interpreted as a person being reincarnated.

If a man's wife or wives are all deceased, it is the responsibility of the youngest son to take care of his father. This is usually not a problem since the Bajju live together patrilocally with their extended family.

Inheritance

Following a man's death, there are two types of property to be divided through inheritance. These are moveable property, such as money, clothing, animals, contents of barns, bows and arrows, and immovable property, such as land, economic trees, houses, sacred groves. In the inheritance of immovable property, the history of the use of land is always taken into account. Land is held by the clan, with individual plots of land allocated to people within the clan according to who farmed that land in the past. It only becomes an inheritance problem when land has been leased from one person to another, with the sons being unaware of the terms of the lease. There are elaborate rules that apply to leased land that must be followed. For example, a lessee must not plant economically productive trees on someone else's land. If there are already economically productive trees on the land, he is entitled only to a small amount of the harvest from such trees with the majority of the harvest going to the land and tree owner.

The man who clears a field is the one who has rights to that field, rights that may be inherited by his sons. Land is not a commodity that is bought and sold, as land belongs to individual clans. Only in very rare instances is land ever sold.

The order of inheritance is as follows:
1. Sons, all of whom inherit equally, with the oldest son choosing first what he wants to inherit. Each son chooses in turn.
2. When there are no sons, brothers of the deceased inherit.
3. When there are no brothers, nephews, and uncles inherit.
4. When there are no nephews or uncles, cousins inherit. (Sanke 1977:20)

As seen in the above order of inheritance, property passes to men within the patrilineage. The following proverb expresses this well: "Smoke does not go from one house (patrilineage) to another" (Sanke 1977:29). Women inherit only moveable property from other women, such as their real or classificatory mothers, mothers-in-law, and sisters. If a woman owns livestock, at her death the animals go to her sons. (Sanke 1977:29)

The division of an estate occurs after the mourning period, specifically forty days after the death. This includes the thirty days of mourning by the deceased's widow. If there are questionable claims to property, those claims are settled through oaths.

The oldest capable son becomes the head of the household. This is a very responsible position that a father often grooms his son for. The one in this position makes decisions for those under him within the household. If it was a lineage head who died, again the oldest son inherits that position.

Children of the deceased are cared for by the man who inherits them, whether his oldest son, brother, uncle, etc. That person must feed them, clothe them, see that they are educated, and be involved in their marriages. That person may also inherit a brother's wife or wives. However, women have the option to decide whether or not they want to be inherited (see under "Second and subsequent marriages" above). If they choose not to be inherited, they must leave their children with the man within the patrilineage who inherited them. The youngest son is usually responsible to care for his mother, the wife of the deceased.

Summary

This chapter addressed the life cycle that people pass through. It moved from birth, marriage, first pregnancy, and death. The Bajju practices are similar to those of neighboring related ethnic groups, such as the Atyap, Agorok, Bace, and Irigwe. Their multiple marital practices often resulted in their having a poor reputation with other ethnic groups. The coming of Christianity to their area has changed their marriage patterns. The practices of wife stealing and of polyandrous polygynous marriages have both disappeared. In fact, monogamy is more common today than polygyny. With Christianity the status of women has risen and marriages have become more stable than previously. However, there is also a rise in single young women becoming pregnant out of wedlock and other problems that have come as a result of very rapid culture change and the relaxation of some of their moral values. Many of the more mature Christians are very concerned about what they see happening with some young Bajju men and women.

The following chapter discusses some of the traditional Bajju taboos.

10

Taboos

Within Bajju culture a number of taboos were followed. The word *taboo* derives from the Polynesian word *tapu* or *tabu,* meaning forbidden and sacred (Crapo 1993:245). Taboos place restrictions on the behavior of people in society, requiring ritual avoidance of whatever is specified in the taboo. They often serve as means of maintaining social control, avoiding illness, and regulating human behavior. Some include positive actions that result in human courtesy and moral benefits to people within a specific culture. Though arbitrary within a specific cultural context, they give both ideals and prescribed behavior that help maintain the social order. As such they help to keep the community ritually clean of negative consequences that might result if they are broken. In general, taboos are found in areas of sex, food, rites of passage, sacred objects, and sacred people (see also the section "Taboos related to *nkut*" in chapter 6).

Bajju state their taboos together with the negative consequences that result if they are not followed. Those consequences involve both the physical and spiritual realms. These two realms are and continue to be intricately interwoven within the daily life of the Bajju. The consequences of violating a taboo often bear a similarity to the violation. For example, there is a close relationship between meat and recently deceased bodies. If a person ate meat of which he or she did not know the source, it might be meat of a deceased human obtained through *nkut* activities and thereby contributed to the person's own illness. From a Bajju perspective the tie between the violation and the consequences might be direct or seen later once something negative occurs. Some taboos apply to children, while others apply to women and men.

Today as Bajju society is in the midst of culture change some of these taboos are breaking down while others continue to be held. In any event, in areas where there was previously a taboo, even if it is no longer adhered to, people frequently comment on it. Taboos are still within people's conscious thought even when they are no longer practiced.

Taboos for children

Food of the small invisible spirits

Bajju told their children not to go outside during the heat of the midday.[1] If they did so, perhaps the *nạtenyrang*, the small invisible spirits that resided nearby, would entice them with food that would make them sick. Kunhiyop reports:

> As a child, the author was restricted from going out on a bright and sunny day because of the fear that he might trespass into the territory of these evil spirits. These evil spirits are believed to cook delicious food and display it in the open in order to tempt greedy people. The person who offends these demons is struck by severe fevers, mental sickness and *rwon nceng* (convulsion) [epilepsy]. (1993:69)

Note that Kunhiyop begins by stating "as a child" and then continues by stating that this taboo applies to children and greedy people in general. The phrase in Jju that describes greediness is *ạrou dissi [nkut]*, literally, "too much eye" or in free translation, "stingy, coveting someone else's things." Bajju teach against stinginess through taboos such as this one.

Meat

Bajju teach their children not to eat meat that people offer them at households other than their own. The fear is that it might be meat obtained through *nkut* activities and, if they eat it, they might be eating the meat of a recently deceased person. This is true especially if someone has recently died.

Taboos for women

A number of taboos applied specifically to women. A few of them were briefly mentioned in the previous chapter, and they are expanded on here. There were taboos related to reproduction, practicing *nkut,* relating to

---

[1] This taboo reminds one of the common saying that only mad dogs and English men go out in the midday sun.

males, menstruation, taking grain from granaries, and hitting people with brooms.

Food taboos

Women were not to eat eggs. To do so meant they would also "eat" their own eggs and thus not be able to conceive or give birth to children. It also meant to practice *nkut* against their own children, thereby causing their illness or death. I well remember giving a cookie to an elderly woman. As she ate it, she remarked on how good it was. Then she asked me if there were eggs in it, and when I answered yes, she promptly spit out what was in her mouth. I quickly realized that if I had been more thoughtful, I would not have placed her in such an awkward situation.

Bajju forbade women to eat certain meat, including chicken and birds in general, hyena, monkey, and monitor lizard. This included not eating gizzards of chickens or other fowl. Gizzards symbolize authority and therefore it is men's food. For a similar reason, women did not eat animal heads as these too symbolize authority and consequently were reserved for men.

Bajju forbade women to eat food they prepared for the *ɑbvoi* men's organization. If the food needed tasting to check on its saltiness, a woman had to call an initiated boy or man from that compound to taste it.

During pregnancy a woman was to refrain from eating sugar cane or other sweets in order to keep her baby from growing too large. Further, if she ate sugar cane during childbirth, she would lose too much fluid.

Menstrual cycle and childbirth

During the time of women's menstrual cycles, they were considered unclean; consequently women were not to cook for their husbands during that period. Another of a man's wives or some other woman or girl in the compound had to cook. Further, for seven days following childbirth women did not cook or perform any farm activities. The reason for this was the belief that any medicine in the household would not function if the woman touched it. The husband could not even receive water from his wife. The new mother also refrained from going to any farm containing growing produce because it would cause the crops to fail.

Greeting men

If a woman was home alone and a man came to visit, she was not allowed to answer his call. She might ask either a boy or a young man to respond. And if no one else but herself was home, then she would answer, "There is no man in the house" (Asake 1982:6). Their concern was that perhaps another suitor would snatch her and take her away.

Granaries

The grain in Bajju granaries represented the blessing of the household. The mark of a well-to-do man was that he had sufficient grain to feed his family for a year. Since women marry into patrilineal families, they were not allowed to climb into granaries to get grain out. The reason for this prohibition was that if a woman entered the grain storage bin in her husband's household, then left her husband and married elsewhere, they believed that she might take the blessing of that household with her. If a woman is home and her husband is not, and she needs to begin cooking dinner using grain from the granary, she has to call a boy or young man from that household to get the grain for her. She could also call an unmarried female from that household to get it out for her. By this means the blessing remains in the household.

Some people put medicine into the granary before putting the grain in it. If a woman entered the granary, especially during her menstrual cycle, it would destroy the power of the medicine. She might also see how much grain was left, something her husband might not want her to know.

While granaries were very common, even in the 1980s, today with the rectangular-built houses, one room is often devoted to grain storage. Fewer compounds now have the round granaries than previously.

Hitting

Women are forbidden to hit people, especially men, with brooms. To do so meant that they would sweep away all of men's charms and power (Asake 1982:4). To hit a boy or girl with a broom made it difficult for that person to marry, as it swept away the blessing. Likewise they were not to hit anyone with a pestle.

Women were also forbidden from hitting the wall of their houses either with their hands or with food. If they did so, it meant that they were calling the masquerades (*dodo* H.) to come.

Women were forbidden to hit a child while they wore the mushroom-shaped ornament used to indicate mourning (*tswandyik*). To do so meant that a woman was beating the head of a child in the underground world, *ayabyen*.

Women in mourning

As mentioned previously, during the month-long mourning period following the death of her husband, a woman kept her eyes lowered out of respect for his spirit. She also had to walk softly on the ground so that she did not disturb his recently buried spirit.

A woman in mourning would not talk to the brother of her husband. The reason was that she was grieving her deceased husband. She did not know which of her brothers-in-law might inherit her.

Taboos for men

Male taboos involved activities such as shaving their heads, refraining from eating food prepared by menstruating women, being careful about what they ate or drank, and wearing skins when entering the *ǫbvoi* shrine.

Shaved heads

No Bajju man would allow his head to be shaved only halfway. The Bajju believed that if that occurred, spirits would come at night to finish the job and the man would go mad.

Unclean food

Men would not eat food prepared by a menstruating woman, for she was in a state of impurity. To do so would expose a man to dangers such as blindness and bad luck in hunting. By eating that food, his charms were rendered powerless and his vision would be impaired so that he could not see an animal from far off when hunting.

Headload rings

Bajju women prepare head rings, termed *nǫkat* (*dikat,* sing.), to place between their heads and their headboards. These round doughnut-shaped grass rings help to stabilize their headloads. No man was to eat porridge or drink water that a woman had carried on her head without having a head ring between her head and the container. To eat such food or drink such water raised the fear that someday someone would come kill him by cutting off his head (Asake 1982:5).

Skins and *ǫbvoi*

When men entered the ancestral shrines, they wore animal skins, the past Bajju male attire. They were forbidden to wear other clothing such as the cloth robes worn by the Hausa. Contrastively, when men went to Christian churches, they were forbidden to wear skins and had to wear cloth robes. Women also had to wear cloth wrappers rather than leaves when they went to church.

For men to wear clothes in the *ǫbvoi* shrine was to bring Christianity into it. At first men were forbidden to wear blankets into the shrine as well, though later it was allowed. The use of clothing made the distinction clear between those who followed traditional religion and those who were Christians.

General taboos

Taboos that applied to everyone concerned a number of matters, including relationships with spirit snakes, meat, whistling, relating to spirits, and manners.

When not to greet

People were forbidden to talk while eating. If a guest showed up while people were eating, he was not greeted until after people had finished eating. The reason is that if people became used to talking while eating, they might not hear when the call for war came and thus their enemies might have an advantage (Asake 1982:5).

If a person hears someone calling in the night, no one was allowed to answer or to reply. The reason was that they were afraid of a day when death would call. If one answered it, it meant that the person would die. It was as through death was calling.

Spirit snakes

Spirit snakes are believed to have the spirits of people in them. The Bajju believe that people's spirits may leave their bodies while they sleep or when they have a fever, and those spirits may enter the bodies of specific snakes. Consequently, Bajju do not kill a spirit snake because if they did so the person whose spirit is in it would quickly be in agony and die. Types of spirit snakes include the following:
1.   A python (*cong*).
2.   A small, harmless, striped tree snake (*kazzwan* or *zzwak*).
3.   A large python-like snake that lives by the river (*cencong*). The Bajju fear this snake because they equate it with a water spirit, the *gajimale*. A diviner (*akut*) might work in conjunction with this snake. The Bajju believe that she might take this snake into her house and feed her children to it. In return for giving it food, it helped her become rich.
4.   A male cobra (*angbaktssuk*, literally, a rooster snake; the female is a *tssuk*). Only a diviner would eat this snake. If others did so, they would experience problems.

Meat

Because of the close association of meat with meat sold in the marketplace of the spirits, people must be careful about the meat they eat. One old man who contracted smallpox attributed his sickness to having been given *nkut* meat. Though he realized its source and thus refused to eat it, he still contracted smallpox, allegedly because he had held the meat in his hand.

Whistling

People were not to whistle at night. To do so would call the evil spirits (*nɑtenyrang*) to come. People also did not whistle in the house of a hunter. To do so would keep his hunting charms from functioning. Additionally when he ate food it would only fill his stomach, but it would not satisfy him.

Reverence and respect

As mentioned in chapter 8, in walking, a person should not look up too much, out of reverence towards God. Also when an adult disciplines a child, that child is not to look up at the adult. By looking down he or she demonstrates respect.[2]

Food

If a visitor came to one's house, and the hostess gave him food, he would not eat it alone. A child or another person from that compound would be sent in to eat with the guest to show that the food was safe to eat, that it had not been obtained through *nkut* activities, and that it was not poisoned. A stranger would not eat all of the food but leave leftovers, whether he was satisfied or not. This is seen as a courtesy, not a taboo per se. To fail to leave leftovers indicated that the person was too hungry.

Bajju are not to blow on their food in order to cool it. If a person does so, he or she would be calling the spirits.

Heads and beds

When people lie down on their beds at night, their heads must be closer to the door than their feet. Only a dead body had its feet closer to the door. Again, since death comes at night, by having one's head closer to the door, the person will be awakened and able to deter death. If one's feet are closer to the door, a spirit would come and count his toes. Since there are only ten toes, the spirit could quickly count them and then kill the person. But if one's head is closer to the door, the spirit would not finish counting the individual's hairs by morning, and the person would live.

---

[2] This contrasts with a Western tradition where a mother will tell her child to look at her when she disciplines him. By looking at her he is giving her his full attention and respect. This is the opposite of what Bajju parents want from their children.

Hunting taboos

As mentioned in chapter 5, no one is allowed to step over the bow or arrows of a hunter. However, if one does so inadvertently, he or she has to then step over them backwards. If the person does not do so, the hunting charms of the bows and arrows will be ineffective. Also a person should not cross arrows.

In order to be in a state of purity for hunting, a man has to refrain from engaging in sexual intercourse the night before. If he did not do this, he would spoil the hunt.

Cocks

A cock that crows between dusk and midnight must be killed. It is a bad omen. It is not only waking up the sleeping inhabitants of the compound, it is also calling the spirits. It also reveals the location of people around an area, especially if there were enemies during wartime, or today thieves or armed men. By crowing it means that something terrible is coming.

No beating of virgins

If a young woman was mature and still a virgin, no one was allowed to beat her. If she is beaten, it tended to break her virginity.

Shaved heads

In the past men, women, and children plaited their hair and put ornaments into it to make them look more beautiful. Young women discontinued doing so when they married. Young men continued doing so for a while and married women began to shave only one side of their heads. This served to discourage other suitors. However, Christian young women continued to plait their hair, even after marriage, until they stopped doing so, probably because of missionary influence.

Men, women, and children had their heads shaved. This custom kept them cool, avoided problems with head lice, and, according to Bajju belief, avoided headaches, as long hair could cause them. Many Bajju continue to have their heads shaved regularly, though increasingly due to influences from outside the area, especially women no longer have their heads shaved.

Widely shared taboos

Bajju share some taboos with other groups, particularly the Hausa and Fulani. For instance, the left hand is reserved for unclean activities. One does not hand something to another person with the left hand; to do so insults that person.

Elderly women have a taboo that prescribes extreme diffidence, border-
ing on avoidance, with their eldest son. It is a means of showing respect
to the person who one day will be head of the compound. This avoidance
parallels that of the Hausa where a woman cannot be in the presence of or
speak to her oldest son. Typically the Hausa foster their first son to their
husband's mother.

If someone needed to leave his load on a path or road briefly, he or she
placed shea tree leaves on it. Then no one would touch or steal their load
as this placed supernatural sanctions on the load. A woman would not even
pick up her load until a man had removed the leaves. This was so in the past
but today people no longer use the shea tree leaves. Also a farmer might
put up shea tree leaves and other items in a medicine bundle on a short
pole placed on the side of his field. No one would steal the harvest because
of supernatural sanctions associated with this medicine bundle. They may
also put a medicine bundle on a tree to keep others from harvesting its fruit.

Taboos in perspective

Within the Bajju taboo system various themes recur. One is that of conta-
gion. For example, the head touching a headboard with food on it without
an intervening head ring can cause a potential problem with the head of the
person who eats that food. Another theme is that of defilement or dirt. This
is illustrated in a man's refraining from eating the food prepared by a menstruating woman or from eating *abvoi* food tasted by a woman. This is also
illustrated by the taboo of men avoiding sexual intercourse prior to hunting.

One element of Bajju culture that runs through a number of these
taboos is that of the intertwining of the sacred with daily life. In particular,
a number of taboos help people avoid calling the spirits. The Bajju do not
whistle at night, or sleep with their feet closer to the door than their heads.
They are careful to know the source of the meat they eat, and they prohibit
their children from eating meat at other compounds where its source may
be questionable. Children also avoid eating beans that the *natenyrang* may
have given them.

While this chapter has dealt with specific taboos, there are taboos
related to other aspects of Bajju culture. They relate to illness and the entire
Bajju medical system. They relate to the spirit world and in particular the
activities of the *natenyrang*. There were various prohibitions placed upon
women during periods of mourning. The Bajju culture, like any culture,
must be viewed holistically in order to see the integration of its various
components.

The taboos or prohibitions of specific behaviors foreshadowed the widespread adoption of Christianity by the Bajju, particularly the legalistic type
of Christianity brought by early SIM Christian missionaries. Christianity
looked like what a true religion should look like. It too had various taboos,

which the Bajju referred to as the rules of following. For example, a man should not have more than one wife. He should not be a horn blower in contexts that related to traditional religion, he should not wear skins in church, and women should not wear leaves in church, and so forth. It was these Christian "taboos" that convinced some early Bajju that Christianity was a true religion and should be taken seriously.

11

Values

If you have, you will have friends. If you don't have, you will have no
friends. (Bajju proverb)

Having described much of Bajju culture, in this chapter I briefly discuss
some Bajju values. Values are accepted or normative ideals of behavior
within a culture. They involve judgment, such that behavior and actions
may be evaluated by people who share a culture. They define what a culture
perceives as right and wrong, and what is moral and immoral. They are the
basis of many decisions that people make. As such, a culture's values are
part of daily living.

The Bajju value their community, with achievement important by vir-
tue of being part of the community. One proverb states "Blessed is the person who has people." By contrast, individualism is not valued. In fact, one
Bajju friend found American individualism problematic. From his perspective Americans' individualism is killing their society.[1]

Other members of the Bajju community often determine a person's
behavior. For example, one young teacher, from the senior primary school
across the road, came to tell us goodbye. He was leaving the next day to
study at an agricultural school. We asked him if he wanted to study agriculture. How was the application handled? He responded that his uncle
had decided what he would study, had applied for him, and had received
the acceptance. His uncle had just informed him that he was going to study
agriculture. It had not been that teacher's choice, but he readily accepted

[1] My friend was living in Portland, Oregon, when he made this statement.

his uncle's decision concerning this next step in his life. Just as that teacher valued his uncle's decision, respect for those over one, whether family, teachers, elders, authorities, or the supernatural is important to the Bajju.

Respect for the supernatural

It was believed and practiced that when one was walking he should not look up too much in order to show respect and a high regard for God. Further, a person should not turn to look back too much, especially at night, as a small spirit, a *kạtenyrang*, or people of the underground world, *bạnyet yabyen*, may be following. They may have either good or bad intentions for an individual, but since the person does not know which, he or she should be careful.

People pray to God for the things they value. The Bajju pray to God for his blessings in giving them children, good crops, animals, wealth, good hunting, and rain. If there is drought and farmers need rain for their crops, they pray for rain at one of the high places known as being significant for this activity or in a church meeting for Christians.

The ruling elder of the village may call a meeting to pray to God to ask his blessing on their land. Prior to planting grain, people may call a meeting to ask for God's blessing. During the rainy season they pray that no deaths will occur, as well as for good health and good crops. Formerly, they prayed that any illness would go to the wooden handle of the hoe so that if it broke, it could be replaced. If sickness did occur, they had a meeting to ask if anyone was responsible for the sickness. When an epidemic occurred, the ruling elder prayed and warned people to desist from witchcraft activities. If anyone knew that he or she was "eating" another person through witchcraft, then that person should stop or God would catch him or her. The elder declared that from that day forward the epidemic would stop. He then beat the ground with his staff. After that he gave a blessing. They also gave an ill person or persons medicine or took the patient(s) to a dispensary or hospital.

In the Bajju worldview there is the belief that if God loves you, things go well with you. Today this leaves Christians open to the prosperity gospel and health and wellness beliefs. This way of thinking involves both some truth and some falsehood. God does bless people with material things and with good health, but then their focus is often on what God has given them rather than on God himself. The Bible teaches that it is only in heaven that we are promised no sickness, no sorrow, and no tears. However, the prosperity gospel fits well with Bajju traditional beliefs. If things are not going well, then someone is practicing witchcraft against the person.

Each evening a parting greeting is "May God raise us," or when on a journey "May God go with you" or "May God keep you in health" or "May you arrive well" (see chapter 8). People live with a daily awareness of God's presence.

Respect for one's husband

A good wife is submissive to her husband, shown by curtseying to him when handing him something. She cooks food for him and does his laundry. Since he is the head of the household, she defers to him in making decisions that affect the entire household. This includes identifying with the religion of her husband. While women's social status has risen with the coming of Christianity, as seen in their active participation in church services and activities, it is still not equivalent to that of men.

Respect for one's family

In speaking about respect for one's family, it is presupposed that a person marries. As I discussed in chapter 9, marriage is highly valued because it brings completeness, status, respect, and responsibility. Kunhiyop states, "Marriage is the most important activity of man's existence" (Kunhiyop 1982:22). Once people marry, they begin their family, a family that they show respect for. Within the family, children show respect to their parents and elders by looking down when they are being disciplined. If a child fails to show respect, for example, through hitting his parents or verbally abusing them, his or her parents may put a curse on the child. To undo that curse, there must be repentance and forgiveness, which occurs through the forgiveness ritual, *sswa bạtwak*. Later in life if a person experiences problems, for example, fails to have children, that person must either go to his parents, or if the parents are deceased, go to their graves, to ask for forgiveness. Reverence and respect for the ancestors are a natural extension of Bajju respect for their parents and family when they were alive.

Just as children respect their parents, parents also value children. A couple is rich if they have a large family. Typically this involved having a large polygamous family. Each child a couple has is warmly welcomed. If health workers hold a women's clinic, women will come largely to find out how they can conceive another child. More-educated couples are aware of the cost of educating all their children, so they tend to limit the number of children they have.

Discipline of children is shared by the community. Any adult can discipline any child. It is only for very serious problems that another adult would take a child back to his or her parents for discipline. If it were not so serious, that adult would have disciplined the child him- or herself.

Having a son to continue the household and patrilineage is very important. If a wife fails to have a son, a man may choose to marry another wife with the goal that she will have a son to continue the patrilineage. This value explains why the life of a barren woman is so difficult. Having children is the reason for marriage, so if a wife fails to have a child within a reasonable period, she may be sent back to her father's household since she has been unable to have a child to continue the patrilineage. Today being married to one wife is important for Christians. This results in a potential conflict between the value of having sons and the Christian value placed on monogamy. As mentioned in chapter 9, if it is determined that the barrenness is the husband's fault, he may ask has brother to impregnate his wife, something that would ordinarily be considered adultery. If there is no child, that couple may foster another's child or children.

Respect for elders and others

Bajju elders are the repositories of wisdom and knowledge. Those who are mature have gained wisdom from experience and knowledge such that they are able to lead others. They are respected, listened to, and obeyed. Respect is shown by one's posture, with bowing, curtseying by females, kneeling, and even lying prostrate on the ground[2] for those who are deeply respected within the culture.

The value of respect also extends to leaders. There is respect for the paramount chief of the ethnic group, district heads, village chiefs, the head of each household, teachers, pastors, government officials, the head of state, etc. Some younger people assert that when they are in positions of authority, they will do things differently, but while the current leaders are governing, they will obey them. This attitude reflects the basic value of respect for those in authority.

The value of respect also includes extending warm hospitality to strangers. The Bajju were known to be very kind at home. When someone comes to another's house, the host or hostess is expected to give some gift to the visitor. That gift may be a beverage, such as a cup of coffee or tea, food, or something else.[3]

---

[2] While an A̲tyap man was visiting us in Duncanville, Texas, I introduced him to the elderly, white-haired grandmother who was living with her son and his family next door to us. The A̲tyap man immediately laid prostate on the sidewalk in order to show her respect, which as an elder she deserved! Since she had significant memory loss, his display of extreme respect was no doubt lost on her. As mentioned in chapter 1 the A̲tyap are closely related to the Bajju, both being descendants from the same Proto-Plateau ethnic group.

[3] This contrasts with what happens in American culture where a guest often brings a gift to his or her host or hostess.

Respect for elders is seen when decisions made are carried out. The consensus decision-making process allows anyone at a meeting to express his or her opinion. Gradually a group consensus emerges. The person with the most respect, whether from wisdom, education, wealth, age, or office, expresses that decision. That person is largely silent throughout the discussion. He listens and ascertains when the group reaches a consensus, then summarizes that decision. After that, no one else speaks. All those present are responsible for implementing that decision.

Maintaining good relationships

Figuratively speaking, feeling heat or being hot is identified with anger or being upset about something. This is often indicated by a person putting his arms and hands on the back of his head, as when walking, to tell you by posture that he is upset.[4] To be cold indicates peace, calmness, and a good relationship with others. No woman with a hot temper would be allowed to bring food to those who were smelting iron, an activity that Bajju men used to do. Further, an angry person is more apt to be accused of witchcraft than a person who is calm and gets along well with others.

It is very common that men, when outside their own home, associate primarily with other men who are around their own ages. Women likewise associate with other women who are around their ages. This meant that men associated with their age mates, those they had gone through initiation with. Likewise children associate with their own age mates who are around their own ages and the same sex.

In village churches men tend to sit on the left-hand side of the church and women on the right side. Further, the seating is age-ranked with the younger children in the front rows, the teenagers next, with adults following. Male elders sit up front. Very young children sit with their parents or others who want to hold them. If an infant needs nursing, the infant is passed from person to person until it gets to its mother. Increasingly in urban churches sex and age ranking is no longer practiced.

Guests are warmly welcomed when they come to greet. In fact, it is sufficient reason to go to someone's house just to greet. When guests leave, the host and/or the hostess walks them out to their car or a certain distance along the path. It shows their guests respect, hospitality, and well wishes for their journey.

---

[4] Such posture in an American context indicates that the person is very relaxed, not that he is angry and needs some resolution to a problem.

Stinginess and sharing

There are negative values to be avoided. Being stingy is one of them. To be stingy is termed *arou dissi,* literally, "too much eye." If one tries bargaining too hard to get the best price for something in the market, that person may be accused of being stingy (cf. chapter 10, "Taboos for children").

Just as stinginess is a negative value to be avoided, sharing is a positive value that is very important to the Bajju. What a person has is shared with others. If a guest comes to visit at any hour of the day or night, the host or hostess provides food and drink for that person. If they need to stay over-night, the host and hostess will find a place for them to sleep. Once we were staying with a Bajju couple who have three children. So they pushed two single beds together for our two daughters and their three children to sleep on. Then more guests arrived. In the morning I asked our oldest daughter how many had slept on those two single beds the previous night. She said eight children!

Dreams

Dreams in which an ancestor appears to a person are taken seriously. Such dreams give direction to the living or warnings about things to be avoided. Dreams can initiate or validate conversion, whether to Christianity, Islam, or some other religion. Christians and Muslims often have dreams that cause them to think carefully about their faith. The content of a person's dreams gives guidance for current behavior. Some dreams give positive guidance while others indicate that something negative will happen to a person.

Some consider dreams as personal thoughts that grow out of peoples' waking experiences, anxieties, and desires that the mind continues to work on while one is in the lighter phases of sleep. When considered from this perspective, dreams do not need to be interpreted. However, when viewed from the perspective of being prophetic, then a dream needs to be inter-preted and acted upon. The Bajju recognize that not all dreams need to be interpreted; some deal with the mundane aspects of daily life. Dreams where an ancestor appears need to be interpreted.

One example comes from a hunting elder who had a dream in which he saw people bringing a corpse to him on a mat. After he awoke, he called the people together to tell them about his dream. Among those who listened to him was a hunter. After hearing the content of the dream, he went hunting. When he saw an animal, he shot at it twice, but each time he missed the ani-mal. When he returned home, he told the hunting elder that it was the elder's fault that he had missed hitting the animal. If the elder had not told them the content of his dream, the hunter would not have missed hitting it. Generally, if an elder has a dream in the evening, he would call people together to reveal it in the morning. However, if it is a bad dream, he should not reveal it.

Education

Education is highly valued among the Bajju. The goal is to go as far as one can. If a person is accepted into a school, then the community will come together to help that individual financially. Once that person has a job he should help the next person with his or her education.

For example, a Bajju teacher, who was single, paid the school fees for sixteen children from his village. We asked if it bothered him to be responsible for so many children, especially when none of those children were his. His response was no; it did not bother him because whenever he decided to pursue further education, the community would help him pay for that education.

With education comes prestige. The titles gained by education are important as they indicate one's status within the community. A person with a PhD degree is respected. The titles Dr., Rev., or Rev. Dr. indicate status a person has within the community.

Time

Bajju, like many Africans, distinguish between African time and Western time. On invitations the time of an event is usually specified. However, it is important to understand which time is to be followed. The most important person will often arrive about an hour after the stated starting time. This gives everyone else invited a chance to be there. It is not appropriate to arrive after the most important guest.

Some events occur when everything is ready ... and not before. Once we were invited to a wedding that the invitation stated started at 2 p.m. Having lived in the village long enough, we did not show up at 2 p.m. We reasoned that the wedding would not take place until the bride and her friends and relatives had arrived. So we waited until 4 p.m. when their vehicle passed by on the road near our home. Even then we had to wait for perhaps another hour before the wedding took place.

Today there is a tendency to stick closer to Western time more than to African time, though it depends on the event. Time is variable. We found it helpful to bring a good book along to read as well as to spend time talking with people while waiting for an event to occur.

Teaching values through proverbs

Values and wisdom are taught through Bajju proverbs. These short, pithy statements often have moral didactic purposes. They are multivocal, and as such they can be used in any number of situations. The following proverbs illustrate some Bajju values as well as aspects of their worldview.

1. *Arau ka̱nu̱, nu a̱mi a̱ cong A̱kpat.*
   The one who speaks quickly (too much) is always involved in trouble.[5]
   In other words a person should think before speaking.
2. *A̱byyi ba̱nyet a ya dikan shan ba'.*
   One who has people does not need a policeman. Here the value of having people is stressed.
3. *Ka byyi, a byyi ba̱rywai.*
   If you have (wealth, possessions, etc.), you will have friends.
4. *Ka byyi ba', a byyi a̱rywai ba'.*
   If you have no wealth, you will not have a friend. These last two proverbs speak of the importance of having wealth and possessions to share with your friends (McKinney and McKinney 2003:170–173).

Teaching values through oral stories

The Bajju have short folk tales and stories that teach moral lessons. Stories often end with the moral of the story. One example is "The Lion and the Fire." Note that it ends with a proverb that gives the value taught by the story.

Zaki bu Rong
The Lion and the Fire

Ka a ryi a̱yin na̱ tyong a̱ bu nwa an dong, kyang a ku nying i ku rau rong a.

Nyyai a̱yin a̱ yi sshyi keyak a̱ hwok zaki ku uwrum bai, na̱ kai a̱nok a̱ rot a̱ tyong a̱ si nwa ka̱yat a̱sshim. Zaki na kun dyi na̱ nwa a a̱sshim a ni, ku seyak. Ka̱ram ka zaki na ku n seyak ni a̱ntyok keyak a̱yyu a̱ cat ryen uwruk a ka̱yat a̱sshim ka, ku seyak. A̱ shyi ba' Ka̱ram ka ka̱won nu ka ka ba, ka̱ret mpfong ka ni, a̱ bu shya a̱tyyi nu ka̱yat a̱sshim, na̱ shyi i ka̱nak. Ka ku zzim sisak ji na̱ yya nwa a̱sshim a ni. A̱tyyi nu a̱ ku kok sisak ji.

Ka̱won ka gaan a̱ drok ba̱ nyong a̱ si sook som ba̱pyyi a̱ bu rot. A̱ cat a̱doma a̱tyyi nu, a̱ sook tswam ndong gaan, a̱ tyyak tyyi ba̱pyyi ba a̱ si sook a̱ ta a̱tyyi nu mi.

Ka̱ram ka a̱tyyi nu na̱ hwok rywei ndong a ni, na̱ ta̱kwang bi ncyi a̱ uwruk ka̱yat a̱sshyim ka. Ka̱won ka a̱ si hywa da̱ nu, "Dikwu a̱mi a bu tyong nwa ka̱yat a̱sshim ka. Nwan bu tyong dikwu u uwruk." (Adapted from McKinney and McKinney 1972:13–14, 2003:179–181)

---

[5] The word *A̱kpat* refers to the Hausa people. Here it is translated as "trouble."

If you see a person flee and enter a fire, the thing that is chasing him is greater than the fire. Long ago a person was farming when he heard a lion come roaring, he dropped his hoe and ran and entered a thorn patch. When the lion saw that he entered the thorns, he passed by. When the lion had passed, the farmer looked for a way to get out of the thorns, but he did not find one. He began to cry. When his child came to the work place, he found his father in the thorns crying. He asked him how he entered the thorns. His father told him how. The child then left quietly; he then took a bundle of grass, which he dropped. He looked for a match in his father's bag. When he found it, he took a match, struck it, and put it on the grass. He then took it and threw it to his father. When his father heard the noise of the fire, he struggled and ran and came out from inside the thorns. His child then said to him, "You fled death by entering into the thorns. You fled death again when you came out."

Summary

This chapter addressed a few Bajju values that involve respect, hospitality, maintaining good relationships in the wider society and with those in authority, and showing respect for the supernatural. These values indicate that maintaining relationships, especially peaceful ones, are of central importance. Relationships are more important than one's work.

12

Indirect Rule in the Precolonial and Colonial Contexts

A discussion of Bajju ethnohistory would not be complete without a discussion of the wider context in which they live. Earlier I addressed their relationship to the ethnic groups around them, particularly those with whom they engaged in interethnic warfare. The wider context includes relating to two Hausa-Fulani emirates and the British during colonialism. As mentioned in chapter 1, both involved people seeking to rule them indirectly.

The phrase "Indirect Rule" refers to the governing of one group by another through the governed group's own leaders. In the relevant historical context here, it refers to the governing of the Bajju by representatives of the Hausa-Fulani emirates farther north in Nigeria, who in turn received their direction from the British colonial government. While this was theoretically what should occur, this is not in fact what happened. Neither the Hausa-Fulani nor the British investigated carefully, if at all, the local political structure that could have been used to govern the minority ethnic groups in this area. Rather, the Hausa-Fulani emirate structure was imposed on the non-Muslim minority ethnic groups in the Middle Belt with chiefs appointed by the Hausa-Fulani, Hausa-Fulani district heads placed over them, and judicial courts set up, which were largely based on the shari'a law. When the British took over Northern Nigeria, they placed themselves over the Hausa-Fulani emirates and sought to govern the minority ethnic groups through the emirates. So the people who formerly slave-raided, taxed, and plundered them were now formally over them, backed by the colonial West

African Frontier Force. The term "Indirect Rule," popularized by the British during colonialism, could also be applied to what the emirates tried to use in relating to the minority groups in precolonial times.

In the sections below I first discuss how Islam arrived in Northern Nigeria, then Hausa-Fulani emirate relations with the minority ethnic groups, followed by British colonialism, and more current conflict between Muslims and non-Muslims in this area.

Islam in Northern Nigeria

Islam arrived in Northern Nigeria through Islamic clerics who accompanied caravans from North Africa to various destinations in Sub-Saharan Africa. They provided various services to the settled populations such as record keeping, medical care, and a religious system, which provided a unified ideology that assisted with trade. Islam provided safe passage for caravans whether or not people could communicate well with each other due to having different languages. Islam reached Kanem Borno in the eleventh century and spread from there into the various Hausa states. It provided a link between Sub-Saharan Africa, North Africa, and the Middle East. At first Islam was limited to the elite of the settled urban populations. In the sixteenth century al-Maghili, an Islamic scholar and traveler, wrote a treatise on the Islamic governing of Kano, a Hausa city.

Zazzau and Jema'a Emirates and Southern Zaria

From 1804 until 1812 Usuman ɗan Fodio led a jihad in Northern Nigeria. It was an Islamic reform movement, which sought to purify Islam as practiced by the Hausa and Fulani. He was a Fulani Islamic cleric from the settled Fulani (*Fulani gidan,* H.). He was distressed over the corrupt practices of those around him, particularly those of the Hausa leadership, such as excessive taxation, bribery, the exclusion of Fulani from government, not living in accord with Islamic principles and the shari'a law, and economic problems. In his jihad he gave flags to those who were to conquer areas in his name. The campaign resulted in the emirates of Kebbi, Gwando, Sokoto, Zazzau, Kano, Katsina, and Gobir. Mallam Musa, the emir at Zaria from 1804–1821, claimed that Sokoto Emirate had given the southern region to him, so when Mallam Usuman[1] sought a flag as his insignia of office for the new emirate of Jema'a na Daroro, Mallam Musa gave him a flag symbolizing that this new emirate was subordinate to Zazzau Emirate. This indicated that Mallam Usuman could wage war for Zazzau Emirate, which resulted in Jema'a Emirate becoming a vassal state of Zazzau Emirate. Jema'a joined Zazzau's other vassal states of Keffi, Doma, Kajuru, Kauru, Lapai, Lafia, and Nassarawa.

---

[1] This was a different Mallam Usuman than Usuman ɗan Fodio.

After the jihad of Usuman dan Fodio, he divided the rule of this large caliphate between his son and his brother. His son Mohammed Bello was over Zamfara, Kano, Zazzau (Zaria), Daura, Katsina, Bauchi, Katagum, and Sokoto; and Usuman dan Fodio's brother Abdullahi was over the Nupe, Borgu, Dendi, Ilorin, and Kiptako. Mohammed Bello resided at Sokoto, the seat of administration of this large caliphate. Much of this territory was outside of the caliphate's control. It was an area where minority ethnic groups resided; representatives of the caliphate used it as a source of slaves, as well as for economic and political expansion. Even Mohammed Bello recognized that Zazzau Emirate encompassed "many places inhabited by barbarians" (Mohammed Bello in *Infakul Maisuri,* as quoted in Ochonu 2014:29).

Following the jihad campaigns, slave markets emerged. Adamu attributes the shift in marketing of slaves from home sales to slave markets to three factors: (1) the drying up of the Atlantic slave trade following the abolition of slavery by European and trans-Atlantic powers, (2) the decrease in the number of slaves sold into the trans-Saharan route, and (3) the increase in the number of slaves obtained following the jihad campaigns (Adamu 1978:171–172). This increase in slave acquisition resulted in a lower population density in the Middle Belt of Nigeria (Mason 1969). The Middle Belt is the U-shaped portion of Nigeria that lies between the Yoruba and Igbo in the southwest and southeast respectively, and the Hausa-Fulani in the north. It encompasses the region where numerous minority ethnic groups reside, including the Bajju. Both Zazzau and Jema'a Emirates claimed the Bajju to be under them.

The various Hausa-Fulani emirates depended upon slave labor for farming. Lovejoy asserted that the various emirates had a slave mode of production (1983:275). In order to obtain slaves, each dry season the emirates sent out expeditions to capture and/or buy slaves from the non-Muslim population around them. These raiders captured slaves, extracted taxes, and plundered the non-Muslims. So dependent were they on slaves that by 1860 Sokoto Caliphate had approximately four million slaves (Lovejoy and Hogendorn 1993:1), many of whom came from Southern Zaria. This was the situation that the British colonialists found when they colonized Northern Nigeria. The Hausa also appointed chiefs among the local people, chiefs who were basically go-betweens between the emirate officials and the local people. Each time the raiders came, the local people fought them. There was no direct control by the emirates over the local population.

Colonialism

In 1857 the British occupied Lagos and soon thereafter established the Protectorate of Southern Nigeria. On January 1, 1900, the British established the Protectorate of Northern Nigeria. On January 1, 1914, it combined these two protectorates, and named the combined territory the Colony and Protectorate of Nigeria. Its reasons for doing so were: (1) the Protectorate of Northern Nigeria was poor, and thus had to have a subsidy from the government of the Protectorate of Southern Nigeria, which had a surplus in its treasury. This helped fulfill the British goal that each of its colonies be financially self-sufficient. (2) The British wanted to unite the railway systems of the two protectorates; linking the two governments made this feasible. This linkage facilitated transportation of commodities from the north to the south for export.

When the British colonized the north they applied the emirate model of government to most areas. One can question why they did so rather than examining the existing political structures of the minority ethnic groups. Basically, they relied on information obtained from the British travelers, first Major Denham, then Hugh Clapperton and Walter Oudney (see Denham et al. 1826), who reached Sokoto Caliphate in the 1820s, and on the Hausa-Fulani assertion that these areas belonged to them. Clapperton talked with Sultan Mohammed Bello who asserted that the caliphate extended all the way to the confluence of the Niger and Benue Rivers. This information was carried back to the colonial office in England. It had an impact on the British colonialists, who felt that if this were the case, then to place themselves over the Hausa-Fulani Caliphate would result in their being able to govern this area effectively. Ochonu (2014) terms what the British did to the minority ethnic groups as colonialism by proxy.

It is also important to understand the socio-cultural evolutionary theory that was prevalent in the late 1800s and early 1900s, which divided people into various categories according to their stage of development. Some groups were seen as backward, pagan, and lower on a cultural evolutionary scale than other groups. Some British colonial administrators accepted such theories. They saw the Hausa with their organized emirate structure, wearing of clothes, and monotheistic religion of Islam as further evolved than the people who wore skins and leaves. Further, British colonialists came from a class-conscious society. One administrator compared the emirs to the barons in British society and stated that the peasantry looks to their barons for protection (NAK: ACC 873 638, 1937). They carried this class consciousness over into their administration of Nigeria. The British recognized no leaders in Southern Zaria above the head of the family who had political authority (NAK ZarProf 3465). The traditional leaders in this area combined religious and political power (Yahaya 1980:16), but they were never recognized during the colonial era.

Temple, who served with Lugard first as the Resident of Bauchi Province and later as Lieutenant-Governor of Northern Nigeria (1914–1917), espoused a similar viewpoint when he stated,

> The native is a human being like ourselves, but in a different
> stage of development. Some natives are, even to-day, in the
> stage of our Druidical ancestors, whereas others are in the
> stage which we passed through in about the Middle Ages.

> The whirligig of time has brought us about five hundred to
> a thousand years ahead of them in the process of evolution,
> that is all. (Temple 1918:31)

Charles Temple considered the Hausa-Fulani emirates in the northern provinces of Nigeria and the Yoruba chieftaincies in the southern provinces to be more advanced along the road to civilization than "the even greater sections of the native community which are more backward" (Temple 1918:61).

When colonialism was established in all the colonies in Africa, the generally accepted reasons were to advance civilization, bring Christianity, and engage in commerce. A fourth "C," that is not usually mentioned, was conquest of lands that belonged to the indigenous populations. In Northern Nigeria the British initially sought to suppress slave raiding, slave sales, and opposition. Slavery itself was not outlawed by the British administration until 1936.

The Hausa-Fulani emirate officials termed the Bajju and other non-Muslim minority ethnic groups "pagans"; the British also used that term. In the National Archives in Kaduna, British documents are stamped as either Mohammedan policies or as Pagan policies. Clearly the pagans were at the bottom of the socio-cultural evolutionary scale. They were less developed, did not wear clothes such as the Hausa did, and had practices that both members of the Hausa-Fulani emirates and the British saw as less developed and primitive.

Throughout the colonial period, the Bajju had no political representation in the government, though they repeatedly requested it. Their first effort in the 1930s was led by Musa Marsa, who sought to be chief of the entire ethnic group. He together with his followers went to Madakiya to request the chieftaincy from the emir. Allahmagani, a respected elder at Madakiya, supported his request. However, before Musa Marsa arrived, the emir heard that he was coming. When he arrived, the emir ordered his arrest. Musa Marsa died shortly after his release from prison.

A second major effort was led by Usman Akangnet Sokwak (1900–1953),[2] an interpreter at the government hospital in Kafanchan. He took Musa Marsa as his role model (NAK ZarProf 3465). In the early 1940s Usman worked towards the establishment of a chieftaincy position among the Bajju. He claimed that his father was the leader (*magaji*) at Sokwak, his relatives were descendants of Baranzan at Dibyyi, and that therefore either he or one of his older brothers should be appointed to this position. Usman sent a number of petitions to the colonial administration requesting the establishment of this position. He engaged an attorney to write his petitions. In one of his numerous petitions, Usman mentioned the possibility of his being appointed as chief, and the leading elder (*gado*) at Dibyyi being

---

[2] In the archival records his name is alternately spelled Osuman Sokop and Usuman of Sokop Kaje (NAK ZarProf 6/1942). My spelling conforms to Bajju pronunciation.

appointed as the district head. His basis for this request came from the Bajju founding charter. Baranzan, the Bajju founding father, resided at Dibyyi, and A̲nkwak, the founder of Sokwak, was Baranzan's eldest son. The *gado* at Dibyyi had long been recognized as the most important elder among the Bajju.

The colonial administration repeatedly told Usman that any change of administrative structure such as he was requesting had to receive the consent of the emir. So Usman, together with some of his followers, traveled by train to Zaria to request the position of chief for the Bajju from the emir. Usman had a limited knowledge of Hausa, so he found himself at a disadvantage when the emir questioned him about what exactly he was requesting. In the midst of a number of questions that Usman was able to answer affirmatively, the emir asked him if he was requesting a *lardi* (H.), a "province." Usman did not know the word; however, in the total context of questions, all of which Usman could answer in the affirmative, he responded "yes" to that question too. That response was clearly unacceptable under the colonial administration, and he was promptly arrested. When Usman and his followers found out the meaning of that word, they felt they had been tricked.

Usman continued his efforts to have the chieftaincy position established. He was again arrested in September 1942. Either during the arrest or shortly afterwards he was beaten. The colonial medical doctor confirmed that he had been beaten; however, the administration chose to take no action. They said that if he chose to pursue the issue, they would take action. They charged him with refusal to obey a lawful order from the Native Authority in whose area he resided and with conduct liable to cause a breach of the peace. They convicted him on the first charge and acquitted him on the second.[3] He spent two months in jail for that conviction.

In 1946 Usman Sokwak and twelve others were arrested on the charge of causing a riot.[4] This time he and his associates received sentences of twelve months with hard labor. The administration considered permanently exiling him from the Bajju area to remove him from his base of popular support. However, the attorney general in Lagos advised against such action because Usman had engaged a lawyer and sought change through peaceful

---

[3] Yahaya points out that the courts often became tools for suppressing critics of the Native Authority (NA) (Yahaya 1980:11). In the case of Usman Sokwak he was not criticizing the NA as much as he was requesting the position of chief, such as other ethnic groups had. Nevertheless his request was a threat to the status quo; the British as well as the NA felt that his movement had to be suppressed.

[4] Those arrested with him were Kwasu Sanke, Abobo Aruwan, Kantiyok Shinkut, Bawwom Bidam, Jatau Bidam, Usman Bvayan, Tanko Kato, Kahuwei Sheyin, Nkut Didam, Laya Sana, and Kwasu Niyrin. Mamman Swam was not arrested with them, but when he heard of the arrest and imprisonment of his colleagues, he trekked to Zaria to join them in prison. All were respected leaders among the Bajju who opposed emirate rule (see Kaburuk 2014).

lawful means (NAK ZarProf 6/1942). He was clearly a thorn in the side of the local administrators.

A recurring theme in the archival material is that if a British resident, district officer, or assistant district officer devoted more time to Southern Zaria, the continuing problems, such as the unrest that surrounded Usman Akangnet Sokwak's efforts to have the chieftaincy position established, would disappear. One colonial officer's response to this perception was to state that he had spent 309 days that year in Southern Zaria. Clearly, the problems in Southern Zaria were deeper than could be remedied by a colonial officer residing in the area; the problems related to structural inequality. Until this changed, there was little possibility of smooth administration of the area.

Independence

Nigeria achieved its independence from British colonialism on October 1, 1960. October 1 is now celebrated as Independence Day, a national holiday in Nigeria. Nigeria's first president was Dr. Nnamdi Azikiwe.

Soon after independence Muslims made various efforts to spread Islam, particularly in the north. Sir Ahmadu Bello, the premier of the Northern Region, desired the north to be "one people, one religion" (Kukah and Falola 1996:42). For that homogeneity to develop, Christians and pagans needed to convert to Islam. During 1964–1965 Ahmadu Bello conducted various conversion campaigns to spread Islam throughout the north. He built mosques, gave gifts (for example, copies of the Qur'an, a pamphlet on Islamic teaching, rosaries, pennies, and cloth) to men, and offered job opportunities to people to induce them to convert (Paden 1986:567, 571). After his conversion campaigns, he left the follow-up to local imams. He also established the Jama'atu Nasril Islam to propagate Islam and to spread Islamic education. He was killed in the 1965 coup.

Discussion

This chapter began with a discussion of the precolonial era, during which two emirates, those of Zazzau and its vassal state of Jema'a, claimed this area. Basically, their claim was based on their slave raiding, plundering, and demanding taxes from the local people. The local people responded by fighting the raiders whenever they entered this area. They were in the slave catchment area for these emirates. As such, the Hausa and Fulani made little effort to convert these people to Islam. Theoretically, Muslims cannot enslave other Muslims, so if they had proselytized this area, their source of slaves would have dried up.

When British colonialism came to this area, they placed the emirates formally over the minority ethnic groups in the Middle Belt. So the ethnic groups who were once slave-raided, plundered, and taxed by the emirates were now placed officially under them. This was reinforced by the presence of the West Africa Frontier Force who had weapons superior to those of the local population. Throughout the colonial era the local people had no political representation, though they repeatedly requested it. This was the situation when missionaries first entered this area. Thus began the Christian era for many Middle Belt ethnic groups, including the Bajju.

13

The Christian Era

When colonialism was first established, the British promised the emirs and their followers that they would not interfere with the practice of Islam. Hence Christian missionaries were shunted into minority areas. The colonialists saw the "pagans" in need of what missionaries had to offer. Many missionaries, who had the goal of reaching the Hausa and Fulani with the message of Jesus Christ, chafed under the prohibition of their working in Muslim areas; however, the minority groups benefited enormously by their work among them. Missionaries brought education, medical work, Christianity, a new world-view that benefited the minority groups, and new occupations, which the colonialists failed to provide for them. Missionaries taught that all people were created by God in his image, and that they were equal before God. This challenged the emirate model that the colonialists applied to the minority ethnic groups. In fact, Turaki (1982) asserted that the colonial administration institutionalized the inferior status and socio-political role of the non-Muslim groups during the colonial era. They were called "pagans" and were at the bottom of the class structure that the British imposed upon them. Those who formerly slave-raided them were now officially placed over them, with the West African Frontier Force used to enforce colonial policies.

The arrival of Christian missionaries

Thomas and Grace Archibald, a Scottish missionary couple, first arrived in Nigeria in 1921 and worked at two other mission stations prior to moving to Kagoro in April 1927. They set up an SIM mission station and dispensary at the foot of the Kagoro Hills. Tom spoke of poison arrows being shot at them through their open windows when they first arrived. It was from this mission station that the gospel of Jesus Christ initially spread to the Bajju. Gradually people began to respond to the Christian message, with the first Bajju Christian conversions occurring in 1929.

This initiated the Christian era among the Bajju. Slowly and steadily many converted, with young men being the first to do so in many areas, followed by the wider population. In 1968 we observed a baptismal service at the Atacap River near the bridge at Unguwar Rimi. While we watched, sixty people were baptized with more waiting on the riverbank. This took place for one denomination in the southeastern part of the Bajju area. Similar baptismal services also occurred for those in other denominations. From a missiological perspective, we were in the midst of a people movement to Christ as large numbers of Bajju were converting.

Other missions soon followed SIM into what was then referred to as Southern Zaria Province. People from other ethnic groups, such as Yoruba and Igbo, came to work on the railroad. The Port Harcourt–Kaduna line of the Nigerian Railroad runs through Kafanchan and through various villages in southern Kaduna State. At Kafanchan the railroad split; one way leads to Kaduna and the other runs through Jos. The northwestern route goes through Madakiya, Zonkwa, Fadiya, and Kamuru Station before going to Kaduna. The northeastern route goes to Jos. There is a section of Kafanchan known as Garaji, after the English word "garage," which developed when the railroad line was being constructed. The Nigerian Railroad has been beset with problems, and it now runs very irregularly, if at all.

Those who came to work on the railroad brought with them the churches they were familiar with from their home areas. For example, they brought Christian Missionary Society (CMS) churches and Baptist churches. Some missionaries from those denominations came to this area. Roman Catholic priests came into the area through a practice they referred to as "doing the line." They rode the train and stopped at various train stations, including at Kafanchan, where they established mission stations. These priests sought to build a mission station at Kagoro. Their request ran counter to SIM work, which had already been established at Kagoro. SIM actively opposed the priests building there. Further, initially the colonial administration subscribed to the concept of spheres of influence for each mission. If the Roman Catholics built a mission station at Kagoro, this would conflict with the work of SIM. However, over time the priests were able to build a large station there. It became the center where new priests came who were to work in Northern Nigeria. They would spend six months there learning Hausa, be introduced to their church's work in Nigeria, and begin to understand the culture around them.

The development of Christian denominations

Still other missions and church denominations soon followed, including the Cherubim and Seraphim and the United African Church, now called First African Church Mission, Inc. These two churches integrate traditional practices with Christianity. They allow men who are married polygamously to be pastors, elders, and deacons in their churches. They also allow drinking alcoholic beverages, though when a person becomes an alcoholic they tell that person to stop drinking. This was also what happened in their pre-Christian society.

There are now the following denominations in the Bajju area:

Anglican Church
Apostolic Church
Assemblies of God
Baptist Church
Celestial Church
Cherubim and Seraphim Church
Christian Redeemed Church
Church of Christ in Nigeria
Deeper Life
Evangelical Churches Winning All
    (ECWA, formerly Evangelical Churches of West Africa)
First African Church Mission, Inc.
    (formerly United Native African Church)
Grace of God Church
Jehovah's Witnesses
Living Faith
Methodist Church
Roman Catholic Church
Seventh-day Adventist

The differences between denominations in the area are largely based on how churches deal with issues such as polygamy, drinking alcoholic beverages, dreams and visions, altered states of consciousness, whether or not people wear white robes in church, and forms of worship. The differences are largely not based on doctrinal issues, in contrast to the case in many Western denominations. All Christians in the area use the same Hausa Bible and the same Hausa hymnal, even where Scriptures in Jju are available. Some missionaries have characterized the differences between denominations as liberal versus conservative. However, this distinction comes from their home cultures rather than Christianity as it is practiced among the Bajju.

Christians locally are termed "people who follow" (*Baɲyet Tssup*). The form of Christianity first introduced into the area consisted of a number of dos and don'ts. It was a fundamentalist type of religion with various rules and regulations. So Christians were those who followed those rules and regulations. Today they are people who follow Jesus Christ. In fact, it was precisely those rules and regulations that convinced Bajju that this is a true religion. Their pre-Christian religion also had a number of dos and don'ts. Hence Christianity looked like a true religion to them. Further, there was little in their pre-Christian religious beliefs that ran contrary to Christianity. They knew there was a God, whom they call *Kaza* (also spelled *Kạdza*). What Christianity did was allow them to know God, the God whom they already knew exists. They knew there was an afterlife, but they did not know that God would be there.

Christianity is highly valued by the Bajju. The church is central to their social, political, and religious life. Many go to some church meeting on a daily basis. Knowing a person's denomination is one piece of information Bajju want to know about each other. At a celebration of a new house, as the name of each individual was called to go into the house, the person's denomination was included as part of his or her introduction.

Every Bajju village has one Christian church in it, and usually more. Churches are now an integral part of most Bajju's lives.

Language use in Christian churches

While initially missionaries began learning the local languages, they stopped using them when the Bible became available in Hausa in 1932. Missionaries made the decision that all missionaries would use only Hausa at their various mission stations in northern Nigeria. Gradually the belief grew that "everyone knows Hausa," something that we often heard as we struggled to learn Jju. Use of Hausa allowed missionary administrators to move personnel from mission station to mission station without having them learn any of the local languages. One missionary cited the case of Gwari, where SIM missionaries spent over fifty years translating the Bible into that language; he asserted that it was never used. In fact, in checking on his assertion we found that this early Gwari translation was being used even though it was quite a literal translation. That missionary also told us that we would be wasting our time to translate the Bible into Jju. The people were without excuse for not becoming Christians as they had had the gospel preached throughout the area in Hausa. He told us this just prior to our moving to the Bajju area where we would be working on Jju language learning, language analysis, and translation. After talking with that missionary, we spoke to a Nigerian principal at the school across the road from that missionary's house. His response was quite different. He said that he had been back into the Bajju area and he found that many did not understand Hausa. He was glad we were going to work on Bible translation in Jju.

Missionaries have been instrumental in spreading the Hausa language into areas where few people initially understood it.[1] Until today Hausa remains the language used in Bajju churches throughout their area, whatever the denomination of a church. All use Hausa, even when the pastor is Bajju and all the people present are Bajju, and even when the New Testament is available in their own language. At the same time Bajju are writing to each other in Jju on Facebook (a current popular social networking site). Clearly this is not a dead language, but one that is flourishing while use of both Hausa and English is also expanding.

In terms of languages used, Jju, Hausa, and English (the official language) are widely used by the Bajju. In interviews carried out in 1984, we found that only five percent of the population was monolingual in Jju. These speakers consisted largely of women who were 40 years of age or older. They could not understand Hausa as used in the churches. This was a linguistically neglected population within the Christian churches. Further, sixty percent of the population of 266 individuals in the 1984 sample asserted that they spoke Hausa only at the market level. As such, many of the concepts taught in Scripture would be difficult for them to understand. In 2009 we again administered the same interview schedule to persons in both rural and urban contexts. That sample consisted of 63 Bajju. In that sample Hausa is mostly spoken in church, market, and medical contexts. Over eighty percent assert that they spoke Jju in their homes. In the 2009 sample we found a smaller percentage of people monolingual in Jju.

While the language of church is Hausa, Jju continues as the language used in most Bajju homes. It continues as an oral language even though it is now written. At this point in the development of Jju, there is limited literature written in Jju. Faith Comes by Hearing recorded the Jju New Testament in audio format; the New Testament is listened to more than it is read. In church contexts a group of children or adults may memorize a Scripture portion in Jju, which they recite in church.

The Bajju look forward to having the entire Bible in their language. The Bible provides guidance for many Bajju. It influences and impacts their daily lives, replacing and supplementing many of their traditional religious practices and beliefs. A Bajju leader stated that they had wanted education to get out from under the oppression they were experiencing both from the Hausa-Fulani emirates and from the colonial administration, but when they received Christianity, they got something far more valuable.

---

[1] See McKinney 1983 for further discussion of the advantages of using the language of wider communication as well as advantages of using minority languages.

Christian churches

In contrast to the Bajju pre-Christian religious system, Christian churches welcome everyone into their services. This includes men, women, and children. By including women, Christianity has raised their status within the Bajju community.

The form of preaching in Bajju churches has been strongly influenced by a Pentecostal style. At some point in most sermons the pastors shout into the microphone to make their point. Since the amplitude is often turned up high on the public-address system, what the pastor is shouting becomes incomprehensible. I asked one pastor what people got out of the incomprehensible part of the sermon. He said that they got a feeling. A further problem with having the amplitude turned up so high is that it can injure people's ears. I observed young mothers with their babies on their backs often go sit outside during the sermons. This certainly helps preserve theirs and their infants' hearing. I also inquired how this could change such that people can understand all of the sermons preached. The response one pastor gave was that it needs to become part of the curriculum at the seminaries where pastors are trained. It is also at seminaries that the issue of which language to use in church services needs to be addressed. Bible translation projects are in progress in several languages in southern Kaduna State, the results of which could be effectively used in church services; but however great the need for such translations, they are unlikely to be widely used in churches in the present context of seminary training with its emphasis on preaching in Hausa. During pastoral training, more emphasis could be placed on use of minority languages in church services.

Christian teaching on local religious beliefs

As Christianity has developed in this area, it answered one set of questions while the Bajju pre-Christian religion answered another set of questions. There is a need for Christian teaching to address the same issues that the traditional religion addressed. For example, how does Christianity explain evil? While there are a host of spirits that the Bajju believe in, there is not one ultimate evil spirit, such as Satan, who is the source of evil. Hence questions arise, such as, why do people become ill, why do people die, why do people suffer misfortune? In their theology about God, he is good and sends only good things to his people. The exception is his punishment of people who do what is wrong. So if God is good, but people continue to become ill and die, why does this occur? The local answer is that we do it to each other through witchcraft (*nkut*). Our spirits leave our bodies during sleep and meet with other spirits in the spiritual realm to cause evil, misfortune, illness, and death for other people in the physical realm. Is this because an evil spirit enters a person and causes their spirit to leave their body during sleep? Witchcraft explains the intersection between when and why a person becomes ill and dies. While there is recognition of the immediate cause of a problem, it is the ultimate spiritual reason that is most important.

As far as Christianity and mourning rituals are concerned, Kunhiyop has expressed his concerns as follows:

> The prohibition of burial and mourning rites without a means of dealing with those cultural needs and values was a handicap in making Christianity relevant. Burial and mourning rites were special occasions where people expressed their emotions because of separation from the deceased and above all the bereaved were incorporated into society. In traditional society, the life of the deceased, especially the elderly, were dramatized, emphasizing the great things he had done. Unfortunately older Churches condemned these rituals without providing a means of dealing with these serious issues. The bereaved were prohibited from weeping because that symbolized a sign of unbelief. What happened in many occasions is that these emotions have been shut in and do more harm than good. Such rituals could have been contextualized or Christianized. (2005:164–165)

As mentioned earlier in this chapter, the differences between Christian denominations in the Bajju area are based on moral issues, and largely not on theological issues, such as occurs in Western churches. Among other matters, differences between denominations relate to the roles that those who are married to two or more spouses can have within the church. Can polygamously married men be baptized? Can they take communion? Can they be pastors and church elders? Should they send away all but one wife as some missionaries have advocated? When a man has two or more wives, is he still "living in sin" as I heard one missionary state? What qualifications should pastors, elders, and deacons have? Concerning polygamy in the ECWA church, if a polygamously married man converts to Christianity, he is baptized and may receive communion. SIM missionaries originally taught that a polygamous man should divorce all but one wife. African pastors no longer require men to do so. It divides a family, resulting in the mother leaving her children behind with their father, and children need their mothers. Many men who are married to more than one wife prior to their conversion to Christianity decide that they will care for the wives they have, and that they will not marry any more wives. Being married polygamously does mean in most denominations that such a man may not become a pastor or an elder in the church.

A further issue is the role of dreams and visions in the church. Should people share their important dreams in the church? Do people go into altered states of consciousness and have visions in church services? If so, are those visions taken seriously?

What is each denomination's perspective on fasting? How long should a fast last? How do people in the church help or monitor a person who undertakes a long fast?

Another issue that churches must deal with is sex that occurs outside of marriage. This has resulted in infants being born to single women. A single woman who has already given birth will often find that either she marries the infant's father or she becomes a second or subsequent wife to a man who is already married. It also explains why adultery committed within an extended family or clan is treated so harshly.

With regard to these issues, how each question is answered often is determined by the denomination the person chooses to affiliate with. Table 13.1 presents some broad, general answers to these questions. The answers represent trends only within each denomination. It is very difficult to give specific responses for each denomination, as individual pastors and elders for specific churches may hold a different position from what is included in the table. Hence the table represents general tendencies only. Other denominations have entered this area more recently; unfortunately I do not have data on them in this table.

Table 13.1. General trends in six denominations

Denomina-tion	Marriage	Leaders	Dreams	Trances & visions occur in services	Fasting
Baptist	Monogamy preferred	Polygynously married men may be baptized but they are excluded from leadership and communion	Not a central focus	No	Not a central focus

Cherubim and Seraphim	Polygamy allowed, but only one wife is formally recognized	Polygamously married men may serve as pastors and other leaders	Yes, they are valued	Visions are important	20 days allowed for long fasts with the church caring for that person
CMS (Anglican)	Monogamy preferred	Only a man with one wife may be an elder or pastor	Not a central focus	No	Not a central focus
ECWA	Monogamy preferred	Only a man with one wife may be an elder or pastor	Some believe they are important while others discount them	No	Not a central focus
First African Church Mission/ United Native African	Polygamy allowed	Polyga-mously married men serve as pastors and other leaders; if a convert has more than one wife, he should take care of his wives, not divorce all but one.	Yes, they are valued	No	?
Roman Catholic	Monogamy preferred	Only a man with one wife may be an elder	Not a central focus	No	Not a central focus

Summary

This chapter addressed the Christian era, which began in December 1929 with the first Bajju conversions and continues until today, as this area is now Christian. During this time there has been very rapid cultural change. The next chapter presents other areas where cultural changes have occurred.

14

Bajju Cultural Change

Over the last one hundred years, the Bajju have experienced very rapid culture change in many areas. This chapter examines several areas of cultural change, not including their adoption of Christianity, which I covered in the preceding chapter and more fully in another book, *Bajju Christian Conversion* (2019).

Settlement patterns

In the precolonial era, Bajju built houses on the tops of rock hills for defensive purposes. When colonialism came, they moved from their hilltop compounds down to locations nearer the roads, which allowed people to take their produce to weekly markets, markets which began after the cessation of interethnic warfare. Moving also allowed people to live closer to their farms.

Just as the location of villages changed, Bajju house types have also changed significantly. Knowledge of early house types comes from Tremearne (1912), who photographed Bajju houses in the early twentieth century; see figure 14.1. The Bajju built round houses with low mud walls that were gradually built up by adding layers of mud applied in the morning, noon, and evening to form circular walls. These had slanted thatched roofs and low doors.

Figure 14.1. Bajju house, early 1900s (Tremearne 1912:288).

Figure 14.2. A̲gorok (Kagoro) house (Meek 1931:90).

The Bajju houses and compounds were very similar to those of other minority ethnic groups in the area. Figure 14.2 shows an Agorok house and figures 14.3–5 are diagrams of Atyap compounds in 1931, which were the same as Bajju houses and other minority ethnic groups in this area.

THE KATAB AND THEIR NEIGHBOURS 19

The following is a plan of a typical Katab compound :—

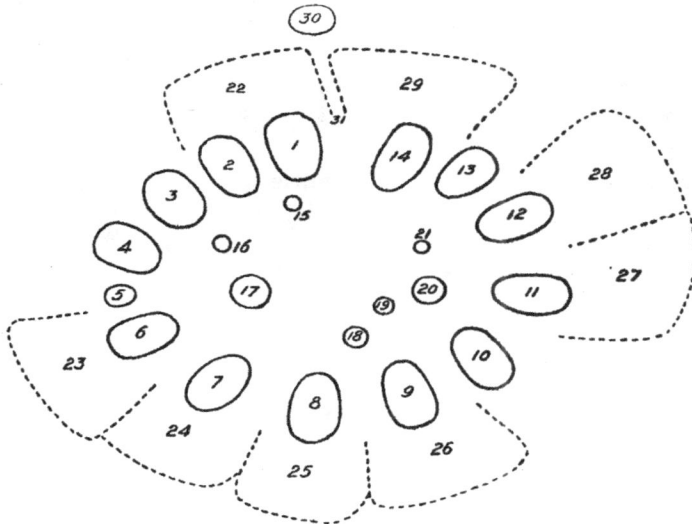

KEY.

(1) Hut of the master of the compound.
(2) Hut of the second wife of the master of the compound.
(3) Empty hut of runaway wife of master of the compound.
(4) Empty hut of runaway wife of master of the compound.
(5) Disused hut built to fill in space between (4) and (6).
(6) Hut of first wife of elder son.
(7) Hut of second wife of elder son.
(8) Hut of mother of the master of the compound.
(9) Hut of first wife of younger son.
(10) Empty hut of younger son's runaway wife.
(11) Hut of second wife of younger son.
(12) Hut of third wife of younger son.
(13) Hut used by master of compound and his two sons as a common meeting room and dining room.
(14) Hut of the principal wife and mistress of the compound.
(15) Small granary containing grain for use of master of the compound.
(16) Small granary containing grain for use of elder son.

(17) Large granary containing grain belonging to elder son.
(18) Goat pen belonging to elder son.
(19) Goat pen belonging to younger son.
(20) Large granary containing grain belonging to younger son.
(21) Small granary containing grain belonging to younger son.
(22–29) Bean gardens of the various wives and of the mother of the master of the compound.

———

(30) Hut common to all female members of the compound for grinding grain.
(31) Entrance to compound.

———

Young male children sleep in mother's hut until age of 5. They then get huts of their own. Female children remain in mother's hut until they marry.

———

Figure 14.3. Atyap compound (Meek 1931:19).

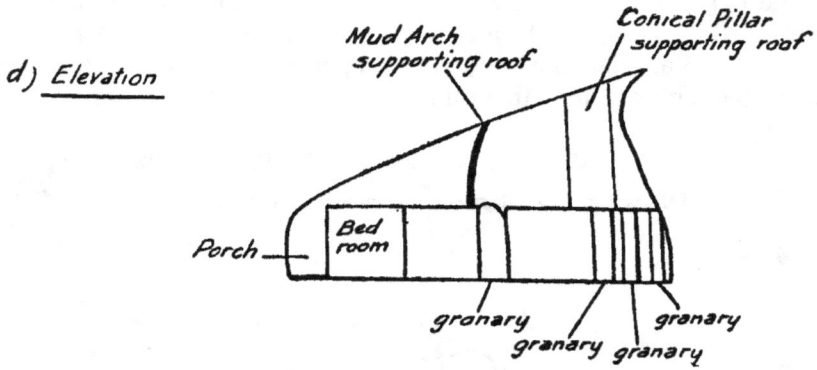

Figure 14.4. Diagram of an A̲tyap house similar to that of the Bajju
(Meek 1931:53).

Katab House

a) General View

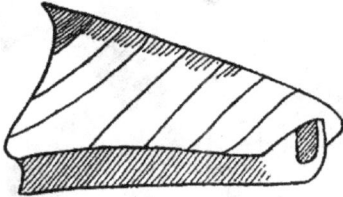

b) Plan of Ground Floor

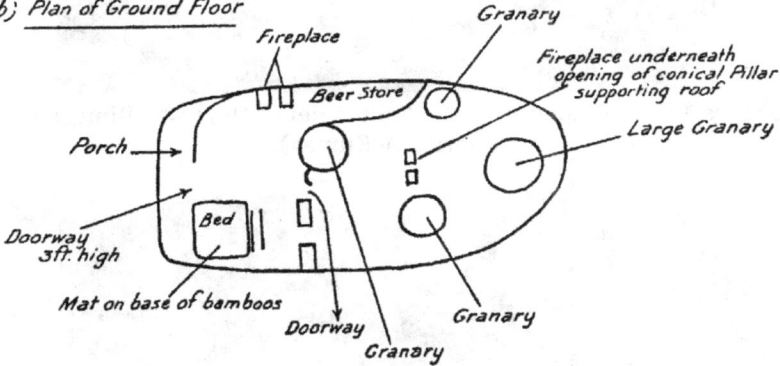

Fireplace

Granary

Fireplace underneath opening of conical Pillar supporting roof

Beer Store

Large Granary

Porch

Doorway 3ft. high

Bed

Mat on base of bamboos

Doorway

Granary

Granary

c) Plan of 1st Storey

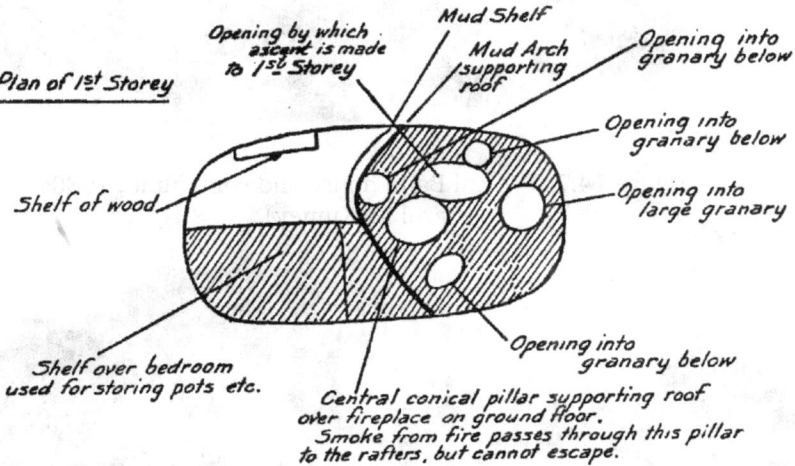

Opening by which ascent is made to 1st Storey

Mud Shelf

Mud Arch supporting roof

Opening into granary below

Opening into granary below

Opening into large granary

Shelf of wood

Shelf over bedroom used for storing pots etc.

Opening into granary below

Central conical pillar supporting roof over fireplace on ground floor. Smoke from fire passes through this pillar to the rafters, but cannot escape.

Figure 14.5. Diagram of an Atyap house similar to that of the Bajju (Meek 1931:52).

Figure 14.6. Compound of the Bajju chief of Unguwar Rimi, 1970s
(Norris McKinney).

Figure 14.7. Typical Bajju house and compound, 1980s
(Carol McKinney).

Figure 14.8. Bajju compound in 2010,   Figure 14.9. Bajju compound in 2010,
front view (Carol McKinney).   courtyard view (Carol McKinney).

Missionaries introduced building with mud blocks, resulting in construction of rectangular houses. In most Bajju compounds each room in the compound opens onto a courtyard. Some continue to have a round house or two as part of the compound, though rectangular houses now predominate; see figures 14.8 and 14.9.

The Bajju built round granaries to store guinea corn and millet. Their construction is described in chapter 1. Here I include pictures of early granaries as well as current ones. Since the grain in the granary represents the blessing of the household, granaries occupied an important part of any compound. Granaries were built on a mud base with openings so that chickens could go under them to eat any insects attempting to enter and eat the grain. Compare the 1912 Bajju granary with that of the Atyap in 1931 (figures 14.10 and 14.11).

Figure 14.10. Bajju granary in 1912   Figure 14.11. Atyap granary
(Tremearne 1912:146).   in 1931 (Meek 1931:45).

Today many Bajju no longer build granaries but devote one room in one of their rectangular houses for crop storage; however, some who farm millet and guinea corn continue to build them. Those who farm maize first hang it on string around their compound to dry, then they put the maize into sacks in the storage room in their compound.

Figure 14.12. Bajju granary, c. 1970. Note the thatch in front
for rethatching the granary (Norris McKinney).

Social change

Numerous social changes have occurred during the past one hundred years.
These include changes in scarification patterns and practices. When Meek
visited the area in the early 1920s, he reported that Bajju practiced facial
and body scarification for ethnic identity. Today many Bajju have one
slanted scar under the left eye, and two small parallel scars beside each eye,
though many children no longer receive their scars. The barber, in addition
to shaving people's heads, also does scarification and male circumcision.
Figure 14.13 shows an earlier Bajju scarification pattern.

One friend did not have his scars, so we inquired why. He related that
his mother would give him a few pennies to go have his scars done, but he
took the money and bought candy instead! Another friend related that his
mother sent him to the battlefront during the Biafran War to check on his
uncle, her brother. Since he did not want to be mistaken for an Igbo and
potentially be killed, he received his facial scars prior to going.

(1) Male

FOREHEAD = 21 on one half
20 on the other
CHEEK = 9 on each side
JAW = 24 on each side

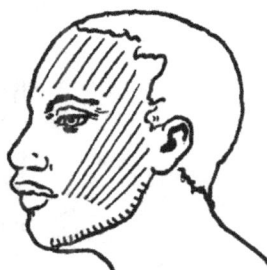

(2) Female

FOREHEAD = 33 on one half
32 on the other
CHEEK = 17 on each side
JAW = 26 on each side

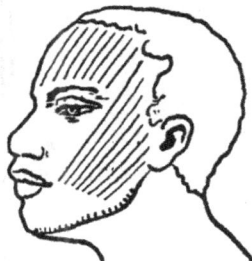

I was unable to discover where these markings originated. The Kaje are regarded as the most skilful markers. The incisions are made with a knife shaped thus :—

Figure 14.13. Scarification among the Bajju, together with the instrument used in applying their scars (Meek 1931:56).

Women also received scarification on their faces as well as on their chests and backs approximately one month after marrying, a practice similar to that of the Baronga of South Africa (figure 14.14). The right image in figure 14.15 is identified by Meek as tattooing, though tattooing was not significant for this population while scarification was. Hence I question his identification of what was occurring.

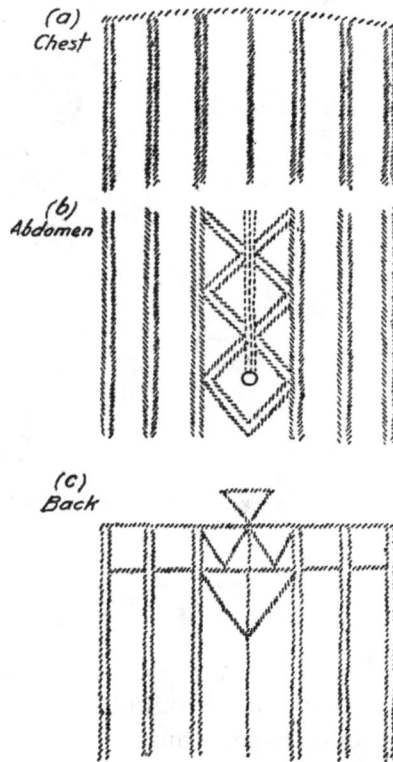

(a) Chest

(b) Abdomen

(c) Back

N.B.—Designs of the above type are common throughout Africa. For example, M. Junod in describing the body marks of Baronga women (S. Africa) says : " On the anterior part of the body four triangles are drawn under the breast leaving a square place of which the navel occupies the exact middle." And again : " The patterns are triangular, the upper triangles meeting with the lower ones at their apex."

Figure 14.14. Scar designs for the chest and back from the Baronga women in South Africa (Meek 1931:57).

When a Bajju young woman turned eleven or twelve, two small red wooden lip plugs were inserted, one just above her upper lip and the other just below her lower lip. As she grew older, larger lip plugs were inserted, 6.5 millimeters to 13 millimeters (1/4 to 1/2 inch) in diameter. Lip plugs were worn by a number of groups in the area, including the Bajju, Atyap, Agorok, and Asholio. The lip plug marked the groups that readily intermarried with each other. Today only very elderly women wear lip plugs and even some of these women have discontinued this practice. Now some women have allowed the holes for their lip plugs to grow closed.

A further practice is that of removing the uvula in order to clear the passage and prevent colds. A small hook is used to do so. Formerly common, this practice is no longer done.

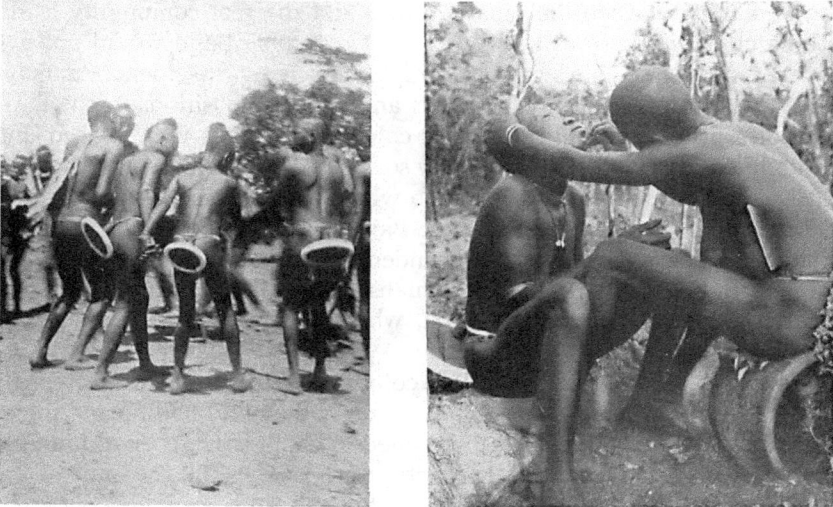

Figure 14.15. A̱tyap (Katab) girls and youths dancing on left, and tattooing (scarification?) on right (Meek 1931:35).

Bajju men wore their hair plaited. As they got older, they had their heads shaved. Elderly women also had their hair shaved off. As mentioned in chapter 10, one Bajju taboo stated that if a man had only one side of his head shaved, the spirits would come at night and shave the other half. However, when women first married, they had only one side of their hair shaved in order to make themselves less attractive to other men. This hair pattern indicated that they were now married. While having one's head shaved is still practiced, particularly by elderly men, having one half of one's hair shaved for women is no longer practiced.

Political change

The political structure of Bajju has changed from governance by the elders (*ba̱gado*) of each village and of the entire ethnic group within a loose confederacy to having a Bajju paramount chief with chiefs of each village. In the precolonial era the elders had both political and religious functions within the community. In their political function they dealt with problems in their own compounds, in their sections, and problems that affected the entire Bajju community. They assessed fines (*tyyi gbang*) and required sacrifices for actions the community defined as contrary to their law. (See chs. 2, 4, and 10 for further discussions of their political and legal system.)

Beginning with Hausa-Fulani interaction and continuing into the colonial and postcolonial eras, Bajju began to have village chiefs. Initially chiefs were intermediaries between the outside world and the real community leaders. To be a chief was seen as a dirty job that reputable Bajju would not want. However, over time chiefs gradually replaced rule by the elders. Elders have now moved into the position of chiefs and advisory positions to chiefs with their roles primarily political. Under colonialism chiefs were placed under district heads. In Southern Zaria, now southern Kaduna State, there was one district head located at Zangon Katab who was over chiefs in a number of different ethnic groups, including the Bajju. Until independence the district head was a Hausa man. When independence came Bala Gora, an A̲tyap man, occupied this position. During colonialism the district heads in this area reported to the Hausa emir in Zaria, who was located approximately 400 kilometers (250 miles) to the north.

As mentioned above, the British colonialists' idea behind Indirect Rule was to govern the people through the leaders they had had during the pre-colonial era. Unfortunately, as mentioned in chapter 12, they did not carefully investigate what that political structure was. While the emir at Zaria and the emir at Jema'a told the British that this area answered to them, in fact the relationship of the local people with the emirates was a contentious one. The British accepted the emirates' assertion that these non-Hausa, non-Fulani, and non-Muslim people belonged to them. In governing them the British set up both "Mohammedan" and "pagan" policies with the non-Muslim "pagan" population at the bottom of the socio-political hierarchy.

After Nigerian independence in 1960, the local governmental structure continued with the district head answering to the emir in Zaria. In 1984 there were three district heads appointed instead of one at Zangon Katab, as well as a chair of the administrative district who was over these district heads. Gwani Dogo, a Christian and the son of one of the first Bajju Christians, served as chair. He had earlier served in the emir's council at Zaria. The Bajju rejoiced over his appointment, but he was still answerable to the emir in Zaria.

Under head of state General Sani Abacha, who was in office from 1993–1998, the political structure of southern Kaduna State changed. He established a committee on state creation, local government, and boundary adjustment. The result of that committee was that the Bajju finally received their independence from Zaria and Jema'a Emirates. Brigadier General Tanko Ayuba was in charge of the state as a whole under General Abacha. Following him, Colonel Jafaru Isaha served as an administrator of Kaduna State. These two men seemed to understand the problems of the minority ethnic groups in southern Kaduna State. Colonel Jafaru Isaha had to receive authority from Abacha in Abuja in order to give these groups independence from Zaria Emirate. The response of the emir at Zaria to their independence was that it was as good as cutting off one of his fingers. By this response he was indicating his disapproval of the Bajju no longer being under him politically.

In 1995 a law passed that created four chieftaincies: those for the Bajju, Atyap, Gong, and Animwem (Numana). The position of the Bajju chief began in 1996 with a Grade 3 position, the lowest level. This changed in 2000 when the Bajju chief was upgraded to Grade 2. In 2007 the Bajju chief finally was promoted to Grade 1, the highest class for all the senior chiefs in the state. It is the same level as that held by the emirs of Zazzau and Jema'a. Other ethnic groups had to wait longer for their chieftaincies. The Angwan and Bakulu received their chieftaincies in 2002, beginning with Grade 3 positions.

When the Bajju finally received their chieftaincy position, they set up a committee to select their new chief. Members of this committee took an oath on Baranzan that they would not publically discuss their deliberations. They selected three candidates for the office of Bajju chief, one from Unguwar Rimi, one from central Bajju, and one from Dibyyi, the location of Baranzan's grave and part of the Baidwang *kwai*. The man from Unguwar Rimi was rejected because one of his ancestors had agreed to the Bajju being placed under the Hausa. The Bajju believe the consequences of his action followed down through the family until someone retracted his words. After the candidate from Unguwar Rimi was rejected, he retracted the words of his ancestor through the *sswa batwak* ceremony.

Nuhu Bature from Dibyyi was selected to be the first Bajju chief. However, the committee agreed that the chieftaincy position would rotate between the different sections (*kwai*) of the Bajju. Thus one of Nuhu's sons would not automatically assume this position at his death.

His Royal Highness Nuhu Bature was born in July 1939 in Dibyyi to Mallam Madaki Bature and Malama Kutuk. He began his career working at Challenge Bookstore in Jos under SIM. After leaving Challenge, he set up his own book and stationery supply store in Jos, which proved to be a successful venture (see figure 14.16). He handled books ordered for various schools in the area, books in general, stationery, and other office supplies. When he assumed the chieftaincy position, his sons continued to run the bookstore until their deaths.[1] Another relative currently runs the bookstore while he also devotes full time to his chieftaincy responsibilities.

---

[1] Two of Nuhu's sons have now died, one from illness and one from being shot in an armed roadside robbery.

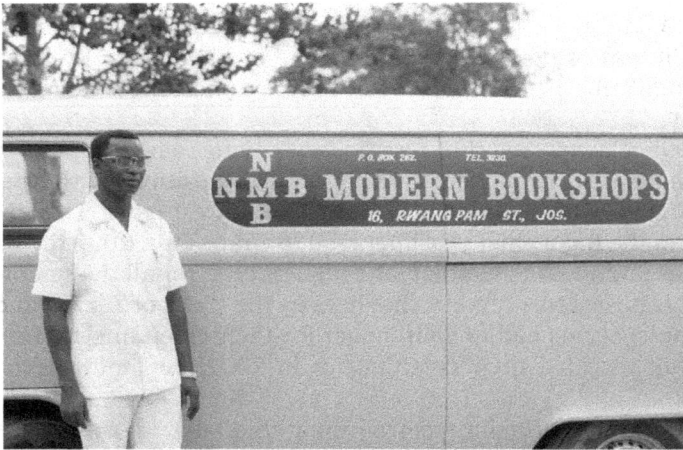

Figure 14.16. Nuhu Bature by his bookstore van in the 1970s
(Norris McKinney).

In addition, there are now eighteen district heads (DH) located throughout the Bajju area. The district heads are over the village chiefs. There are
currently district heads in various Bajju villages; see table 14.1.

Table 14.1. Bajju villages with district heads

Abet	Kamarum (DH lives at Kurdan)
Adwan	Kpunyai-Cincuk (DH lives at Katssik)
Afana	Madakiya
Atat (part of Madakiya)	Marsa
Ayagan	Tsorang
Dibyyi	Unguwar Rimi
Fadan Kaje	Zitrung
Fadia	Zonkwa
Formang	

The Bajju chief appoints district heads, including one for the Kamantan,
which was under the Bajju. Two of them were turbaned[2] in Zaria, but when they
returned to their home area, His Royal Highness Nuhu Bature turbaned them
again. Since then further district heads were selected by His Royal Highness
Nuhu Bature, then their position was recognized by the state government. After
that, the Bajju chief turbaned them. He meets frequently with the district heads
at his home at Dibyyi.

---

[2] The white turban was a sign of political office, such as was worn by chiefs,
paramount chiefs, district heads, and emirs.

Figure 14.17. His Royal Highness Nuhu Bature's house, 2010
(Carol McKinney).

When Nuhu Bature first received his position of a Grade 3 chief in 1996, the Bajju area was still under Zaria. Since their independence from Zazzau Emirate, there has been peace in the area until the post-presidential election violence in April 2011.[3] The area was so peaceful that on November 26, 2010, the Bajju chief received a peace award in Kaduna.

His Royal Highness Nuhu Bature provides for his people in whatever way he is able to. For example, each November he calls the widows to his compound where he gives each woman several yards of cloth to take to a tailor to sew a new outfit for Christmas. Christmas is the time of year that many Bajju wear new clothes. Since widows do not have husbands to provide for them, the Bajju chief has taken care of them by giving them cloth and food products once a year.

---

[3] Following the presidential election, the supporters of Muhammad Buhari, the Congress for Progressive Change candidate, who lost to the People's Democratic Party candidate Goodluck Jonathan, rioted in Zonkwa, Madakiya, Kafanchan, and Unguwar Rimi, all located within the Bajju territory, as well as elsewhere in northern Nigeria.

Figure 14.18. Rev. Iliya Ahuwan, left, and
His Royal Highness Nuhu Bature, 2010 (Carol McKinney).

Economic change

Economic change came to the Bajju with the introduction of ginger and
rice growing by the colonialists. Missionaries also contributed to the economic development of this area. For example, SIM introduced building with
mud blocks, high-grade cheap salt, maize growing, economically productive trees, hog rearing, schools, churches, and various occupations that are
today understood as typically Christian (for example, carpentry, teachers,
pastors, mechanics, etc.). Today parents expect to send their children to
school. After primary school, students seek whatever further educational
opportunities they can find. Education has led to economic advancement
for people from southern Kaduna State, who are now scattered throughout
Nigeria. They serve in government, in the ports, in the army, in teaching
positions, as nurses and doctors, in commerce, pastors and local leaders in
churches, in the petroleum industry, etc. These positions were not possible
under colonialism; however, the Bajju were preparing for them through
education. Today many Bajju have PhD, MA, and BA degrees from univer-
sities locally and in other countries. At the same time there are people in
villages who are completely illiterate and monolingual in Jju.

To understand how much change has occurred, one only has to recall
that in the late 1800s it was not possible for outsiders to enter this area
for fear of having their heads taken in warfare. There were no markets, as

it was not safe to travel through this area. Today there are daily markets at Zonkwa and Kafanchan and weekly markets in some villages. Roadside stands are ubiquitous in the area.

Jju, the language of the Bajju, now has its own orthography that has been approved by the federal government. The Bajju have government permission to use their language in primary schools, though English continues as the language of education. The Bajju Language and Translation Association has its office in Zonkwa where they continue to develop material in Jju. Specifically, they have concentrated on translating the Old Testament into Jju and revising the Jju New Testament with the goal of having the entire Bible in Jju. They have one person specifically assigned to Jju literacy, a venture that is necessary if people are to read material written in Jju. Agriculture continues to be the main subsistence base in the Bajju home area. While industries could be set up to process the crops grown in this area, this has not occurred.

Religious change

As discussed in chapter 13, within a fifty-five-year period (1929–1984) the Bajju moved from having no Christians to almost one hundred percent Christian. This is enormously rapid religious change. The Hausa-Fulani influence in the area and the colonial presence undermined their traditional religion, especially the influence of the *ạbvoi* organization. Men directed the community through the *ạbvoi* by maintaining the belief that the *ạbvoi* was everywhere and was all knowing. But events occurred that the *ạbvoi* was unable to control. The colonial administration identified this organization as the source of problems they encountered, including an attack on the emir and his party in 1915; consequently, the West African Frontier Force destroyed the *ạbvoi* shrine at Katssik. Further, missionaries condemned the *ạbvoi* organization and required new Christians to leave it.

Bajju Development Association

The Bajju Development Association (BADA) has been set up in various urban areas with various aims and objectives, including the following according to its Abuja website, http://bajjugarki.blogspot.com (2009):

Aims and Objectives

1. To organize, maintain and protect the interests of its members.
2. To promote and encourage free exchange of ideas among members and between the Association and similar associations within and outside the Federal Capital Territory.

3. To develop and foster a corporate spirit, social, intellectual and cultural relationship aimed at bringing together the activities of its members towards a common goal.
4. To provide moral and material assistance to needy members and Kajju land in general.
5. To stimulate interest and active participation in all matters of growth, development and unity in Kajju land and the society at large.
6. To preserve and protect the good image of the Association and the prestige of the Bajju people in general.
7. To foster mutual co-existence and understanding among members and the general public.
8. To achieve the above mentioned through legitimate means and in accordance with the provisions herein and those laid down rules and regulations of the Federal Capital Territory and the country at large.

The motto of BADA is *Zi Tung Dung* 'we just meet' (literally, 'we meet meet'). Formerly *Zi Tung Dung* was the name of this organization. There are BADA branches in most of the main cities of Nigeria, especially in northern Nigeria where Bajju meet monthly to promote the Bajju and to help those who live in Kajju. Other ethnic groups have similar community development groups in cities throughout Nigeria, which promote the welfare of their people, help with their development, and in general contribute to the wellbeing of their ethnic group. In a country without a social security system for most of the population, such organizations provide valuable assistance to people who need it. Further, such organizations provide a sense of belonging and solidarity with one's ethnic group.

Education and medical care

Cultural change occurs all the time at various rates and in diverse areas of culture. This has certainly been true for the Bajju. They assert that there are two primary reasons for the rapid cultural change that has occurred in their area: civilization and Christianity. Concerning civilization bringing change, the Hausa-Fulani emirates and the British colonial government both insisted that the Bajju have chiefs, positions that were foreign to them. The elders (*bagado*) lost the important roles that they had played within the community. Their two functions, governing and spiritual guidance, were given to chiefs and pastors. The pastors today have more than just spiritual functions; they are also involved in solving problems within their communities.

Civilization also came through education. Schools were first located at Kachia and Zangon Katab. Christian students were required to shave off their plaits before they were allowed to enter these schools. Government schools were for the most part reserved for Hausa and Fulani students, not for the indigenous population of the area.

Christian missionaries set up the majority of the schools for the minority populations in southern Kaduna State. They required students who came to schools to wear school uniforms rather than leaves for females and skins for males. Further, they required those who attended mission-ary-founded schools to be Christians. So education and Christianity came together. However, many became literate before they really understood what Christianity was all about. The Bajju perceived that Christian mission-ary schools were superior to government schools in the area. It was not until the 1950s and 1960s that the government became interested in educating the minority populations in northern Nigeria.

Missionaries set up dispensaries, many associated with mission stations, and a hospital in the area. At Zonkwa, Catholic missionaries set up St. Louis Hospital. In the Bajju area there is one government hospital at Kafanchan. The care at the missionary-founded dispensaries and hospital was superior to that of the government hospital. Although people had to pay at the mis-sionary-established medical facilities, while care was theoretically free at government-established health facilities, the personnel at the latter often demanded bribes for service and medicine. The care at the government hospital in Kafanchan has improved over the years, often dependent on hospital leadership. When we first moved to Unguwar Rimi in 1968, there was one doctor who ran the government hospital. The local people felt that they basically went to the hospital to die. Over time the number of doctors increased and the level of care has improved.

Islam and southern Kaduna

Southern Kaduna has never been an Islamic area, although there are pockets of Muslims resident in various places in this area, such as at Kachia, Zonkwa, Kafanchan, Unguwar Rimi, Zangon Katab, and elsewhere. However, the rela-tionship of the minority people with the Islamic emirates has always been problematic. In the precolonial era representatives of Zaria and Jema'a Emir-ates slave-raided this area each dry season, plundering it, and demanding taxes from the local population. To obtain slaves and plunder, the Hausa-Fulani emirate officials had to fight with the local population, who never recognized their authority over them.

A few mosques have been built in this area where the Hausa and Fulani attend (see figure 14.19). The local people, as Christians, do not attend them.

Figure 14.19. Mosque in the A̲tyap area, 2010
(Carol McKinney).

More recently the area of the Emir of Jema'a has been elevated to that of an emirate. The indigenous local people do not recognize this emirate. The emir's position is over the settlers of Hausa-Fulani origins. The indigenous population resent that he was appointed an emirate within their territory, since the territory where he lives and theoretically governs never belonged to him. He was originally located at Gidan Wiya, then moved to Madakiya, and finally to Kafanchan, where members of multiple ethnic groups reside. The original inhabitants of the area where he currently lives were the Fantswam, a closely related group to the Bajju. The colonial officials mistakenly identified this as a Hausa-speaking Muslim area.

Religious conflicts

Since independence, multiple conflicts have occurred between the Hausa-Fulani Muslims and Middle Belt minority ethnic groups. Umaru (2013:56–64) lists twenty-nine conflicts between 1980 and 2011. These conflicts have occurred for various reasons, such as assertion of political dominance over others; taking or protecting land; anger over elections results; location of a new church, mosque or market; teaching and preaching by a Christian evangelist or Muslim cleric or prophet; conflict over selling pork in a market context; ethnicity; perceived economic advantage of one group; adoption of shari'a law; religious conflicts; Islamic problems elsewhere that result in local conflicts (for example, Danish cartoons perceived to insult Mohammed); perceived blasphemous remarks against Islam; attacks and reprisal attacks; and attacks on churches and Christians on Christian holy days. In these attacks there has been loss of life, burning of homes, churches, mosques, schools, markets, etc., and general animosity. For a fuller treatment of Muslim-Christian relations see Ochonu (2014), Kukah and Falola (1996), and Umaru (2013).

Conflicts that impacted the Bajju and other minority ethnic groups in southern Kaduna State include the March 1987 conflict that began at the College of Education in Kafanchan. The Muslim Students Society began it in response to the Young Christian Students group's meeting where a convert from Islam was the major speaker at their meetings. The conflict spread from Kafanchan to other areas in northern Nigeria, including to Kaduna, Zaria, Funtua, Gusau, Malumfashi, and elsewhere (Kukah and Falola 1996:144–148). Thousands of people lost their lives in this Muslim-Christian conflict. The local emir of Jema'a, the Muslim Student Affairs officer of the college, and various teachers (*mallams*) sought to quiet the conflict, but to no avail. The local minority people set up roadblocks where they screened people in cars that drove into the area. They allowed anyone who spoke one of the local languages to pass, but not others. Their goal was to keep more weapons from entering the area.

In May 1992 another conflict occurred between the Kataf and Hausa-Fulani. This conflict began over the location of the market at Zangon Katab. Muslims wanted it to be within their walled location used by traders and emirate representatives (*zangon*), while Christians felt that it had outgrown the limited space there. That was the immediate cause. Umaru stated that the cause was "deep-rooted community conflicts centered on ethnicity, domination, interrelations between the Hausa and the Kataf ethnic groups, as well as economic and political issues" (2013:58).

Another conflict in the area occurred in April 2011 following the defeat of the Muslim candidate Buhari in the presidential election. As a result, Muslims rioted, beginning in the town of Kafanchan in southern Kaduna State, where they burned the market, a number of homes, and churches; Christians retaliated by burning mosques and killing Muslims. The rioting spread to the villages of Zonkwa, Unguwar Rimi, and elsewhere in southern Kaduna State. The riots also spread to the states of Bauchi, Gombe, Katsina, Kano, Kogi, Niger, Sokoto, Taraba, and Zamfara, as well as elsewhere within Kaduna State. Umaru classified these riots as post-election political-religious violence (2013:64). In Kafanchan prior to the riots the Muslims had sent their wives and children away as the riots were planned. Because the Hausa-Fulani were one of the smaller populations in this area, they suffered the most. They began the riots, but because they ended up suffering with many killed, they accused the local people of genocide. The local people told them they could return to the area under three conditions: (1) they come with their wives and children, (2) they recognize the local political authorities, and (3) they recant the negative things they had said about the local population.

There have been efforts to bring about understanding and cooperation between Christians and Muslims. These include the Nigerian Interreligious

Council set up in 1999 with both Christian and Muslim leaders, and the Interfaith Mediation Center. On the Christian side, the Christian Association of Nigeria has sought to negotiate peace and to analyze conflicts that occur. On the Muslim side, there is the Nigerian Supreme Council for Islamic Affairs, Jemalata-Nasril Islam, and the Council of Ulema. When there is a conflict the government typically sets up a commission to investigate the causes. However, few have been held responsible or jailed for their part in the conflicts as a result of those various commissions. This has led to real frustration and even a cynicism towards commissions.

A goal of Muslims since the jihad of Usuman ɗan Fodio has been to have shari'a law adopted. At each constitutional convention for Nigeria, Muslims have wanted shari'a law to be part of the constitution. Christians have strongly objected to this, and the constitution itself does not include it but is neutral concerning religion. Twelve northern states have now officially adopted shari'a law: Bauchi (2001), Borno (2000), Gombe (2001), Jigawa (2000), Kaduna (2000), Kano (2000), Katsina (2000), Kebbi (2000), Niger (2000), Sokoto (2000), Yobe (2001), and Zamfara (2000) (Umaru 2013:69). Individual states adopting shari'a law has caused concern, uneasiness, and fear among Christians. While Kaduna State now officially has adopted shari'a law, in many ways it is not applicable to the southern part of the state, which is largely Christian.

Technological change

Today many Bajju have cell phones, enabling them to contact friends, family, and others. Some have computers and televisions. The use of modern technology has privileged the use of English rather than Hausa or Jju. So today many know English as well as Jju and Hausa.

Summary

This chapter has described some of the cultural changes that have occurred in the broad area within which the Bajju live. Christianity contributed significantly to the changes brought to this area. At the same time a number of their traditional beliefs have been retained by Bajju Christians (see also *Bajju Christian Conversion,* 2019). Hence in this book, those traditional beliefs have been extensively discussed.

Appendix A: Hausa and Jju
Terms for Other Ethnic Groups

Hausa, English Terms Ethnic group	Jju Terms Ethnic Group	Jju Terms Language	Jju Terms Person
Atakar, Atakad, Attaka	Batakat[1]	Takat	Antyok Batakat
English, white (red) persons	Bashong	Shong	Shong, Antyok Ashong
Fulani, Fulbe, Fulfulde, Fula, Peul	Babita	Bita	Abita, Antyok Abita
Hausa	Bakpat	Kpat	Akpat, Antyok Akpat
Ikulu	Bayinkrum	Krum	Antyok Bayinkrum
Jaba, H., Ham, Hyam (Ham language)	Bada	Da	Antyok Bada
Kagoma	Bayinmang	Mang	Antyok Bayinmang
Kagoro, H., Agorok	Bagro	Gro	Antyok Bagro
Kaje	Bajju	Jju	Antyok Bajju

[1] *Ba-* is the plural noun class prefix for people.

Kamantan	Babyrek	Byrek	Antyok Babyrek
Kataf, Katab, H., Atyap	Batyap	Tyap	Antyok Batyap
Moroa	Bashoriya	Shoriya	Antyok Bashoriya

Appendix B: Villages in Bajju Sections (*Kwai*)

Villages among the Bajju are not strictly defined by geographical boundaries; they are also defined by political allegiance to particular chiefs. This came about because of their horticultural practices where over time the land became exhausted, resulting in people moving their residence to more fertile land, but even after moving they owed their political allegiance to the same chief. This is illustrated in table 1, for example, by the various village sections of those listed under A̱zitrung.

Tables 1–6 below list the Bajju and Hausa names of each village in each Bajju section (*kwai*) in Kajju. Names in parentheses are alternative spellings that have been used in the literature. Where a Jju name is listed but no Hausa name is given, it is likely that the Hausa did not recognize it as a separate village from a nearby one so did not give it a name.

Table 1. *Bɑyindwang kwai* villages

Bajju name	Hausa name
Azansak (Azansak)	Madauci (Madaci)
Azunkwa (Azunkwa)	Zonkwa
Azitrung (Zuturung, Azuturung)	Zitrung
Azitrung Pama	Zuturung Fama
Azitrung Kayi	Zuturung Daji
Azitrung Karyi	Zuturung Gida
Azitrung Mago	Zuturung Mugu
Dibyyi (Dibiyi)	Kurmin Bi

Table 2. *Bɑtɑdon kwai* villages

Bajju name	Hausa name
Adom	—
Akong	—
Amankwo	Mafili
Asanson (Sansun)	Bonkwa
Atityen (Atutiyen)	Atat, Bodari (Abodari)
Azenkyrwa (Azankirwa)	Madakiya
Azuhwwo	Asiho
Bvonkpang (Bonkpang)	Kauraje
Dicedon	Ziti
Dinyring (Diyiring)	Andom
Hurgyam	Furgyam (Hurjam)
Kamantsok	Dawadi
Katakntrum	Kataktrum
Kukwan	Ayagan
Kpong	Kpon
Twan	Dando
Zzat	Galadima, Matsirga

Table 3. *Bayintsok kwai* villages

Bajju name	Hausa name
Abak	Tabak
Atagom, Yaribvam	Zagom
Rwap	Rumpa
Kahom	Kafom
Dihogwei	Fadan Kaje
Jei Karyi	Fadan Gida (Fadiya Bakut)
Jei Cwang	Fadiya Tudan Wada
Jei Yazanom, Jei Yazanu	Fadiya Yazanu
Jei Bwasan	Fadia Bosan
Kanshwa	Tsohon Gida, Ngwabarai
Nhok	

Table 4. *Banyehwan kwai* villages

Bajju name	Hausa name
Akudan	Kurdon
Azauru (Azauru)	Zauru
Angbakpat (Abarkpat), Ungwar Rimi	Unguwar Rimi (Gidan Tagwai)
Arikayakon, Aarikawan	Rikawan
Asakwak	Sakwak (Sokwak, Sokwap)
Byet, Bebyet	Abet
Bvontwap	Bontang
Byena	Afana
Ncenccuk (Chancuwuk)	Cencul (Cancuk, Chanchu, Chenchuk)
Dihwan (Duhwan)	Farman
Dihwan Jjim	Fanjim
Kamrum	Kamuru Kaje (Kamurm)
Kamarsa	Marsa
Kanyem	Kanyem (Kanem)
Katssik	Katsit
Kpunyai	Kynyai (Kunyan, Kunye)

Table 5. *Bɑyinbyin kwai* villages

Bajju name	Hausa name
Ạbvwan (Ạbuwan)	Aduwan
Ạkadon (Ạkadon)	Kankada
Ạrebvok (Ạrebok)	Mafili Bebok
Ạwadon (Ạwadon)	Wadon
Tsoryang	Tsoriyan

Table 6. *Bɑyintrung kwai* villages

Bajju name	Hausa name
Ạbvong	Abong
Byet	Abet
Bvontwap	Bontong (Vontong)
Dihwan (Duwhan)	
Dihwan Jjim (Duhuwan Jiyim)	

Appendix C: Jju Numbers

àyrung	one		
àhwa	two	nswang hwa	twenty
		nswang hwa bu yirung	twenty-one
àtat	three	nswang tat	thirty
ànai	four	nswang nai	forty
àpfun	five	nswang pfun	fifty
àkàtat	six	nswang àkàtat	sixty
àtirung	seven	nswang atiryung	seventy
àninbvak	eight	nswang aninbvak	eighty
àkumbvrung	nine	nswang akumbvirung	ninety
swak	ten	cci	one hundred
swak bu yirung	eleven		
swak bu hwa	twelve	ccyi sswa	two hundred
swak bu tat	thirteen		
swak bà nai	fourteen	cci kop	one thousand
swak bà pfun	fifteen	kopp sswa	two thousand
swak bu àkàtat	sixteen		
swak bu atiryung	seventeen		
swak bu anaibvak	eighteen		
swak bu àkumbvirung	nineteen		

Appendix D

Jju–English Glossary

Glossary abbreviations

adj.	adjective	NP	noun phrase
adv.	adverb	pl.	plural noun; multiple action
H.	Hausa		verb
J.	Jju	sing.	singular noun; single action
L.	Latin		verb
lit.	literally	v.	verb
n.	noun	VP	verb phrase

ạbibyyi, n. Bad, ugly, evil.

ạbibyyi nkut, ạkạtuk nkut, NP. Use of spiritual power for evil purposes.

Ạbrak, n. Name given a male infant who returned (for example, was reincarnated).

ạbvoi/ạbvwoi/ạbwei/bvai, sing.; *bạbvoi,* pl., n. (1) Men's secret ancestral organization. (2) Ancestral spirit; members of this society communed with the spirits of the departed male ancestors. (3) *Abvoi* Name given to an infant boy born when this ancestor organization was celebrating.

ạbvok, sing.; *bạbvok,* pl., n.(1) Diviner who was clairvoyant and on occasion could become spirit-possessed in order to ascertain the cause of and solution to some problem within the community. (2) Medical practitioner, both traditional and modern; Bajju doctor; seer; prophet; healer-diviner. Such persons were able both to treat illnesses through herbal medicines and to see the ultimate cause of an illness. They were also consulted before some activities, such as hunts and war. They used a variety of means, including throwing rocks or cowries to foresee the outcome of an activity. (3) Sorcerer, sorceress.

ạbyo, sing.; bạbyo, pl., n; H. *mazo* Musical horn made from the horn of a bushbuck.

ạbyyai, n. Woman's headboard used for carrying her load. It can be turned over and used to sit on. In the past women gave birth on their headboards.

ạcongong, sing.; bạconcong, pl., n. Water spirit that lives in clear still water, as well as in the bush, in trees, in a forest, or in caves.

ạgba, sing.; bạgba, pl., n. Musical horn.

ạgbaryi, n.; H. *mariri* Musical horn made from the horn of an oryx.

Ạgorok, Agworok, n. Closely related ethnic group located northeast of the Bajju, also known as the Kagoro.

ạgumkpap, n. Large, hard black seed that was covered with a spider web, which men of the ạbvoi blew to magnify the sound. From ạgum, referring to the pod

of the *Oncoba spinosa,* L., a tree that grows near streams, and *kpap* 'hard'.

ạgwam, sing.; bạgwam, pl., n.; H. *sarki* Chief, king. Derived from the English word *govern*.

Ạgwam Kạza, NP. Lord, Lord God.

Ạgwam Tazwa, NP. Chief of heaven or the sky, God.

ạgyashak, n.; H. *dodo* Dancing masquerade, the wife of ạkusak, also a dancing masquerade; originally borrowed from the Kagoma, the southeastern neighbors of the Bajju.

ạhwa, n. Small calabash, often used to drink beer from.

ạhwwuk, n. (1) Co-wife, rival. (2) Jealousy.

ạjrang, n. Cleansing, as to cleanse the community of the consequences of a trespass; to rinse; purification ritual.

ạjjwa, n. West African hartebeest musical horn.

ạkạtuk wun, NP. Evil spirit.

ạkinkyim, sing.; bạkinkyim, pl., n. Clay pot drum that comes in various sizes, some so large that they are set on the floor while played. These are women's instruments usually played in church and other Christian contexts.

ạkusak, n.; H. *dodo* Dancing masquerade, the husband of *ạgyashak*. He wore a woven grass outfit, and other men sprinkled water on him with shea tree leaves to cool him. The *ạkusak* danced with women; he also disciplined them by beating them for allegedly breaking a rule of the men's organization.

ạkut, sing.; bạkut, pl., n. (1) Witch, one who has the power to harm others in the spiritual realm. One who causes evil, physical illness, misfortune, or death; one who practices witchcraft; one who eats human flesh in the spiritual realm. (2) Diviner.

ạkwwuk n. Widow. A woman was known as *ạkwwuk* for one month after the death of her husband. After that time, she was free to remarry. During this period she was not allowed to speak with the brother(s) of the deceased. If she did not remarry after one month, she was known as the wife of the deceased, not as *ạkwwuk*.

ạkpatyok, n. Bachelor, spinster, or a widower who does not remarry, lit. 'an empty person'; a derogatory term symbolizing loneliness and incompleteness.

ạmampfwa, n. Meningitis.

ạmbyring, n. Woman, wife.

ạna, n. Mother.

Anang, n. Infant girl's name, 'gift'.

ạnạkwu ạmbyring, NP. Barren woman.

Angan, n. Ethnic group located west of the Bajju, also known as the Kamantan.

ạnguma, n. Poison made from the *shing* tree used in hunting. It is placed on the tips of arrows.

ạngbaktssuk, n. Male spitting cobra. Only diviners eat this snake. A female spitting cobra is termed *tssuk*.

ạninyet, sing., bạninyet, pl., n. Tall spirit.

ạnok, sing.; bạnok, pl., n. Hoe.

ạpyya, n. The loved wife in a polygynous household, the favorite wife.

ạrak, n. The rejected wife in a polygynous household.

ạrendwan, n. Enemy. This term refers to enmity or rivalry between brothers. It also applies to the relationship between two men, one of whom has taken the other man's wife in marriage.

ạrentong, n. (1) Worthless person, bachelor. (2) Shooting star. (3) *Arentong* Name given to an infant born at the time of sighting a shooting star. Such an infant is believed to be a reincarnated person.

arna H., n. Pagans, a term applied by Muslims to non-Muslims.

ạrou dissi nkut, ạrou dissi, NP. Stinginess, greediness; lit. 'too much eyes'.

ạshishik, n. Ugly, evil, death, an evil or terrible thing.

ạshishik ạyin, NP. Ugly person.

Ạsholio, n. Closely related ethnic group located northeast of the Bajju, also known as the Moroa.

ạtakwo, n. Grain stalks that remain after the grain is harvested and are used for animal feed or fuel.

ạtanrang, n. Ringworm; used euphemistically in a patient's presence for leprosy in its early stage, characterized by white spots on the skin.

Ạtatad, n. Closely related ethnic group located northeast of the Bajju, also known as the Atakad.

ạtro, sing.; *bạtro,* pl., n. Cloth, clothing.

ạtutwan ạyin, NP. Blind person.

ạtsatsak, adj. Good.

ạtsatsak nạtenyrang, NP. Good small spirits.

ạtsatsak nkut, NP. Protective discernment such as an elder may have that allows him to ascertain if someone is seeking to harm a person within his family.

ạttyi, n. Father, father's brother.

Atyap, n. Closely related ethnic group located north of the Bajju, also known as the Katab or Kataf.

ạyabyen, n. Underground world where the ancestors reside; residence for those who fulfill their roles in society following death; world of ancestral spirits; the afterlife.

Baranzan, n. Bajju founding father and apical ancestor.

Bạjju, n.; H. *Kaje* People who speak the *Jju* language and live in *Kạjju,* their territory.

bạkạmbvon Baranzan, NP. Daughters-in-law of Baranzan; women who marry Bajju men.

bạkut ạtacci, NP. Witches with eyes; persons who use their spiritual eyes for evil purposes.

Bạnyet Tssup, NP. People who follow. Christians. Initially, Christians were people who followed rules and regulations. Today, they follow Jesus Christ and know God, *Kạza.*

bạnyeyabyen, bạnyet yabyen, NP. Ancestral spirits, the living dead who are believed to be alive. They are invisible and care for the welfare of their offspring by protecting them from evil. However, if a person sees one, it is believed that he or she will die. They must be appeased if they were wronged during their lifetime. A person and elders then go to the grave of the deceased to pray for forgiveness and offer wine or beer. A person may swear by his ancestral spirit.

bᶏsoza, n. Fever.

bᶏzzak ba, n. Dream.

bᶏzzwak, pl. n. Man's maternal relatives, such as mother's brother; in-laws.

bvori, n.; H. *bori* Spirit possession cult which received its name from the village of Bori in northern Benin.

Bvvoᶏbying, n. Infant girl's name meaning 'she has delivered again'.

cat, v. (1) Like, need, want, desire, love. (2) *Cat* Name given to a desired son.

cei, n. Age mate, men initiated together.

cet, n. Strength.

Cincong, n. Infant girl's name meaning 'little', given an infant girl born prematurely.

cong, n. Python.

cong, v. Walk.

crwang, n. Beniseed, sesame seed.

ccuk, n. Leopard.

Dambvvo, n. Name meaning 'would that they knew'; a name that might be given an infant boy when people harmed others.

dangi, n. People who are of the same stock, a term that refers to the Bajju, Jarawa, and Irigwe and reflects their common Plateau origin.

Dankpari, n. Husband of Zᶏbya, the furious ancestral spirit who did not dress in a masquerade outfit. People never saw him; they only heard his voice.

dibyit, n. Light-colored place on the skin that may indicate leprosy.

dibyit ᶏtanyrang, NP. Early stage of leprosy.

Dibyyi, n. (1) Name of the village where Baranzan originally settled and where his grave is located. (2) *dibyyi* grave.

dikat, n. Ring used for balancing a headload, placed between a woman's head and her load.

dikok, n. Red-flowered kapok tree, *Bombax buonopozense,* L.

dikum ccuk, NP. Musical horn.

dikwai, n. Vine growing by the river that produces fruit every year. A very scratchy vine used to treat leprosy.

dikwu, n. (1) Death, epidemic. (2) *Dikwu* Name given to an infant girl born during an epidemic. Since she is already "dead," the goal of giving her this name is to ensure she will live.

dikwu Kaza, NP. Death because of God's judgment.

dikwuk, n. Fallow field.

dimyak, n. Man dodging, moving cautiously and stealthily, crouching, hiding behind trees, and so forth. This posturing was used for both warfare and hunting.

dison, n. Child who does not thrive and who is believed to be a river spirit. This child may be returned to the river from where he or she is believed to have come; a form of infanticide.

ditun, n. (1) Bitter leaf. (2) Beniseed paste used for religious purposes.

ditun kawha, NP. Bitter leaf given to a young woman by her family when they found that she was pregnant for the first time; lit. 'paste of the stomach'.

dodo H., n. Evil spirit, goblin, men's ancestral cult, masquerade.

Fantswam, n. Closely related ethnic group, also known as the Kafanchan.

gado, sing.; *bagado,* pl., n. (1) Respected elder, ruling elder, priest; religious, political, and jural leader. (2) Custom.

gado abvoi, NP; H. *magaji, magajin dodo* Elder in charge of the

men's ancestral organization in a particular village.

gado kankrang, NP. Ruling elder of a village.

gado kapyyi, NP. (1) Hunting elder. (2) Priest who examined the body of a deceased individual to determine the cause of death.

gado karyi, atyyi karyi, antyok karyi, NP. Ruling elder of a household; head of a household.

gado kwai, NP. Ruling elder of a section of the Bajju.

gado nkpang, NP. (1) Ruling elder of stones; religious, political, and judicial leader of a section (*kwai*) of the Bajju. (2) Ruling elder of all the Bajju people who was located at Dibyyi.

gado sot, NP. Ruling elder of a clan.

gajimale, n. Spirit that lives in clear still pools of water, in trees, bushes, caves, or under mountains. It can also reside in one's room. It can appear as a beautiful woman to a man or as a handsome man to a woman. While it can transform itself, it cannot transform its toes, which are like those of horse hooves. The Bajju believe that to see one can cause blindness.

gbaam, n. (1) Broth made from the stomach of an animal. This was usually made at the hunting elder's house. (2) Cooked medicine.

gbap, n. The later stage of leprosy characterized by the disease having entered a person's fingers.

gida, gidan H., n. House, compound, settled population, as *Fulani gidan.*

gunki, n. Roan antelope.

Gyong, Gong, n. Ethnic group located southeast of the Bajju, also known as the Kagoma.

Ham, n. Ethnic group located south of the Bajju, also known as the Jaba. They speak the Hyam language.

hung ayin, NP. Reserved person, as a future spouse, whether male or female.

hung kaneyang, hung kaseyang, NP. (1) Reserved bride or groom; promised/betrothed person. (2) Arrangements made for a person to marry a specific individual when older.

Hyam, n.; H. *Jaba* Language spoken by the Ham people.

hyyu, n. Sickness.

hyyu anok, NP. 'Feed the hoe', a ritual of sacrifice of the first yams harvested to thank the hoe for its part in farming them.

hyyu batwak, NP. Sickle cell anemia.

Jju, n. Language spoken by the Bajju, a Central Plateau language within the Benue-Congo language family, part of the larger Niger-Congo family of languages; also called the Kaje language.

kasiseyang ka, n. Early wet season when farming begins.

kadak, n. Garden in the area adjacent to the compound, where women farm sponges, broad beans, various greens, tomatoes, okra, and other plants for sauces.

kahwa atang, NP. (1) Dysentery; lit. 'thief of the stomach', formerly believed to be caused by witchcraft. (2) Cholera.

Kajju, n. Geographic area where the Bajju live. This word is likely the origin of the term *Kaje,* the term formerly used by outsiders for this ethnic group and their language.

kamanda, n. Potash.

kanak ka, n. Crying, mourning, funeral.

kanak bapfo, NP. Funeral, memorial service with dancing, which occurred after an elderly person died a natural death.

kanak bassi, NP. Funeral with tears for a child or youth.

kaneyang, sing.; *naneyang,* pl., n. Girl, unmarried woman of any age.

kaneyang ambyring, NP. Married woman without children.

kạnshrya, n. Flute made from bamboo or reed.

Kạrik, Kạrick, n. 'Division in the household'; name given an infant son born into a troubled household.

kạrom, n. Ram, male goat.

kạron, n.; H. *dorawa, dorowa* Locust bean tree, *Parkia filicoides,* L.

kạryi, n. House, household, compound.

kạryong, n. True, truth.

kạryong ạmi, NP. 'It is true', a phrase used in place of other oaths by Christians.

kạsap, n.; H. *baska* Type of poison made from the *loofah* plant *Luffa acutangula,* L., *aegyptiaca* (Bargery 1934:93) that is placed on arrowheads.

kạsham, n. (1) Beautiful, good. (2) *Kạsham,* name often given to an infant girl by Christian parents.

kạshyen, n. Long musical horn with a gourd at the end.

kạtenyrang, sing.; *nạtenyrang,* pl., n. (1) Small white or black spirits that are invisible to everyone but diviners. (2) In the Jju Bible, 'Satan' is translated as *Kạtenyrang.* This expands the meaning of this small spirit to the ultimate evil spirit who is responsible for evil in the world.

kạtyenkon, n. Cleared enclosure used for a ritual or festival.

Kạyit, n. (1) Name given an infant son when born outside the house, as on the farm. (2) *kạyit* bush, outside.

Kạza, n. (1) God, Supreme Being. (2) Name given an infant son as a shortened form of 'God sees them'. It refers to someone practicing *nkut* against a woman, but she conceived and bore a son in spite of *nkut.* (3) *kạza* up, tall, above. (4) North.

Kạza ạbiryi, NP. God will see.

Kạza ạ cyyang, NP. God sees.

Kạza ạ maai, NP. God is sufficient.

Kạza ạn sshi, NP. God exists, God is present; an expression used to acknowledge God's omnipresence.

Kạza an tun, NP. God preserves, God protects me.

Kạza ntazwa, NP. God of heaven.

kạzzwan, zzwak, n. Small harmless striped tree snake.

ke, locative. Where.

kobo, n. Penny.

kon ạgbaryi, NP. Wooden musical horn.

kop, v. (1) To ripen. Refers to fruit ripening on a tree or elderly individuals who have ripened and are ready for death. (2) Unearth.

kwai, n. Large territorial unit or section. See appendix B.

Kyung, n. Related ethnic group, also known as the Kaninkon.

madauci H., n. Important position or official in the emirate held by one of the emir's chief slaves.

magaji dodo H., NP. Leader of the *ạbvoi* organization; he was in charge of the ancestor cult shrine.

mạsham, n. Leaves of shea tree; leaves that women formerly wore; leaves that symbolized the men's secret organization.

mpfu, sing.; *ạmpfu,* pl., n. Shrine of the men's ancestor organization, *ạbvoi* building.

nat wei rong, VP. Two- or three-month period after the birth of a child that the mother and child spend with her family; lit. 'go warm oneself by the fire'.

nkut, n. (1) Spiritual power used to harm or protect, spiritual power, the power of medicine, witchcraft. The Bajju distinguish two types: *ạtsatsak nkut,* 'good protective witchcraft', and *ạbibyyi nkut* 'evil witchcraft'. (2) Evil person. (3) *Nkut* Name given an infant boy so that an evil spirit's power cannot hurt him. The logic is that if he is already *nkut,* no further *nkut* can harm him.

nkwwa, n. Guinea corn beer.

nom, temporal (1) Sun. (2) Day.

ntwak, n. Salt.

nwap, n. People, nation.

nwap nyreng, NP. People you might marry, a phrase told to a baby girl at her naming ceremony.

nwap nzwang, NP. People with whom you might wage wars, a phrase told to a baby boy at his naming ceremony.

nyon, n. Chicken, hen.

rong ncen, rwong ncen, NP. Epilepsy, convulsion; lit. 'fire of the river'; having sexual relations with a demon.

rong ndong, NP. Bride's initiation into a family when her mother-in-law puts cooking utensils out for her. From that day she cooks for her husband herself; lit. 'fire fire'.

ryi, n. Bridewealth.

ryik, sing.; *ndyik,* pl., n. Rope, snake.

ryok, v. Stop.

sak ạmbyring, VP. To inherit a widow in order to keep the family together; lit. 'keep a woman'.

shrywa, sing.; *shrywa,* pl., n. Hollow reed flute.

song kata, NP. Dance of the arrow. In this dance male hunters act out a hunting scene, which is accompanied by drumming and flute or horn blowing. One man may pretend to be a lion while another man acts as the hunter who stalks him. The hunters perform this inside the circle formed by the horn-blowing musicians, while outside the circle others dance and sing.

sot, n. Clan; a named exogamous totemic group of lineages. Bajju clans are patrilineal.

sshi, v. To swear, used for minor transgressions. A person can do so privately without others present.

sshi anok, VP. To swear on one's hoe, a man's oath.

sup ji, n. Large pot used to store water. It may also be used to cook food for a feast.

ssuk, v. To renovate, to make new again.

sswa, v. (1) To drink. (2) To swear.

sswa abvubvu, VP. To swear an oath on the goatskin that a woman used to carry her child on her back, a woman's oath.

sswa abyyai, VP. To swear an oath on a woman's headboard, a woman's oath.

sswa atro, VP. To swear an oath on the cloth that a woman carries her baby in on her back. Formerly women swore on the goatskins they carried their babies in.

sswa Baranzan, VP. To swear an oath on Baranzan; an oath used for issues that affect the entire Bajju.

sswa bamyyi, VP. To swear an oath on hot oil.

sswa batwak, VP. To swear an oath on ashes; lit. 'to drink ashes', 'to repent', 'to lick ashes'; repentance. This was a means of retracting an oath. It is a means of repenting from one's acts or words or from one's ancestor's words or actions.

sswa kasa, VP. To swear an oath on the world.

sswa kata, VP. To swear an oath on one's arrow, a man's oath.

sswa katssong, VP. To swear an oath on a woman's axe; a woman's oath.

sswa mbyen, VP. To swear an oath on the ground, to take an oath on a grave, to swear on the farm dirt.

sswa mbyin, VP. To swear an oath on a drum; a type of oath used for very serious issues, such as land disputes.

sswa nak, VP. To swear/drink an oath, to swear an oath; this is taking oaths that are on the more serious end of a continuum. *Sshi* is used for less serious transgressions. Other persons must be present as witnesses when a person takes this oath. Today this occurs only in a court of law.

Tsam, n. Closely related ethnic group, also known as the Chawai.

tson, n.; H. *acca*. White variety of hungry rice, *Digitaria exilis,* L.; a cereal grain. Also used as a generic for any type of hungry rice.

tssuk, n. Female spitting cobra.

tsun, n.; H. *acca* Red variety of hungry rice, *Digitaria exilis,* L.

tswa ɑbvoi, NP. Members of the men's secret organization; lit. 'seeds or offspring of the ancestral spirits'.

tsswa ɑssi, NP. Spirit eyes that can cause illness or death through *nkut.*

tswandyik, n. Small ropes, lit. 'spirit ropes', that were given to women to wear around their waists during a mourning period. These indicate that they were not to marry and not to divorce their husbands during the time they wore them. This mushroom-shaped ornament hung down in back of a woman over the leaves she wore; it was suspended by a small rope.

tun kɑnu, VP. To confess.

tun zei, VP. Ritual performed by a child from the household of the *gado.* He would sprinkle medicine on a large, recently killed animal's head and stomach in order to take away the evil part of the animal that had the power to harm a hunter for killing it.

Tungzwang, n. Name given an infant son born when people are gathered for war.

tyong tsaab, VP. Elopement; lit. 'horse trot'.

tyyi gbang, VP. To pay a fine.

Tyyibvwak, n. Name given an infant son meaning 'to hold in one's hands'.

yaryi, n. (1) Village or section of a clan that was formally one/ unified but has now been divided such that intermarriage is now allowed. Intermarrying units, formerly from the same clan. (2) Term of address to a bride from one's *yaryi.*

yi, pronoun. Second person plural subject pronoun.

yyuk, v. To ululate, a sound used to express excitement, joy, happiness, and praise; a high-pitched warble, often done by women.

zaki, n. Lion.

zat, n. Buffalo.

Zabya, n.; H. *Zabiya* Wife of Dankpari; this masquerade led the singing within the *abvoi* hut.

Zataat, ashya, n. Name given an infant girl meaning 'You have reached us' or 'She has found us'. If it has been a long time since a woman conceived and then she has a daughter, she may be given this name.

zei, n. Evil part of an animal that has the power to harm a hunter for killing it.

Zigwai, n. Name often given an infant girl by Christian parents, meaning 'We are thankful, we are happy'.

zinzom, n. Two-stringed guitar; reed rattle.

Zi Tung Dung, NP. 'We meet meet; we just meet'; the motto for the Bajju Development Association.

zumunta banyring, NP; H. *zumunta mata* Women's Christian fellowship. Each church has its own *zumunta mata.*

zumunta bantyok, NP. Men's Christian fellowship.

zzu shan, VP. To beat with a stick; a means used to assert that the decisions reached by the elders are final and will be fulfilled.

References

Archival References from the National Archives of Kaduna (NAK)

NAK ACC 873 638. 1937.
NAK K 2985 Kaje Tribe, Anthropological Notes on. 1914.
NAK ZarProf 312 9 (also 3316) Notes by P. F. Brandt, On the Social and Economic Organisation of the Tribes in Southern Zaria. 1939.
NAK ZarProf 607 Zangon Katab, Notes on. Report by Mr. M. V. Spurway. 1932.
NAK ZarProf 1024 Conflict between Christian and Pagan Customs. n.d.
NAK ZarProf 3465 Confidential Dispatch No. C8/1946, Usman Sokop Kaje: Petition by (1940–1949). n.d.
NAK ZarProf 6/1942 Osuman Sokop Kaje. 1942.

Textual References

Abraham, R. C. 1962. *Dictionary of the Hausa language*. Second edition. London: University of London Press.
Adamu, Mahdi. 1978. *The Hausa factor in West African history*. Zaria, Nigeria: Ahmadu Bello University Press.
Ahuwan, Iliya. n.d. Migration of Kaje people to Kaduna City. Ms.
Ames, C. G. n.d. *Archibalds and Kagoro*. SIM archives.

Ames, C. G. 1934. *Gazetteers of the northern provinces of Nigeria,* vol. IV, *The highland chieftaincies (Plateau Province),* with a prefatory note by A. H. M. Kirk-Green. Jos, Nigeria: Jos Native Administration. Reprint edition. London: Frank Cass.

Asake, Musa Nchock. 1982. Tarihi shigowar bishara a kasar Kaje [History of the Good News among the Kaje]. Kafanchan, Nigeria: Evangelical Churches of West Africa. Unpublished ms.

Asake, Musa Nchock. 1991. An evaluation of the historical development of Christianity among the Bajju of northern Nigeria with special emphasis on selected ethical-doctrinal tensions. ThM thesis. Dallas Theological Seminary.

Asake, Musa Nchock. 1998. An exposition of 1 Timothy 3:1–7 and Titus 1:5–9 with application to Bajju ECWA churches in northern Nigeria. PhD dissertation. Dallas Theological Seminary.

Bargery, G. P. 1934. *A Hausa-English dictionary and English-Hausa vocabulary.* London: Oxford University Press.

Bajju Development Association. 2009. Aims and objectives. http://bajjugarki.blogspot.com/. Accessed 12 October 2018.

Bayei, Yabo. 1983. *Gan Bajju* [Bajju proverbs]. Jos: Nigeria Bible Translation Trust.

Bendor-Samuel, John, ed. 1989. *The Niger-Congo languages: A classification and description of Africa's largest language family.* Lanham, MD: University Press of America.

Berger. Iris. 1976. Rebels or status-seekers? Women as spirit mediums. In Nancy J. Hafkin and Edna G. Bay (eds.), *Women in Africa: Studies in social and economic change,* 157–181. Stanford, CA: Stanford University Press.

Besmer, Fremont E. 1983. *Horses, musicians, and gods: The Hausa cult of possession-trance.* South Hadley, MA: Bergin & Garvey.

Blench, Roger, and Mallam Dendo. 2004. The Benue-Congo languages: A proposed internal classification. Ms.

Bourguignon, Erika, ed. 1973. *Religion, altered states of consciousness, and social change.* Columbus: Ohio State University Press.

Conant, Francis Paine. 1960. Dodo of Dass: A study of a pagan religion of northern Nigeria. PhD dissertation. Columbia University, New York, NY.

Crapo, Richley H. 1993. *Cultural anthropology: Understanding ourselves and others.* Third edition. Guilford, CT: Dushkin.

Dariya, Timothy. 1983. Dityin Bajju [Origin of the Bajju]. Kaduna. Ms.

Datok, Polycarp F. 1983. *A short history of Sura (Panyam): (c. 1730–1981).* Jos: Nigeria Bible Translation Trust.

Denham, Dixon, Hugh Clapperton, and Walter Oudney. (1826) 1985. *Narrative of travels and discoveries in northern and central Africa in the years 1822, 1823 and 1824.* Reprint edition. London: John Murray.

Diamond, Stanley. 1967. The Anaguta of Nigeria: Suburban primitives. In Julian H. Steward (ed.), *Three African tribes in transition*, 360–505. Urbana: University of Illinois Press.

Evans-Pritchard, E. E. (1937) 1976. *Witchcraft, oracles and magic among the Azande*. Oxford: Clarendon Press.

Eyo, Ekpo, and Frank Willett. 1980. *Treasures of ancient Nigeria*. New York: Alfred A. Knopf.

Glick, Leonard B. 1967. Medicine as an ethnographic category: The Gimi of the New Guinea Highlands. *Ethnology* 6(1):31–56.

Gunn, Harold D. 1956. *Pagan peoples of the central area of northern Nigeria*. London: International African Institute.

Isichei, Elizabeth, ed. 1982. *Studies in the history of Plateau State, Nigeria*. London: MacMillan.

Kaburuk, Chidawa. 1976. Polygyny in the Old Testament and the church in Africa. STM thesis. Dallas Theological Seminary.

Kaburuk, Chidawa. 2014. *Prisoners of faith and hope*. Zonkwa, Nigeria: Jju Language and Bible Association.

Kato, Marcus N. 1973. Kaje death and burial ceremonies. *Savanna* 2(2):219–222.

Kato, Marcus N. 1974. A study of traditional social organization among the Kaje with reference to social change during the recent past. MA thesis. Ahmadu Bello University, Zaria, Nigeria.

Kluckhohn, Clyde. (1944) 1967. *Navaho witchcraft*. Boston, MA: Beacon.

Kukah, Matthew Hassan, and Toyin Falola. 1996. *Religious militancy and self-assertion, Islam and politics in Nigeria*. Aldershot, UK: Avebury.

Kunhiyop, Samuel Waje. n.d. Socio-historical setting of the Kaje. Ms.

Kunhiyop, Samuel Waje. 1984. An analysis of the continuity of traditional values in Christian life and practice among Kaje (Bajju) Christians. BA thesis. ECWA Theological Seminary, Jos, Nigeria.

Kunhiyop, Samuel Waje. 1988. Developing the Christian core among the Bajju with special application to the belief in *nkut*. MA thesis. Western Conservative Baptist Seminary, Portland, OR.

Kunhiyop, Samuel Waje. 1993. A theological analysis of Bajju conversion to Christianity. PhD dissertation. Trinity Evangelical Divinity School, Deerfield, IL.

Kunhiyop, Samuel Waje. 2005. *Christian conversion in Africa: The Bajju experience*. Jos, Nigeria: ECWA Productions.

Lewis, I. M. 1971. *Ecstatic religion: A study of spirit possession and shamanism*. Harmondsworth, England: Penguin.

Lewis, M. Paul, Gary F. Simons, and Charles D. Fennig (eds.). 2015. *Ethnologue: Languages of the world. Eighteenth edition.* Dallas, TX: SIL International. Online version: http://www.ethnologue.com/15/. Accessed 12 October 2018.

Lovejoy, Paul E. 1983. *Transformations in slavery: A history of slavery in Africa*. Cambridge: Cambridge University Press.

Lovejoy, Paul E., and Jan S. Hogendorn. 1993. *Slow death for slavery: The course of abolition in northern Nigeria, 1897–1936*. Cambridge: Cambridge University Press.

Mason, Michael. 1969. Population density and "slave raiding": The case of the Middle Belt of Nigeria. *Journal of African History* 10(4):551–564.

Mbiti, John S. 1970. *African religions and philosophy*. Garden City, NY: Anchor.

Mbiti, John S. 1975. *Introduction to African religion*. London: Heinemann.

McKinney, Carol V. 1979. Plural verb roots in Kaje. *Afrika und Übersee* 62(2):107–117.

McKinney, Carol V. 1983. A linguistic shift in Kaje, Kagoro, and Katab kinship terminology. *Ethnology* 22(4):281–293.

McKinney, Carol V. 1992. Wives and sisters: Bajju marital patterns. *Ethnology* 31:75–87.

McKinney, Carol V. 2019. *Bajju Christian conversion in the Middle Belt of Nigeria*. Publications in Ethnography 47. Dallas, TX: SIL International.

McKinney, Carol V., and Norris P. McKinney. 2003. Worldview reflected in Bajju proverbs. In Mary Ruth Wise, Thomas N. Headland, and Ruth M. Brend (eds.), *Language and life: Essays in memory of Kenneth L. Pike*, 163–182. Dallas, TX: SIL International and the University of Texas at Arlington.

McKinney, Norris P. 1978. Participant identification in Kaje narrative. In Joseph E. Grimes (ed.), *Papers on discourse*, 179–189. Dallas, TX: Summer Institute of Linguistics.

McKinney, Norris P. 1984. The fortis feature in Jju (Kaje): An initial study. *Studies in African Linguistics* 15(2):177–188.

McKinney, Norris P. 1990. Temporal characteristics of fortis stops and affricates in Tyap and Jju. *Journal of Phonetics* 18:255–266.

McKinney, Norris P., and Carol V. McKinney. 1972. *Zizwa Jju* [Jju Letters]. Zaria: Institute of Linguistics.

Meek, Charles K. 1931. *Tribal studies in northern Nigeria*. Vol. 2. London: Kegan Paul, Trench, Trübner.

Morrison, J. H. 1982. Plateau societies' resistance to Jihadist penetration. In Elizabeth Isichei (ed.), *Studies in the history of Plateau State, Nigeria*, 136–150. London: MacMillan.

Muller, Jean-Claude. 1976. Of souls and bones: The living and the dead among the Rukuba, Benue-Plateau State, Nigeria. *Africa* 46(3):258–273.

Ochonu, Moses E. 2014. *Colonialism by proxy, Hausa imperial agents and Middle Belt consciousness in Nigeria*. Bloomington: Indiana University Press.

Offiong, Daniel. 1985. Witchcraft among the Ibibio of Nigeria. In Arthur C. Lehmann and James E. Myers (eds.), *Magic, witchcraft, and religion: An anthropological study of the supernatural*, 152–165. Palo Alto, CA: Mayfield. Originally published 1983 in *African Studies Review* 26:107–124.

Paden, John N. 1986. *Ahmadu Bello, Sardauna of Sokoto.* London: Hodder and Stoughton.

Peter, Prince of Greece and Denmark. 1980. Comments on the social and cultural implications of variant systems of polyandrous alliances. *Journal of Comparative Family Studies* 11(3):371–375.

Powell, J. Mark. 1981. Cropping system in Abet: Report 1, cropping patterns. Ms.

Reynolds, J. A. 1950. Report on the Kaje tribe. Ms.

Sangree, Walter H. 1974. Prescriptive polygamy and complementary filiation among the Irigwe of Nigeria. *Man* 9:44–52.

Sangree, Walter H. 1982. Spirit possession cults in Irigwe, Nigeria: An indigenous response to severe separation depression. In O. A. Erinosho and N. W. Bell (eds.), *Mental health in Africa*, 60–75. Ibadan, Nigeria: Ibadan University Press.

Sangree, Walter H. 2008. "Marriage and madness": Marriage stability and demon possession in Irigwe, Nigeria. *Working Papers in African Studies 260*. Boston, MA: Boston University.

Sanke, Daniel Kogi. 1976. Kaje kinship and marriage: A study of adaptation in a changing world. BA thesis. Ahmadu Bello University, Zaria, Nigeria.

Sanke, Simon. 1977. Laws of inheritance among the Kaje. BSc thesis. Ahmadu Bello University, Zaria, Nigeria.

Sargent, Carolyn Fishel. 1982. *The cultural context of therapeutic choice: Obstetrical care decisions among the Bariba of Benin.* Dorcrecht, Holland: D. Reidel.

Shemang, Iliya Usman. n.d. *The Bajju of central Nigeria.* Abuja: Kazlight Global Nigeria.

Smith, Michael G. 1975. *Social organisation and economy of Kagoro.* Occasional Publications 4. Zaria, Nigeria: Sociology Department, Ahmadu Bello University.

Smith, Michael G. 1980. After secondary marriage, what? *Ethnology* 19:265–277.

Smith, Michael G. 1982. Cosmology, practice, and social organization among the Kadara and Kagoro. *Ethnology* 21(1):1–20.

Taylor, John. 1963. *The primal vision: Christian presence amid African religion.* London: SCM.

Temple, Charles L. 1918. *Native races and their rulers: Sketches and studies of official life and administrative problems in Nigeria.* Reprint edition. London: Frank Cass.

Temple, Olive Susan Miranda, comp. 1922. *Notes on the tribes, provinces, emirates and states of the northern provinces of Nigeria,* ed. Charles L. Temple. Second edition. Lagos, Nigeria: C.M.S. Bookshop. Reprinted by London: Frank Cass.

Tremearne, A. J. N. 1912. *The tailed headhunters of Nigeria.* London: Seeley, Service.

Turaki, Yusufu. 1982. The institutionalization of the inferior status and socio-political role of the non-Muslim groups in the colonial hierarchical structure of the northern region of Nigeria: A social-ethical analysis of the colonial legacy. PhD dissertation. Boston University, MA.

Turaki, Yusufu. 2006. *Foundations of African traditional religion and worldview.* Nairobi, Kenya: Word Alive.

Turner, Victor W. 1972. Between: The liminal period in rites of passage. In William A. Lessa and Evon Z. Vogt, *Reader in comparative religion.* Third edition, 338–347. New York: Harper and Row.

Umaru, Thaddeus Byimui. 2013. *Christian-Muslim dialogue in northern Nigeria: A socio-political and theological consideration.* Crossways, Dartford, UK: Xlibris.

Van der valk van Ginnen, P. M. H. 1981. *Land use in northern Nigeria: The Kaje of Abet and land use problems in Abet.* Internal Communication 41. Kaduna, Nigeria: International Livestock Centre for Africa Subhumid Programme.

Vansina, Jan. 1990. *Paths in the rainforests: Toward a history of political tradition in Equatorial Africa.* Madison, WI: University of Wisconsin Press.

Waters-Bayer, Ann. 1982. History of land use and settlement patterns on the Abet plains. Zonkwa. Ms.

Waters-Bayer, Ann. 1983. Day by day: The Fulani of the Abet plains. Kaduna. Ms.

Winick, Charles. 1977. *Dictionary of anthropology.* Totowa, NJ: Littlefield, Adams.

Yahaya, A. D. 1980. *The native authority system in northern Nigeria 1950–70: A study in political relations with particular reference to the Zaria Native Authority.* Zaria: Ahmadu Bello University Press.

Index

SIL International® Publications
Publications in Ethnography Series
ISSN 0-0895-9897

45. **Acclimated to Africa: Cultural competence for Westerners**, by Debbi DiGennaro, 2017, 163 pp., ISBN 978-1-55671-386-6.

44. **The heart of the matter: Seeking the center in Maya-Mam language and culture**, by Wesley M. Collins, 2015, 205 pp., ISBN 978-1-55671-375-0.

43. **African friends and money matters.** Second edition, by David E. Maranz, 2015, 293 pp., ISBN 978-1-55671-277-7.

42. **Ensnared by AIDS: Cultural contexts of HIV and AIDS in Nepal**, by David K. Beine, 2014, 357 pp., ISBN 978-1-55671-350-7.

41. **The Norsk Høstfest: A celebration of ethnic food and ethnic identity**, by Paul Thomas Emch, 2011, 121 pp., ISBN 978-1-55671-265-4.

40. **Our company increases apace: History, language, and social identity in early colonial Andover, Massachusetts**, by Elinor Abbot, 2007, 279 pp., ISBN 978-1-55671-169-5.

39. **What place for hunters-gatherers in millennium three?** by Thomas N. Headland and Doris E. Blood, eds. 2002, 130 pp., ISBN 978-1-55671-132-9.

38. **A tale of Pudicho's people**, by Richard Montag. 2002, 181 pp., ISBN 978-1-55671-131-2.

SIL International® Publications
7500 W. Camp Wisdom Road
Dallas, Texas 75236-5629 USA

General inquiry: publications_intl@sil.org
Pending order inquiry: sales@sil.org
publications.sil.org

About the Author

Carol McKinney with her husband Norris and their four children (Mark, Eric, Susan, and Christy) worked in Nigeria, West Africa, with the Bajju people who live in southern Kaduna State. Completing her PhD in Anthropology from Southern Methodist University, Dallas, Texas, she taught at the Texas SIL school, then at the Graduate Institute of Applied Linguistics, where she was an Associate Professor of Applied Anthropology.

McKinney previously published *Globe Trotting in Sandals, a Field Guide to Cultural Research* and co-authored, with her husband, *Introduction to Field Phonetics*. She has published many articles which largely focus on the Bajju.

She was involved in language development in Jju, working closely with a local Bajju team translating the New Testament. The Bajju themselves are currently working to complete the Old Testament.

Further publications

www.sil.org/contributor/mckinney-carol-v

www.ingramcontent.com/pod-product-compliance
Lightning Source LLC
Chambersburg PA
CBHW071850270326
41929CB00013B/2179